W9-BXJ-289

BLOOD
RUNS
COAL

BLOOD
RUNS
COAL

THE YABLONSKI MURDERS

AND THE BATTLE FOR THE

UNITED MINE WORKERS OF AMERICA

MARK A. BRADLEY

W. W. NORTON & COMPANY

Independent Publishers Since 1923

Frontispiece: FBI photo of the Yablonski home, January 12, 1970.
(Gordon G. McNeill, JAYLCC MD LOC, Box 24)

Copyright © 2020 by Mark A. Bradley

All rights reserved
Printed in the United States of America
First Edition

For information about permission to reproduce selections from this book, write to
Permissions, W. W. Norton & Company, Inc., 500 Fifth Avenue, New York, NY 10110

For information about special discounts for bulk purchases, please contact
W. W. Norton Special Sales at specialsales@wwnorton.com or 800–233–4830

Manufacturing by Lake Book
Book design by Chris Welch
Production manager: Anna Oler

Library of Congress Cataloging-in-Publication Data

Names: Bradley, Mark A. (Mark Andrew), 1956– author.
Title: Blood runs coal : the Yablonski murders and the battle for the
United Mine Workers of America / Mark A. Bradley.
Description: First edition. | New York, NY : W.W. Norton & Company, [2020] |
Includes bibliographical references and index.
Identifiers: LCCN 2020016358 | ISBN 9780393652536 (hardcover) | ISBN 9780393652543 (epub)
Subjects: LCSH: Yablonski, Joseph A., 1910–1969. | Boyle, William Anthony, 1904–1985. | United Mine
Workers of America. | Labor leaders—United States—Biography. |
Murder—Pennsylvania—Case studies.
Classification: LCC HD6509.Y3 B73 2020 | DDC 364.1/523/0924 [B]—dcundefined
LC record available at https://lccn.loc.gov/2020016358

W. W. Norton & Company, Inc., 500 Fifth Avenue, New York, N.Y. 10110
www.wwnorton.com

W. W. Norton & Company Ltd., 15 Carlisle Street, London W1D 3BS

1 2 3 4 5 6 7 8 9 0

For Anna and Robin

Coal is already saturated with the blood of too many men and drenched with the tears of too many surviving widows and orphans.

—John L. Lewis, 1947

Other sins only speak; murder shrieks out.

—*The Duchess of Malfi* by John Webster

CONTENTS

PART II: THE WALLS OF JUSTICE

BLOOD
RUNS
COAL

Kill Them All

It was just after one o'clock in the morning on New Year's Eve, 1969. In less than twenty-four hours, it would be time for Americans to say goodbye not just to a year, but to a decade. For many, the 1960s had seemed awash in chaos and turmoil. But for others, these ten years had shepherded in a much-needed cultural and social awakening.

While the country was deeply divided on what the waning decade meant, nearly everyone agreed it had been bloody, especially for civil rights leaders and politicians who called for change. Between 1963 and 1968, assassins' bullets cut down Medgar Evers, John F. Kennedy, Malcolm X, Martin Luther King Jr., and Robert F. Kennedy. Crimson images, from a rural Mississippi driveway to a crowded Los Angeles hotel's pantry, weighed on the country's psyche. Americans seemed resigned to the fact of assassination as an unavoidable risk for those brave enough to speak out against injustice and inequality. Maybe the 1970s would be different.

In the southwest corner of Pennsylvania, just across Ten Mile Creek in the soft coal mining borough of Clarksville, the lights of the old stone farmhouse on Bridge Street finally clicked off. From the perch of a hill about a mile away, the three men sitting in a light blue Chevrolet Impala could still see it clearly, even as a cold rain pelted their windshield.

This was the home of United Mine Workers of America insurgent

Joseph "Jock" Yablonski, another man who wanted change. He wanted to purge his labor union of corruption and return it to the coal miners it was supposed to represent—and that started with ousting W. A. "Tony" Boyle, the UMWA's despotic president since 1963.

Yablonski shared the eighteenth-century farmhouse with Marg, his playwright wife. Charlotte, their only daughter, had moved back home for a spell after working on her father's campaign. She was a social worker waiting to start a new job in Washington, D.C.

The men chased sips of Seagram's Seven Crown whiskey from a paper carton with a six-pack of Iron City beer. They had been watching the house from their secluded overlook since early that evening. Yablonski had many admirers and a host of enemies, but these men were neither. One, hunched over the steering wheel, was looking to save his crumbling marriage. The other two were looking forward to a big payday they could spend on cars, women, and booze.

With the temperature falling, the rain turning to slushy drops, and the trio's patience running out, their driver shifted the car into first gear. The Impala eased down the slick road and rolled to a stop near a row of firs shielding the house. The fifteen-foot-tall trees made it invisible to the family's nearest neighbor, four hundred yards away.

The men got out of their car and crept closer to the old house. They saw a holiday wreath hanging on the front door and Christmas cards lining the downstairs windows. It took them fewer than ten minutes to cut the outside phone wires, disable the two cars parked in the long winding driveway, unscrew the metal frame from one of the side porch's locked storm doors, and slip inside unseen.

Armed with a stolen .38 pistol and an M1 carbine traded for another pistol and some whiskey at a gun show, the men walked down a short, carpeted hallway and waited. One of them, who had broken into the farmhouse two months before, stepped past the Christmas tree with opened presents still under it, in search of anyone who might be up. When he returned, they took off their shoes and tiptoed up the wide stairs in their stocking feet toward the bedrooms on the second floor. They had come to kill Jock Yablonski and anyone else who got in their way.

The Yablonski murders are the most infamous crimes in the history of American labor unions. They triggered one of the most intensive and successful manhunts in FBI history.

It took the special prosecutor assigned to the cases nine arrests and five jury trials to prove that Tony Boyle ordered the execution of his rival. Boyle is the highest-ranking American union leader ever convicted of first-degree murder.

Yet the assassinations were much more than the last spasms of a decade that ran red with them: they led to the first successful rank-and-file takeover of a major labor union in modern United States history. Three years after the murders, Yablonski's followers transformed the UMWA into the most democratically run union in the country. Their victory inspired workers in other labor unions, especially in the United Steelworkers of America and in the International Brotherhood of Teamsters, to rise up and challenge their own entrenched, out-of-touch leaders.

It was no accident that the seeds that led to Yablonski's revolt took root when they did. Nineteen sixty-eight was one of the most tumultuous years in American history. By then, the country's streets were on fire and its social fabric badly frayed. The year started with the Tet offensive, an appalling surprise that proved to Americans that their government had lied to them about the progress of the Vietnam War. It ended with seventy-eight coal miners killed in a fiery explosion on a cold, windy morning in West Virginia. In between, Martin Luther King Jr. and Bobby Kennedy were assassinated, and Richard M. Nixon was elected president.

America seemed to be coming apart at the seams, its key institutions under attack. Labor unions were no exception. Roughly one-third of the country's nonfarm workers belonged to labor unions in 1968—only 6.4 percent of private workers belong to unions today—but vocal social critics began seeing organized labor as an obstacle to social change instead of an engine driving it. There was more than some truth to that.

The earliest generation of labor leaders had sacrificed their money, liberty, and even their lives to build a movement that gave America's organized workers an eight-hour workday, health insurance, pensions, job security, safer workplaces, and a more equal and humane society. Many of their heirs were not as committed, especially after labor unions became bigger, stronger, and richer. They focused more on keeping their own lush perquisites and maintaining power than on the needs and wants of the men and women they represented.

Big Labor's internal politics grew more repressive and less susceptible to change than those of Big Business as its leaders became more ensconced and entitled. Their lockstep support for the Vietnam War underscored that they were not only out of touch with the social forces sweeping the country but openly opposed to them.

Yablonski, a longtime union insider, witnessed this transformation firsthand, and he wanted to restore the mine workers' union to what it had once been—a powerful force for social good. But from the beginning, his campaign to unseat Tony Boyle had the feel of a Greek tragedy. When he announced his bid for the union's presidency, he may as well have predicted his own death: he knew what Boyle did to "traitors" who challenged him.

The story of his bid to return the UMWA to its rank-and-file coal miners is one of extraordinary courage, raw ambition, shameful betrayal, unspeakable savagery, and blood-soaked redemption. More than anything, it is a story about a pivotal time in American history—one with reverberations still felt today.

PART I

"I CANNOT STAND SILENT"

ONE

A Hazardous Business

Just before midnight on November 19, 1968, ninety-nine men working on the "cat-eye shift" at Consolidation Coal Company's Number 9 mine walked into its bathhouse and began pulling on their thick work shirts and darkly smudged overalls. Superstitious, none of them dared call their 12 a.m. to 8 a.m. turn in the mine the "graveyard shift" or talk about the dangers that waited for them below. Instead, they distracted themselves by chewing Red Man tobacco, talking about hunting, West Virginia University Mountaineers football, and Thanksgiving, just eight days away.

Their chatter stopped after they stepped into steel cages and started their nearly six-hundred-foot drop to the mine's sooty floor. As they descended farther and farther into the darkness, the men became like professional boxers before a big fight: quiet and focused on what lay before them. It was spitting snow, and a face-biting wind was tearing off the last faded leaves from the trees on the sloping hillsides as the men disappeared underground.

The oldest among them was sixty-two, the youngest only nineteen. They lived on narrow, pitching streets in gritty little northern West Virginia mining communities called Idamay, Enterprise, and Shinnston. One had mined coal for forty-two years, another for just eight days.

Dewey Tarley had a mischievous sense of humor. The twenty-eight-year-old roof bolter made $157 a week. This was enough to help take care of his widowed mother, make monthly payments on a white 1965 Ford Mustang, and pump dimes into the jukebox at Meff's, a local hangout in nearby Fairmont, where he nearly wore out Johnny Cash's live recording of "Folsom Prison Blues."

A forty-eight-year-old section foreman, Emilio Megna, had eight more hours to go before he could retire and open a gas station. His son had begged him to skip his last turn in the mine and go trout fishing. Megna said no. He owed the company one more shift.

Hartzell Mayle operated a loading machine. He lived fifty miles from Number 9. He and his wife had sixteen children. To make ends meet, the fifty-one-year-old miner raised chickens and pigs between his shifts inside Number 9.

Many of the men on the cat-eye shift were veterans. By 1968, 1,400 men from Marion County had fought in Vietnam's steamy jungles.

When they reached the bottom, the miners broke into six- to eight-man crews and boarded mantrips—electric train–like vehicles that ran on rails or had rubber tires—that carried them through Number 9's vast network of spidery tunnels to their workstations. For the next eight hours they would cut and load coal. One crew toiled at freeing a large piece of equipment that had been covered with slate and debris during a roof fall while the others clawed coal out of the mine's rich seams.

But earning a living was not the only thing on their minds. They knew that the shift of miners working before them had had to stop digging three times, once for two and a half hours, while the mine's four giant surface fans drew fresh air into its tunnels and diluted deadly methane gas.

They also knew that they were working at the most dangerous jobs in the country for a company that was obsessed with extracting as much coal from beneath West Virginia's rolling hills as it could.

In 1963 the *Atlantic* called coal mining a "mortician's paradise," and for good reason. The federal government first began compiling statistics on coal mining deaths and serious accidents in 1900, and by November 1968, over 101,000 coal miners had been crushed, gassed, electrocuted, or incinerated underground, while another 1.5 million had been seriously injured. Coal mining's injury rate was four times higher than that of any other industrial job in the United States and fourteen times higher than the national average for all workers.

At least another 150,000 active and retired coal miners had pneumoconiosis, or black lung, contracted by inhaling coal dust, which made their lungs as porous as fishing nets and turned them into wheezing wrecks.

The Consolidation Coal Company and the reckless way it operated Number 9 had added to these grim statistics. In 1954, an underground blast killed sixteen miners working on a chilly Saturday in November. Some engineers argued then that the mine was too dangerous and gassy to reopen, but its coal deposits were too rich for its owners to abandon.

Eleven years later, a four-man crew was standing on a scaffold 233 feet inside the mine's 577-foot-deep Llewellyn airshaft when a spark below ignited a pocket of methane gas. The four men were orbited up and out of the huge shaft's mouth as if they had been shot out of a bazooka. Their shredded body parts were found later in a creek, seventy-five feet from the shaft.

Consolidation Coal Company simply wrote off these losses as the price of doing business. By 1968, it was the biggest bituminous coal producer in the country. Owned by the New York City–based Continental Oil Company, Consolidation's honeycombed network of Appalachian mines churned out nearly fifty million tons of coal a year. Number 9, which stretched for nearly twenty-two square miles between the small mining communities of Farmington and Mannington, West Virginia, contributed two million tons to this yearly total. Workers who complained about the mine's poor safety conditions were ignored, and the coal company gave its loudest critics the most dangerous jobs.

The federal government's attitude was no better. The United States Bureau of Mines had only 250 inspectors assigned to watch over the country's 5,400 mines. They had fined only one operator in sixteen years. The bureau was a captive of the coal industry, and its managers fired or transferred inspectors who pushed too hard to close big mines. The Department of the Interior, its parent agency, seemed more concerned about preserving Alaska's reindeer than protecting coal miners.

Worse, the miners' own labor union seemed to care more about its fat coffers than the coal dust–daubed men who filled them. The United Mine Workers of America had a one-man safety division. Its District 31, where Number 9 was located, spent only $14 on safety training in 1968.

Now, even the weather seemed to be conspiring against the cat-eye shift. The temperature at midnight on November 20 was a chilly 35 degrees.

Coal operators dismissed it as hillbilly folklore, but every miner in West Virginia knew that the months of November and December were the explosion season. Cold air accompanied by dizzying drops in barometric pressure dried out mines and caused them to fill with odorless methane gas and mix with thick coal dust, whipped up by giant electric continuous mining machines, with rotary bits as big as a railroad boxcar's wheels. The faintest spark could turn this volatile mixture into something like gunpowder and transform a mine's shafts into smoking barrels of underground cannons.

This had happened at Monongah, only seven miles from Number 9. On a cold clear day in early December 1907, an underground explosion inside the Fairmont Coal Company's interconnected mines Numbers 6 and 8 pulverized at least five hundred men and boys. It likely killed a lot more; no one knew exactly how many newly arrived immigrants, mostly from Italy and Poland, worked in the two mines.

Number 9 burrowed into the same eight-foot-thick, gassy Pittsburgh coal seam as the Monongah mines. It emitted eight million cubic feet of methane gas a day, enough to heat a small city. The mine's four towering surface fans, which ran around the clock, were supposed to draw enough fresh air into the mine's tunnels to dilute and blow away this odorless but explosive gas, but they sometimes broke and shut down for hours.

The miners who worked in Number 9 worried about all this, but they knew they were not going to find any other well-paying jobs in Marion County. No honest workingman in West Virginia's hollows could make as much money as a union coal miner, even though every one of them knew he was gambling with his life each time he clamped on his safety helmet and went underground.

At 4:00 a.m., the men on the cat-eye shift took a short break to eat the packed food they brought with them in the mine's "dinner holes" and rest.

Just as the men had stopped to eat, the Mods Run fan, one of the mine's four huge surface fans, ground to a halt and threw off its blades. While the men ate, Number 9's west side tunnels began filling with deadly, odorless methane gas. Seventy-eight of them would soon be dead.

Number 9's safety system was designed to warn its miners after a fan stopped ventilating. Each fan was connected to a display board in the lamp house, a building near the mine's entrance used to store supplies. When a fan slowed or stopped running, a warning light turned red, an alarm sounded, and the men evacuated. As a fail-safe, the system was designed to cut off all power to Number 9 if a fan was down for more than twelve minutes.

That is, unless someone in the company decided that shutting off power and evacuating the miners interfered too much with cutting and loading coal. Sometime before the Mods Run fan stopped working, a coal company employee disabled the fan's alarm system.

At 5:27 a.m. an explosion so violent that it shook the windows in Fairmont twelve miles away tore through the shaft at the mine's Llewellyn Portal. Billowing mushroom clouds, shot through with orange and blue flames, curled above the mine. The heat was so intense that it scorched several of the miners' cars in Number 9's parking lot. Thirteen men, working elsewhere in the sprawling mine, scrambled to the surface. A crane operator, using a makeshift bucket, extracted eight more.

As the mine belched fire and smoke, word raced through the tiny Appalachian communities surrounding Number 9 that it had blown up. Family members, tears in their eyes, gathered in the mine's cinderblock company store, clustered among its plastic furniture, and stared out at the rolling clouds of smoke. Some of the missing men's wives were grandmothers, others were still in their teens. Those mountain women who had experienced mining disasters before suspected the worst. They gave up hope of ever seeing their menfolk again and went home soon after they arrived. Others previously untouched by underground explosions clung to hope and waited for any news about a rescue.

The grisly drama of a shift of coal miners trapped in a burning hole a week before Thanksgiving attracted the country's biggest dailies and news networks, making this the first major mine disaster in United States history to be nationally televised.

Americans stared in horror at their televisions as Walter Cronkite and other major network anchors, in between clips about the Vietnam War and President-elect Richard Nixon's promise to get the country out of what had degenerated into an unwinnable quagmire, reported on the tragedy unfolding inside Number 9. In eight months, the United States would send two astronauts 240,000 miles into space to walk on the moon, but there was no way to rescue seventy-eight men trapped six hundred feet beneath West Virginia's rumpled hills.

While the first explosion had killed some of the miners instantly, others had enough time to put on their gas masks. Recovery crews later found an open first-aid kit and bodies lying on a sheet of canvas, as if some of the trapped men had lain down together to conserve their dwindling supply of fresh air.

The news cameras were still rolling when apologists for the coal industry trooped before reporters to circle the wagons. Their messages were the same: coal mining was too inherently dangerous to spend any more money trying to make it safer, and men's lives were cheaper than coal. John Roberts, who headed Consolidation Coal Company's public relations department, described the explosion as "something that we have to live with," as did J. Cordell Moore, an assistant secretary at the United States Department of the Interior, and Hulett C. Smith, governor of West Virginia. Smith, who led a state in which there was more debate about whether there should be sex education in its public schools than about safety in its coal mines, lectured the grieving families that "we must recognize that this is a hazardous business and what has occurred here is one of the hazards of being a miner."

But the most astonishing performance was that given by W. A. "Tony" Boyle, wearing his signature Washington uniform of a fedora, a pressed suit, and a red rose in his lapel. His few appearances in the coalfields were usually carefully staged, allowing him time to don a new pair of overalls and shiny work boots, but this time Boyle swooped onto the scene in a helicopter furnished by the coal company.

When he stepped up to the hastily erected podium in the company store, Boyle stunned many of those who had gathered to hear his expected words of sorrow and outrage by instead, in a flat, nasal voice, praising Consolidation Coal Company's safety record and its history of cooperation with the union. He reminded the families, as if they did not already know it, that coal mining was a very dangerous way to make a living.

The public spectacle of the UMWA's president defending the grossly negligent, if not outright criminal, actions of a coal company while seventy-eight of his coal miners lay entombed in its burning mine shocked many of the onlookers. "I hated him right then," Judy Henderson, now a widow at just twenty-one, told the *Washington Post*. "I couldn't believe someone could say that right in front of the mine where all our husbands were buried alive."

Nor could Joseph "Jock" Yablonski, the burly head of the union's powerful District 5 in southwestern Pennsylvania. He felt almost physically sick as he watched Boyle's speech on his television, only an hour's drive from Number 9's roasted portals.

Yablonski thought about John L. Lewis, the larger-than-life former president of the coal miners' union, as he watched Boyle extol Consolidation Coal Company's bottomless virtues. In the wake of an explosion that had killed 119 Illinois miners in December 1951, Lewis had put on a miner's helmet and emerged from underground hours later, his face streaked with coal dust and etched in grief. A reporter captured his emotions in what became an iconic photograph in the Appalachian coalfields.

"That picture just had to make coal miners feel so proud," Yablonski told one of his sons. "But that son of a bitch Boyle. With those people dead in the mine, how could that bastard stand up and praise the company's safety record the way he did?" But as Yablonski stewed, the explosion inside Number 9 was unleashing mighty currents for change across the coalfields.

Many of the families clung to hope until the day after Thanksgiving. On the evening of Friday, November 29, when they gathered to pray inside the James Fork United Methodist Church, John Corcoran, president of Consolidation Coal, stepped forward and told them the time had come to seal the mine. He had already told a group of local ministers on Thanksgiving that there was no hope, but he had not wanted to give the families such awful news on the nation's day of prayer and thanks.

By then, at least twenty-four explosions had ripped through Number 9 and filled its air with poisonous gases. A Catholic bishop said the Lord's Prayer that evening inside the church as a caravan of ninety dump trucks, gorged with 1,600 tons of crushed limestone to snuff out the still-raging underground inferno, slowly rumbled toward the mine. One young man, overcome by sorrow and rage, threatened to shoot anyone who tried to close up the mine. Two ministers led him away as deep, uncontrollable sobs wracked his body. It was going to be a gloomy holiday season in West Virginia's snowy hollows.

The grieving families—235 children had lost their fathers and 74 women had lost their husbands in the underground inferno—had little reason to believe that this latest coal mining disaster would be treated any differently than all the ones that had come before it. The nation's response to tragedies such as Number 9 had always been the same: prayers, an outpouring of sympathy for the widows and children, toothless coal mining safety legislation, and a return to the collective amnesia that allowed things in the mines to go on as they always had.

But the country was changing, even if men like Tony Boyle could not see it. Spurred by the longest period of sustained economic growth in American history, the 1960s brought demands for all kinds of rights to the forefront. The civil rights movement ignited the idealism, egalitarianism, and rights consciousness that galvanized many different groups—African Americans, Hispanics, women, and gays—to challenge the country's social and economic structure.

The increasingly unpopular war in Vietnam, which sparked the most extensive and sustained protests in American history, contributed to this growing willingness to question authority and challenge the status quo. When Viet Cong guerrillas launched the Tet offensive in South Vietnam on January 31, 1968, they shattered the illusion so artfully sketched by President Lyndon Johnson and his generals in the Pentagon that the United States was winning the war. Though the American armed forces repelled the offensive, CBS news icon Walter Cronkite reported a month later that it was "more certain than ever that the bloody experience of Vietnam is to end in stalemate." The fallout from Tet roiled the country's streets and campuses as more and more Americans lost faith in their government's leaders and demanded change.

After the tragedy at Number 9, a spirit of reform finally began seeping into the remote backwoods of Central Appalachia; the region's geographic isolation and one-industry economy could no longer keep it at bay. Coal miners began asking why they had to accept as the price of their jobs getting killed, maimed, or sick. How, they asked, had the union that once protected them from the coal operators become the union that protected the coal operators from them?

Three coalfield doctors had been asking their coal miner patients these questions for a long time. Isadore Buff, Donald Rasmussen, and Hawey Wells Jr. were heart and pulmonary specialists tired of burying patients who died young because they had inhaled too much coal dust. After Number 9 blew up, the doctors barnstormed around West Virginia, waging a vocal campaign against the coal companies and their many protectors in state and local government. Coal executives and the legislators they backed with fat checks had thwarted all attempts to make black lung a compensable occupational disease, which would have required coal companies to pay for the crippling illnesses their underground mining caused. The death rate for miners was nearly twice that for all working men in the country and a staggering 122 percent higher for those coal diggers who were between the ages of sixty and sixty-four.

Coal barons and paid-for politicians were not the doctors' only foes: they tangled repeatedly with West Virginia's conservative medical establishment. Dr. Charles Andrews, the provost of Health Sciences at West Virginia University, blasted the notion that coal dust played a key role in causing black lung, claiming instead that cigarettes were much more dangerous to miners than coal dust. The Cabell County Medical Society joined the chorus, its doctors insisting that black lung was "a condition compatible with good health." The Kanawha County Medical Association attacked the three doctors personally. It condemned them for inciting the miners without first presenting scientifically documented evidence.

The disaster at Number 9 brought the black lung epidemic national attention. Reporters and newsmen, waiting for any word about the fate of the seventy-eight miners, focused their notepads and cameras on the living conditions in the communities that surrounded the burning coal mine. The three black-lung doctors took full advantage of this gruesome opportunity to educate Americans about the ravaged lungs of coal miners.

West Virginia Democratic congressman Ken Hechler was among those listening. Hechler, a former college history professor who held a PhD in political science and American history from Columbia University, a best-selling author on World War II, and a former special assistant to President Harry Truman, represented a district in which 4,500 coal miners resided. After the Consolidation Coal Company converted Number 9 into a tomb, Hechler sat down at his typewriter in his book-lined Capitol Hill office and composed a "Declaration of Conscience." In three tightly written paragraphs, he accused the UMWA of being more interested in making money than in protecting its members, and demanded that Congress intervene and save the miners from the coal operators and their own labor union. He then took the first step by introducing a bill in the House of Representatives that aimed to reduce the levels of coal dust a miner inhaled.

Ralph Nader shared Hechler's outrage; the consumer advocate, who had rocketed to national fame as a muckraker after he wrote *Unsafe at Any Speed*, his 1965 best-selling indictment of the automobile industry's resistance to even basic safety features, had met Dr. Isadore Buff in 1967, and he had seen firsthand in West Virginia what black lung did to coal miners. Ben Franklin, a reporter for the *New York Times*, encouraged Nader to write about the suffering he had seen. The *New Republic* published his article on black lung in February 1968.

Spurred on by Hechler, Nader, and the three doctors, and helped by community activists from Volunteers in Service to America, who were outraged that Big Coal treated the state like a "Third World colony," a group of coal miners from Marion, West Virginia, formed the Black Lung Association in early January 1969. On January 26, over three thousand miners gathered at the Charleston Civic Center to attend the association's first statewide meeting.

Ken Hechler brought them to their feet when he ridiculed the West Virginia Medical Association with the slogan, "Black Lung is good for you." He pulled out a twelve-pound roll of baloney from his bag and shouted, "That is baloney!"

Hechler then read the miners a statement from Nader. The consumer champion denounced the coal industry's chronic neglect of health and safety, which made the lives of coal miners cheaper than the coal they brought out of the ground. After cataloging Tony Boyle's many failings, Nader urged them to choose a new leader. His words electrified the convention hall. Miners across West Virginia began bombarding their state legislators with phone calls and letters, demanding that they pass a bill that provided black lung benefits and more stringent coal mining safety standards.

On February 18, 1969, a miner working in the East Gulf mine near Charleston poured out water from his thermos onto the ground. His simple but universally understood act in the coalfields calling for a walkout started a wildcat strike that spread like wildfire across West Virginia. Within five days, over 40,000 miners had walked off their jobs, shutting down the state's coal industry.

Boyle denounced the Black Lung Association's members as "black-tongue loudmouths." The United States Senate's Labor Subcommittee summoned him to testify. His crude and hot-tempered remarks shocked the committee's members: he branded Hechler and Nader "false prophets," and he threatened to shove a bologna down the West Virginia congressman's throat. He challenged Nader to a fistfight in an alley and belittled him afterwards as a "camel rider from Lebanon."

The miners ignored Boyle's threats and stayed out of the mines. With the strike costing the coal operators over $42 million so far—$305 million in today's dollars—the state legislators capitulated. On March 11, 1969, Governor Arch Moore signed a bill that compensated West Virginia's black lung victims up to $52 a week. Boyle was shameless. He tried to take credit for the legislation just as it was about to become law.

The victory of their grassroots rebellion showed the UMWA's rank and file what their history always taught them: they were not powerless when they united and fought for a common cause. That cause once had been the right to organize and earn a living wage. It was now for a clean and democratic union.

Ralph Nader was right: the coal miners would need a new leader to bring this about, but Tony Boyle was determined to keep his job even if he had to kill to do it.

TWO

That Bastard Will Rue the Day

On September 27, 1946, the nation's newspapers reported that John L. Lewis had suffered an acute attack of appendicitis and had been rushed into emergency surgery at Baltimore's Johns Hopkins Hospital. More likely, he had suffered from a blood clot that blocked his coronary arteries. While Lewis recovered, John O'Leary, his aging vice-president, warned him that it was time the union began moving younger men into its high command.

Lewis had always resisted naming an heir; he was too Olympian to do that. With his thundering voice and rococo rhetoric—seasoned with biblical, Shakespearean, and classical allusions—he had defied presidents, ignored judges, and excoriated coal operators for his miners while singlehandedly molding them into the most influential and feared labor union in American history. In 1943, during the height of World War II, he had led his 500,000 coal diggers out of the pits on a strike for higher wages. While the editors of the U.S. Army's *Stars and Stripes* newspaper damned his "coal-black soul," opinion polls pegged him as the most unpopular man in America, and congressmen demanded that he be charged with treason, Lewis pointed out that mining coal was more dangerous than serving in the country's armed forces during the war. After President Franklin D. Roosevelt threatened to send in the Army to break the strike, Lewis sneered, "They can't dig coal with bayonets." His miners got their pay raise.

By the end of the war, the UMWA's members were the highest-paid industrial workers in America. In 1946, many of the union's soft coal miners made almost $60 a week.

Before Lewis took over the union in 1919—it was founded in 1890 in Columbus, Ohio—its miners worked twelve to fourteen hours a day and saw their children only on Sundays, when they were too tired to hold them. They shoveled tons of coal on their hands and knees in stifling hot "rooms" with ceilings as low as thirty inches and never knew when a roof might collapse, breaking a back, cutting off a leg or an arm, or burying them alive. And, all too often, they lay in narrow tunnels with their shirts pulled tightly over their heads, faces buried in the blackened muck, as the deafening roar of a methane gas explosion signaled they were about to die.

These barbaric working conditions, coupled with the coal operators' often savage reactions to their workers wanting better working conditions and higher pay—union members risked being blacklisted, beaten, and shot—formed the twin pillars of the miners' unwavering belief that the UMWA was all they had standing between them and industrial slavery. Thousands of desperate men, courting death or destitution if they were caught, met on remote hilltops and gathered in the deep woods to swear an "obligation" to the union.

Those who did were not disappointed. Lewis, through his strategic use of strikes to cripple the American economy—coal supplied the lion's share of the country's energy in the middle of the twentieth century—and his repeated threats of industrial violence, won his miners shorter working hours, gave them a pioneering pay-as-you-go welfare and retirement fund, built them a string of ten hospitals dotted across Central Appalachia, and forced Congress to pay at least lip service to their work safety. One newspaper declared that Lewis made his coal miners the "aristocrats of labor."

The UMWA became their religion, and he became their god. Coal miners loved John L. Lewis and for good reason. He gave them something they had never had before—their employers' fear and respect.

His picture hung beside that of Jesus Christ on the walls of their shot-gun houses.

But what Lewis gave his miners came at an exorbitant price. He ran the UMWA with an iron fist. Standing nearly six feet tall and weighing well over two hundred pounds, his leonine head and sheepdog-like eyebrows made him look much larger. He used his booming voice like a policeman's billy club. He shouted down anyone who openly criticized him inside the union, stuffed ballot boxes to ensure his reelection, and drove his foes out of the UMWA after he defeated them. To ensure his continued rule, Lewis turned the union's constitutional conventions into mirages of democracy by stacking them with his own handpicked delegates.

What were supposed to be checks and balances on his authority became rituals of backslapping and rubber-stamping. In the twelve UMWA conventions Lewis chaired after 1936, he did not hold a single roll call vote. Lewis preached to his members that their union had too many enemies; only a permanent state of emergency, with him in charge, could save it.

He alone made all the UMWA's most important decisions and negotiated its contracts with the coal operators. "I work harder than anyone else in the union, and I know more about the problems of miners than anyone else," he once told a biographer. "Therefore, I should think my decisions would mean more than those of anyone else." No one in the union questioned that they did.

Lewis governed the UMWA from his baronial Washington, D.C., headquarters, a former gentlemen's club, where he surrounded himself with obedient yes-men, blood relatives, expensive leather chairs, brass chandeliers, a Chippendale-furnished dining room, and a stone fire-place big enough to swallow six-foot-long logs.

Confined now to a hospital bed and faced with his own mortality, Lewis agreed with O'Leary that Tony Boyle and Jock Yablonski were particularly promising future leaders. The two men were as different as they were alike.

Boyle radiated tension. Some of this sprang from his modest physical appearance: he was tiny and balding, with wisps of graying auburn hair around his ears that pushed outward from his talcum-powdered white face, and his bushy red eyebrows arched up like question marks when he became agitated. He looked more like a scowling elf than the great labor leader he yearned to be.

With his linebacker's neck, a face furrowed with deep creases, beetle-eyebrows, and a gravelly voice, the barrel-chested Yablonski looked as if he had just stepped out of *On the Waterfront*, Elia Kazan's 1954 movie about union corruption. He was tough and expressive. Yablonski could also be mercurial and volcanic, but warm and charming. With a cigarette dangling between his lips, he greeted miners by clasping a calloused hand on their shoulders, pulling them close, and listening intently to what they had to say. Boyle always shook hands with them as if he were wearing white gloves.

Their speaking styles magnified their differences. Boyle read very long, carefully scripted speeches, often encased in plastic. When he did not follow what was placed in front of him, he rambled and was often incoherent. Yablonski was a much more polished public speaker. He characteristically peeled off his suit coat, loosened his tie, and popped his shirt collar. He never used a note, even when reciting statistics, and frequently sprinkled his stump speeches with colorful profanity.

Boyle enjoyed watching television, and seldom read anything other than union reports. He thought of himself as a suave ladies' man, but his female secretaries inside the UMWA's Washington, D.C., headquarters believed he was lecherous. He and his schoolteacher wife filled the rooms of their home with photographs—of him.

Yablonski was a voracious consumer of newspapers, was married to a talented playwright, owned an interest in a harness racing track, listened to opera, and bought an eighteenth-century stone farmhouse in Clarksville, Pennsylvania, where he and his wife raised two sons who were lawyers and a daughter who was a social worker.

Yablonski liked the limelight and welcomed public attention. Boyle, even after he became the UMWA's president in 1963, had an unlisted phone number, looked out on the capital city's McPherson

Square through bulletproof windows, and came and went using a private staircase leading from his second-floor office to the street. A gate barred the main marble stairs leading to his office.

Boyle's insecurities fed his paranoia. He insisted on personally opening all the UMWA's mail. He monitored visitors to the office of John L. Lewis, now president emeritus after he retired in 1960 but still a trustee of the union's cash-rich pension fund. Boyle ordered his chauffeur to drive his black Cadillac—he occasionally rode in the front seat next to his driver to show his common touch—to the union's parking lot whenever he was out of town, so that his employees would not know he was gone. Strangest of all, he developed a habit of jerking his head around to look over his right shoulder, as if he constantly suspected someone was stalking him.

Yet Boyle and Yablonski were similar. Both came from very rough backgrounds, and both were extremely ambitious.

Boyle grew up in the Montana coalfields. Born on December 1, 1901, in what was then the tiny gold and silver mining town of Bald Butte, he was the son, grandson, and great grandson of Irish and Scots-Irish coal miners. His father, tired of being poor, had come to Bald Butte from Scotland to dig for gold and silver, but he should have stayed where he was; both were gone by the time the Boyles arrived. James Boyle went back to mining coal in conditions even more dangerous than those in the British Isles.

Tony Boyle dropped out of school in the ninth grade and followed his father into the pits. He was only twelve when his father died of black lung. Restless, Boyle roamed around the Pacific Northwest, working for a railroad and mining copper before returning to Montana to dig for coal eight years later. An underground accident sheared off the little finger on his right hand.

Cursed with a terrible temper, Boyle often found himself out of work after he clashed with an unforgiving foreman. To stave off unemployment, he became an electrician, but he never liked working with his hands. He also started a correspondence course to become a lawyer, but never finished it. In 1928, he married Ethel Williams, a schoolteacher.

Determined to stay aboveground and wear a coat and tie instead of a helmet and overalls, he became an organizer for the expanding UMWA. He was a tireless worker, and, in 1938, he became the Congress of Industrial Organizations' vice-president for Montana. Two years later, John L. Lewis appointed him president of the UMWA's District 27, which encompassed Montana, North and South Dakota, Alaska, and part of northern Wyoming.

This post was almost as dangerous as mining coal. On his way home from a UMWA meeting in 1941, members of a rival union ambushed Boyle. They knocked out his front teeth and broke his back, putting him in a body cast for nine months. When he got back on his feet, he used what he called the "rough stuff" to stamp out his local foes.

After Lewis brought him to Washington in 1948 as his special assistant, Boyle continued to use the "rough stuff." Lewis regularly dispatched him to some of the country's most vehemently anti-union coalfields.

In 1951, Boyle offered Charles Minton, a UMWA miner, between $25,000 and $50,000 to murder two small-coal operators in Wise, Virginia, who opposed the union, promising him that the UMWA would pay for the finest lawyers if the police arrested him and take care of his family if he went to prison. While Minton excelled at blowing up mine owners' power stations and their coal tipples, he was no killer. When he backed out of the plot, Boyle had him fired and blacklisted, making it impossible for him to earn his living in the coalfields. Minton, who moved to New York State, sued the UMWA, which quickly settled his lawsuit for $25,000. In 1969, all the records of this case mysteriously vanished from the Wise County courthouse.

Physical violence was just one of Boyle's interests: he wanted to make himself and his family rich. The Boyles had slaved for generations for nothing more than subsistence wages, blown-off limbs, and hacking coughs that eventually killed them. He was going to change that.

Boyle pressured state inspectors to close rival coal mines that competed with his brother Jack's mines in Roundup, Montana. In 1957, he persuaded the Montana legislature not to pass a law that required coal operators to install roof bolts. Boyle argued this would be too costly for small mine owners. A year later, four miners were crushed to death in one of Jack Boyle's coal pits after a roof collapsed, but Dick Boyle, another brother and now Tony's handpicked president of District 27, ruled that the accident was "unavoidable."

Yablonski's beginnings were just as difficult as Boyle's. He was the son of a Polish artillery officer who immigrated to Pittsburgh in 1904 after serving in Czar Nicholas II's Russian Army. Five years later, Zdsislaw Jablonski married his first cousin Ludovica Jasinska, a seamstress working in a local factory. Joseph Albert "Jock" Jablonski, their first child, was born on March 3, 1910, in Pittsburgh's Polish Hill neighborhood.

Polish Hill had the highest rate of typhoid fever in the United States, which, along with a job offer to work in the country's biggest soft coal mine, prodded the newly Anglicized "Stephen Yablonski" to move his family an hour down the Monongahela River to California, Pennsylvania, later that year. Jones and Laughlin Steel Company's enormous Vesta Number 4 Mine produced 12,000 tons of coal a day and harnessed 2,400 miners to do it. Away from the cramped, sloping tenements of Polish Hill and its Dante-like view of what one writer described as "Hell with the lid taken off," the Yablonskis were able to afford a house, a cow, and wide-open spaces overlooking the river for their son to enjoy.

A fatal accident marred Jock Yablonski's thirteenth year. In 1923, he killed a neighborhood friend while target practicing in a cow pasture with an old pistol he and one of his brothers found. A coroner's jury ruled the shooting an accident, but Yablonski hated guns for the rest of his life.

In 1925, he dropped out of school and joined his father in a mine known as Vesta Number 4. His mother cried when he entered the mines. She feared he would never amount to anything.

Yablonski entered an industry seething with unrest. That same year, the Pittsburgh Coal Company closed its doors. It canceled the union's contract and cut the miners' wages from $7.50 to $6.00 a day. John L. Lewis ordered his miners out of the coal pits, triggering one of the most violent labor disputes in American history.

Unable to dig coal, Yablonski worked as an elevator operator in a hospital, unloaded baggage and produce cars at the railway station, and toiled as a coil winder for Westinghouse. This lifting and pulling gave the five-foot-six Yablonski a bull-like neck and a thickly muscled chest.

But steady work was hard to find during the Great Depression. At loose ends, Yablonski seemed set on confirming his mother's worry about not amounting to anything. He often got into trouble, especially when he lost what little money he had rolling dice. One of his friends from these days later told the FBI that Yablonski was a very "rough fellow" who often got into violent fistfights.

On September 23, 1930, Yablonski finally went too far. After he got paid for doing some odd jobs, he went to the local Moose Club in Monongahela. He downed several drinks and played the club's slot machines until he lost all his money. Afraid to go home to face his parents without it, Yablonski hid in a backroom until after the club closed and broke into the slot machines, stealing $318—the equivalent of $4,618 today.

The local police arrested him. Yablonski pleaded guilty to breaking and entering and larceny. A judge sentenced him to two to four years in the Allegheny County workhouse. He served eight months.

Chastened, Yablonski returned home, but tragedy struck the family soon after he was paroled. During the early morning hours of March 18, 1933, Stephen Yablonski came limping through the kitchen door after his shift in the Vesta Number 6 mine and vomited. He had been badly hurt while lifting a large chunk of slate. It had broken in two, knocking him to the ground. The fall ruptured his bladder.

He was unable to urinate on his own. A local doctor tasked Jock with changing his father's catheter every morning. Stephen died of blood poisoning and pneumonia two months later.

Yablonski's life continued to spiral downwards after his father died. He married Anne Huffman, a local girl, that same year, but their physical union lasted only two days. Anne's parents believed that Yablonski, with his calloused hands and Polish last name, was not good enough for their daughter. She dutifully broke off the marriage and returned home—but not before she became pregnant.

Boiling over with anger, Yablonski broke into the Huffmans' house and slapped Anne's mother. A justice of the peace made him pay a stiff fine and handed him a restraining order. Anne gave birth to their son Kenneth on February 13, 1934, and a family court judge ordered Yablonski to pay weekly child support.

The UMWA's resurgence under John L. Lewis and President Franklin D. Roosevelt's New Deal pulled Yablonski out of his tailspin. The union needed miners who were fearless and aggressive, and Yablonski was both. In 1934, he began to steadily climb the union ladder. Twelve hundred miners unanimously elected him to be the president of the union's Local 1787. He used the position as a springboard, winning a seat on the governing board of the UMWA's powerful District 5 that same year.

In 1942, Yablonski won a seat on the UMWA's International Executive Board, its twenty-eight-man College of Cardinals. His ability to organize nonunion mines and resolve coalfield disputes made him one of Lewis's most valuable lieutenants. Lewis called him his "right-hand man."

By then, Lewis had made the UMWA the country's wealthiest labor union. Given the stakes of who was going to be his heir, it is not surprising that Boyle and Yablonksi often clashed.

The two men first collided during an International Executive Board meeting in 1946 when they argued over whether the UMWA should establish a welfare and retirement fund for its miners; Yablonski supported the fund while Boyle insisted the money be spent on higher wages. The meeting ended with Boyle ridiculing his rival's position and Yablonski calling Boyle a "no good son of a bitch."

Yablonski was stunned when Lewis, who was retiring because of a series of heart attacks, tapped Boyle in 1960 to serve as the UMWA's vice-president under Thomas Kennedy, his geriatric successor. Yablonski had had more field experience than Boyle and now headed District 5 in southwestern Pennsylvania, one of the union's largest and most important territories. Self-confident, he never doubted that he was more competent or would make a better union president than Boyle.

But Yablonski was also more charismatic, and less likely to fit comfortably into Lewis's shadow. Lewis, always governed by his enormous ego, preferred to turn the union over to a lesser man rather than risk being overshadowed by a dynamic successor. Yablonski's strong personality was not his only problem; he was also Polish, and the union's upper echelons had always been reserved for those whose last names came from the British Isles or Ireland. While Lewis preached that the UMWA was open to all, his rhetoric stopped at the doors of the union's plush headquarters' offices.

Shortly after Boyle's selection, Yablonski and several other UMWA's leaders met in a hotel room in Washington. The others urged Yablonski to contest Boyle's appointment; someone called Boyle a "sheepherder" and other uncomplimentary names. Yablonski realized that challenging Boyle meant challenging Lewis, too, and he was not yet willing to do that, but word filtered back to Boyle about the meeting and the unflattering remarks made about him. He decided that Yablonski was someone he needed to watch even more closely.

Yablonski's disgust grew when Boyle became the UMWA's acting president in December 1962. One of Boyle's first public appearances in his new role was on December 6 of that year at United States Steel's sprawling Robena mining complex near Uniontown, Pennsylvania, after an explosion killed thirty-seven miners. While he surveyed the carnage, Boyle asked, "Did a trapper boy leave the door open?" Boyle's question astonished Yablonski. Trapper boys, who once manned the doors to mine passages to ensure that fresh air continuously flowed through the tunnels, had not been used for decades.

Boyle's heavy-handed display at the UMWA's September 1964 convention only added to Yablonski's sinking feeling that the union had fallen into the wrong hands. He had come to the Florida convention with high hopes: six months before, 18,000 union miners had thrown down their tools and climbed out of the pits, disgusted by Boyle's failure to win more than a two-dollar-a-day raise, seven unpaid holidays, and no sick leave in the UMWA's newly negotiated contract with the Bituminous Coal Operators' Association. Many of the striking miners were from District 5, and Boyle ordered Yablonski to get his men back to work. He did, but he promised his district's miners that their delegates could air their complaints about the new contract.

Boyle became the union's president on January 19, 1963, after cancer killed Kennedy. He did not want to hear about miners' grievances. He wanted to celebrate his coronation and avoid unhappy dissenters.

Boyle decided to move the union's September 1964 quadrennial constitutional convention from Cincinnati, Ohio, near the smoky coalfields, to a thousand miles away from them in sunny Bal Harbour, Florida. He personally approved which delegates could attend: he only wanted those who were willing to glorify him. The union paid all their expenses.

To entertain his admirers, Boyle imported five Appalachian bands to the Americana Hotel. They billed the union $390,000 for their services after they arrived on the special train he had chartered for them. By the time the last filet mignon was eaten, the 1964 convention cost the UMWA $1.4 million, almost $900,000 more than its 1960 convention. Seventy-seven thousand dollars from the union's treasury were thrown away on alarm clocks, Zippo lighters, and transistor radios, all stamped with Boyle's name and picture.

When Boyle, wearing his patent-leather elevator shoes and his signature rosebud in the lapel of his sleekly tailored suit, strode to the podium, the ballroom of the Americana Hotel exploded with wild cheers, thunderous clapping, and band music for nearly fifty minutes before he finally motioned them to stop. Boyle basked in his followers' adulation.

He warned them that any criticism of him was an attack on the UMWA, and reminded the traditionally clannish miners that they prospered best when they listened to their leaders, not to outsiders. Boyle brought his disciples to their feet when he vowed to thrash the union's real and imagined foes because he had no "chicken blood" flowing through his veins.

He imported Albert Edward Pass, the bloodthirsty but always-grinning secretary-treasurer of District 19, and a squadron of his white-helmeted thugs to police the convention's floor. A chunky man of medium height, Pass was widely known in the union as "Little Hitler." He lorded over his territory of Tennessee and six counties in mountainous southeast Kentucky as if it were his personal kingdom. William "Little Bill" Turnblazer Jr. was its president, but Pass was its high priest. He decided who was going to be rewarded and punished in what was the UMWA's most violent precinct.

The second oldest of twelve children, Pass was born on June 30, 1920, in Rockwood, Tennessee. His father was a coal miner and a part-time preacher. A devout union man, Ninevah Pass ended every prayer at the supper table with the refrain "God bless John L. Lewis and the UMWA." He raised his children in a drafty coal-company house in Fleming, Kentucky, on stories about the heroics of Lewis and the mine workers. Pass became as devoted to the UMWA as he was to the evangelical homilies his father preached on Sundays.

Yet Pass was no simple follower. He had an ordered, methodical mind, and grew up reading more than the Bible and Sears and Roebuck catalogs. After he graduated from high school, he borrowed $300 from a local coal company clerk to enroll in Draughon's Business College in Knoxville. He left after only six months, but not before he mastered the fundamentals of bookkeeping and accounting.

Unable to find work doing either, Pass returned to Fleming and became a coal loader for the Elkhorn Coal Company. In January 1941, he leaped at an offer to become a bookkeeper at District 19's headquarters in Middlesboro, Kentucky. He was soon one of the union's most zealous disciples and ruthless enforcers.

Pass was elated when Boyle asked him to police the 1964 convention. His goons on the convention floor wore white miner's helmets emblazoned with "Loyal to Boyle" on one side and "District 19" on the other. Dozens of them menacingly surrounded the floor's microphones. They punched and kicked the first delegate to address the convention after he questioned why coal operators were voting on union matters. He was beaten so badly—an observer said he was bleeding "like a stuck hog"—that the convention had to be recessed temporarily.

Boyle, who wore his own white hard hat and was now an honorary member of District 19, was exhilarated by the bloodshed. He looked on approvingly as Pass's henchmen dragged away the battered offender. No one was going to be permitted to challenge his one-man rule.

Yablonski complained to Boyle about the mauling and threatened to pull District 5's delegates out of the convention if the beatings did not stop. Boyle, who had cowed the convention's dissenters with the bloodletting, reined in Pass. He could deal with Yablonski later. He had other things to do.

Boyle extended his term from four years to five and raised the number of local endorsements needed to challenge him in a presidential election from five to fifty. His self-appointed rules committee blessed these "reforms." The convention's delegates also passed a resolution reaffirming the UMWA's support for civil rights.

When one of his aides begged him to run against Boyle in the union's upcoming December presidential election, Yablonski shook his head. He was not ready for a head-on collision, but he knew his showdown with Boyle was coming. He could not live with himself if it did not.

Their battle lines were drawn once more a year later, when the Pennsylvania legislature began weighing an amendment that expanded the state's workers' compensation laws. The amendment made more workers who suffered from occupational diseases, such as black lung, eligible for payments of $75 a month. Its language would apply to 3,000 miners who toiled in the hard coal or anthracite fields of northeastern Pennsylvania, but Yablonski wanted the amendment to cover all the state's coal miners.

Boyle told him to "not rock the boat"; the amendment would cost the coal industry too much. He was more interested in the tons of coal extracted from the ground than the welfare of those who did it. But Yablonski refused to listen, and he persuaded a gaggle of powerful state senators, and then the governor, to apply the amendment to all Pennsylvania's coal miners. It became law on October 8, 1965. Boyle punished Yablonski for defying him, exiling Leon Yablonski, Jock's brother and a union field organizer in Cleveland, Ohio, to Canon City, Colorado, a distant outpost on the UMWA's fringes.

In 1966, Boyle forced Raymond Lewis, John L.'s brother, to retire as the union's vice-president. He wanted his own man around him, not another reminder of the UMWA's great patriarch. He refused even to consider District 5's resolution that he name Yablonski the UMWA's vice president, elevating George Joy Titler instead.

Titler was no stranger to brute force. A rumpled, barrel-bellied West Virginian with a face the color of dull putty, he was so fat he could not tuck in his shirt all the way. He sported a golf-ball-sized agate ring on his thick, beefy left hand. He once bragged to a magazine writer how he used it: "Usually, I can knock a man unconscious with the flat of my hand, but sometimes you run into rough babies that make a little trouble and"—fingering the ring—"she comes in mighty handy."

He had plenty of experience in dishing out the "rough stuff." Lewis dispatched him to "Bloody" Harlan County Kentucky in 1937 to lead the UMWA's field operations. Open warfare erupted there between the miners and the coal operators. By the time the two sides reached an uneasy truce in 1939, fifty-five murders were still unsolved. Titler survived at least four attempts on his own life.

He was also a master at orchestrating voting fraud. During the union's 1964 presidential election, he held court in the Glass House Restaurant on the West Virginia Turnpike while loyal local union officials brought him their ballot boxes. In between large bites of food, Titler shredded anti-Boyle ballots and substituted new ones, guaranteeing that his patron won the state in a landslide.

In June 1966, Boyle and Titler sent an eight-man commission to Pittsburgh to investigate District 5's finances. When the commission found some "irregularities," Boyle ordered Yablonski to Washington and demanded he resign as the district's president, a position he had held since 1958. If he balked, Boyle threatened to declare the district insolvent, place it under his direct control, and handpick its officers.

On June 21, 1966, Yablonski reluctantly gave in and resigned as District 5's president, sacrificing his position to save the region's long-standing independence; District 5 was one of only four of the union's twenty-three American territories that elected its own officers. But Boyle was not finished with Yablonski—he wanted to drive him out of the union. For months, he gave him nothing to do; when that failed, he dispatched him to Somerset County, Pennsylvania, to organize that notoriously anti-union enclave.

Yablonski brooded over his removal and his mistreatment, vowing revenge. He told one of his sons "that bastard will rue the day" for what he had done. But while he waited for his chance, he dutifully toed the line.

In September 1968, the UMWA staged its forty-fifth convention in Denver, Colorado, which proved nearly as wasteful as the last one in Bal Harbour, Florida. While he spent only $200,000 dollars of his members' money on bands, Boyle made up for it by doling out lucrative convention jobs. About one-fourth of the delegates served on committees and were paid an average of $1,500 each, even though most of the committees never met at all. The thirty-nine-member Committee on Appeals and Grievances cost the union over $40,000, but did not hear any appeals or grievances.

Delegates pushed forward countless resolutions urging Boyle to become the union's lifetime president or to accept a doubling of his $50,000-a-year salary, with unlimited expenses. As Boyle pranced across the stage, a folksinger on whom he had squandered union funds sang "The Ballad of Tony Boyle" to the tune of "The Foggy, Foggy Dew." Its final stanza concluded with "God bless the Union and Tony, too."

Democratic presidential nominee Hubert H. Humphrey spoke at the convention in praise of Boyle's trenchant advice and wise counsel. The country's vice president promised to make the UMWA's president a frequent oval-office luncheon companion as soon as he defeated Richard Nixon in that November's presidential election. After the UMWA endorsed him, Humphrey told the cheering delegates that it was Boyle who had talked him into running in the first place against the Republican Party's nominee.

No delegate was more effusive about Boyle than Jock Yablonski, the convention's keynote speaker and the chairman of its Nominating Committee for the UMWA's International Executive Board. "I lack the words which would enable me to describe the love, the devotion, and the respect I have for our distinguished president," he gushed on the convention's opening day. Several days later, he grabbed the microphone again. "Now what are we going to do with this fellow? He won't accept a gift [a television set]. I guess about the only thing we can do is really try to the utmost of our ability to provide the real, honest-to-God support for him and his administration that they deserve!"

Yablonski hated himself for groveling. When reporters later

questioned him about his extravagant lionizing of Boyle, he justified it by saying "that is what you have to do to stay around." He might have added that he wanted to hold on to his $26,000-a-year salary and his pension. He knew Boyle could erase both with the stroke of a pen. Yablonski was part of a generation of miners who had lived through the Great Depression, and who had experienced firsthand the dread of tomorrow and the fear of financial insecurity that came with it.

He also knew he had to stay in the UMWA if he was going to have any hope of becoming its president. A candidate had to be a member of the union to run for office. Yablonski believed that Boyle would not force him out as long as he was useful and did what he was told.

On April 20, 1969, Boyle launched his election campaign for another five-year term as the UMWA's president. He was facing only token opposition—from Steve Kochis, the underground machine operator whom he'd trounced in 1964, Elijah Wolford, a locomotive driver, and Basil Callen, a coal loader—but Boyle was taking no chances. He gave his first speech in West Virginia, the locus of the black lung revolt. He asked Jock Yablonski, the union's best orator, to join him on the campaign trail to be his opening act.

Many who heard his servile speeches forgot Yablonski had ever criticized Boyle. In countless dreary little coal towns, he praised Boyle's inspiring leadership and lashed out against those miners who allowed themselves to be misled by the UMWA's growing chorus of critics. Boyle fed off Yablonski's lavish encomiums and used the energy they stirred to play to the miners' xenophobia. He blamed Big Oil, insurance companies, and even communists for the union's growing list of troubles.

But Yablonski never relaxed around his rival. Boyle kept pushing him to give up his seat on the union's International Executive Board by not running for reelection in 1970. He tried to entice Yablonski to do that by appointing him the acting head of Labor's Non-Partisan League on April 7, 1969, placing him in charge of all the UMWA's Washington lobbying and legislative activities relating to mining safety. Among his most important tasks was garnering congressional support for what was to become the 1969 Federal Coal Mine Health and Safety Act, groundbreaking legislation, which contained a clause granting miners compensation for black lung.

Yablonski was eager for a new challenge and accepted the appointment, but he always changed the subject whenever Boyle pressed him about giving up his seat on the union's board. Yablonski feared that Boyle, after he won another term as the UMWA's president and no longer needed him, was going to fire him as soon as he resigned from the board.

Yablonski realized he was quickly running out of options. When Boyle had forced him to give up his District 5 presidency in 1966, he promised himself he would make him pay. That day had yet to come, and, as time wore on, looked like it might not. That was about to change.

THREE

Free at Last

While Tony Boyle basked in the 1968 convention's limelight, he and his family looted the union's treasury. Dick Boyle, a brother, raked off $36,000 a year in salary and expenses as District 27's president. Though the entire district had only 870 miners, he routinely billed the union for "organizing" expenses, once in 1967 for $17,000, although no new members were added to the district's membership rolls. Antoinette Boyle Engebregson, Tony's daughter, was the district lawyer. Her salary was $40,000 a year—nearly $300,000 today—as much as the UMWA's general counsel earned. She had so little work that she did not have a union office and kept all her private clients.

When the press confronted him about his relatives on the union payroll, Boyle was dumbfounded. "What the hell do you want me to do?" he snapped at a reporter. "Fire them?"

Ralph Nader, the consumer champion and safety advocate, was not going to let Boyle get away with stealing from the union's treasury and neglecting its miners' safety. He was especially enraged by the UMWA president's comments after Number 9 was sealed. Boyle crowed publicly that he was not going "to destroy the coal industry to satisfy the frantic rantings of self-appointed and ill-informed saviors of coal miners." More pointedly, he told a congressional committee that the UMWA was not going to interfere with the way coal operators ran their mines.

Nader dropped a bombshell on the union boss in a six-page April 26, 1969, letter to Ralph Yarborough, chairman of the Senate's powerful Committee on Labor and Public Welfare. Nader reported that the union's Welfare and Retirement Fund kept $70 million in an interest-free checking account in the National Bank of Washington, of which the UMWA owned 75 percent in stock. The coal miners earned no interest on this money, but while retired miners' pensions and benefits were being reduced or eliminated, the UMWA-owned bank reaped over $3 million a year in dividends. Between 1964 and 1969, Boyle earned over $30,000—more than $215,000 today—in bank director's fees. Bored, he often slept through the bank's board meetings.

Nader also revealed that Boyle had conspired with John Owens, the UMWA's treasurer, to siphon off $850,000—the equivalent of $7 million now—from the union's retirement assets to a special account in the National Bank of Washington, in order to fund pensions at full pay for himself, Owens, and Lewis. The union's soft coal pensioners collected a measly $115 a month. Retirees from northeastern Pennsylvania's anthracite coal fields got only $30 a month.

Nader expected little from Yarborough, a cheerleader for Big Labor, but he did expect the newspapers to pick up the story, and the *Washington Post* and the *Washington Evening Star* published lengthy pieces on his findings.

Boyle unleashed the *United Mine Workers Journal*, the union's notoriously sycophantic bimonthly news tabloid, on Nader, who was branded a "fink" and "instant expert" in front-page stories. While it attacked him, it glorified Boyle. Its May 15, 1969, issue had twenty-eight pictures of him sprinkled among its twenty-four pages.

Throughout that spring, Nader continued to hammer away at Boyle's corruption. From the pages of the *Washington Post* to the halls of Capitol Hill, he accused Boyle of plundering the union's pension fund, enriching himself and his family from its treasury, and turning his back on the health and safety of the UMWA's coal miners.

Yablonski did not know Nader, but his nephew did. Steven Yablonski was a young partner at Rowley and Watts, a law firm in Washington, D.C., specializing in antitrust cases; he met Nader in late 1968 when the firm worked with the consumer advocate on some automobile safety cases.

When Steven told Nader that his uncle Jock Yablonski was upset by how much the UMWA had deteriorated under Boyle's rule, Nader was intrigued. He asked to set up a meeting with Yablonski, and Yablonski agreed. He was astonished that an outsider knew so much about the UMWA's dirty laundry. He was also enthralled. Nader was his hero; the consumer advocate had faced and overcome great odds when he had confronted General Motors so publicly about its callous refusal to build safe cars. Yablonski was ashamed that his union, once a major catalyst for progressive social change, was so openly hostile to one of the country's most brilliant activists.

They met late at night on May 3, 1969, in an office at Rowley and Watts at 1730 Rhode Island Avenue, N.W., in Washington. After both men agreed the UMWA had fallen into the hands of criminals, Nader leaned forward and asked Yablonski if he would run against Boyle in the union's December presidential election.

Yablonski sat in stunned silence while Nader, who made no specific promises, pledged his "all-out support." Star-struck, he never asked Nader what that meant.

When he finally collected himself, Yablonski said something that would haunt those who attended the meeting for years to come: "If I do run, Ralph, they'll try to kill me." Nader, insulated by his Harvard Law School and Washington sensibilities, shot back, "They wouldn't dare—you will be in a goldfish bowl."

Yablonski knew better: those who challenged Big Labor often paid with their lives. Just three years before, corrupt union bosses had gunned down Dow Wilson and Lloyd Green, instigators of a Brotherhood of Painters, Decorators, and Paperhangers' uprising in San Francisco. Shotgun blasts in the dead of night killed both men.

Yet change could happen. Rising resentment among rank-and-file members, brought on mostly by a sense of alienation, had swept at least one powerful union boss out of power. In 1965, I. W. Abel, the secretary-treasurer of the United Steelworkers of America, unseated David J. McDonald, its tweedy, tone-deaf president. The election was badly stained by allegations of voting fraud, but Abel won. He relied heavily on the ballot-challenging provisions of the Labor Management Reporting and Disclosure Act of 1959. Popularly known as the Landrum-Griffin Act—its principal sponsors were Representative Phillip M. Landrum (D-Georgia) and Senator Robert P. Griffin (R-Mich.)—Congress passed it in 1959 to curtail labor union violence and autocratic rule by increasing the democratic rights of rank-and-file members.

Yablonski was encouraged by the law's successes. He was also intoxicated by Nader's promise of support, but he held back as he digested the immensity of what the consumer advocate asked him to do. He agreed to meet with him again, but that was all that had been decided by the time the meeting finally broke up in the early morning.

Yablonski flew to Charleston, West Virginia, that same day to introduce Boyle to a large throng of miners who had gathered to hear him rail against the union's enemies. Yablonski stood beside him with a poker face while Boyle warned them that the UMWA's critics were trying to turn it into a "divided house."

Boyle was about to learn just how accurate his warning was.

Ralph Nader was not the only force pushing Yablonski to oppose Tony Boyle. Personal ambition spurred Yablonski on, in part, but there was a subtler force working on him, as well—an awakening social conscience. Monsignor Charles Owen Rice, who officiated at Yablonski's second wedding, later speculated that what drove him to finally take a stand was a need to give his life more meaning.

Yablonski was fifty-nine years old in 1969, only a year from being able to retire and collect a comfortable pension, but after the explosion inside Number 9 and the West Virginia black lung revolt, he could not walk away while the UMWA was in such corrupt, incompetent hands. After one of his sons questioned why he had to challenge Boyle, Yablonski's answer was emphatic: "By God, I have to do it!" He could no longer remain silent, nor could he push for reform inside the union as long as Boyle was leading it. A retirement spent second-guessing a decision not to run against Boyle would be worse than none at all.

Social forces were also driving him to run, especially the burgeoning antiwar movement. As he watched America's college campuses and city streets explode in fire and rage, Yablonski began seeing militant action as the best way to force social change. He was a lifelong Democrat, but he had broken ranks with most of anticommunist organized labor in 1968 by supporting Senator Eugene McCarthy's Vietnam War peace plank at the party's convention that August in Chicago. Yablonski had seen too many flag-draped coffins returning from the rice paddies to the coalfields to back Hubert Humphrey's continuation of President Johnson's hapless war strategy.

The Chicago Police Department's brutal crackdown on the demonstrators during the Democratic Convention deeply offended him. Yablonski spent hours in Grant Park, moving among the protesters listening to their grievances, and even though he voted for Humphrey over Richard Nixon that November, he continued speaking out against the Vietnam War.

On May 1, 1969, he spoke at a May Day rally sponsored by the Students for Democratic Society at the University of Pittsburgh. After praising the students' willingness to stand up for what they believed in, Yablonski drew the loudest applause of the day when he declared that the United States had to "get the hell out of Vietnam because we have no business there!"

Yablonski's wife and daughter reinforced his belief that his time had come. "Marg" was sick of watching her husband defend Boyle's failings. She berated him for becoming Boyle's "flunky," and urged him to enter the union's presidential race. She had no patience for his reluctance, especially after he repeatedly told her how corrupt Boyle was. Yablonski often used his wife as a sounding board, and she rarely held back what she thought. Her sense of injustice was fed by her conversations with him and by the novels and plays of John Steinbeck and Arthur Miller, her two favorite authors.

Margaret Wasicek was the daughter of Slovak immigrants, born on August 8, 1912, in Fairhope, Pennsylvania. Of medium height, with large dark eyes and long raven-colored hair, which she often tied in a knot, Marg studied English for a year at Grove City College before she transferred in 1931 to nearby California State Teachers College. Her father was worried about her finding work during the Depression, and insisted she become an industrial arts teacher. The college's 1933 yearbook described her as "An ultra-modern miss."

After he divorced Anne Huffman, Yablonski met Marg on a blind date. They were married in 1937. She devoted herself to her husband's career and raising their family. Marg believed in the power of education. She set the tone for the household, even posting poetry on the wall of their home's first-floor bathroom for the children to memorize. She converted Yablonski into a serious reader and an opera lover.

He called her the "Duchess," after the Duchess of Windsor, because of the way she styled her dark hair. Marg enjoyed raising eyebrows. She often sprinkled her conversations with salty expletives.

Marg wrote her first play in 1945. Fueled by coffee and cigarettes, she went on to write several that were good enough to be produced in summer stock and at the Pittsburgh Playhouse. A New York City production company offered her a contract as a screenwriter, but she turned it down; she could not leave the coalfields because of Yablonski's career. Marg continued to write, however, and had written nearly sixty plays by 1969.

Yablonski blamed himself for sidetracking his wife's career. He knew that her education and tastes set her apart from her Clarksville neighbors, some of whom considered her aloof. He brooded about this.

He confided to a relative that he was going to make this up to her once he became the UMWA's president.

While Marg was outspoken in prodding him to run, his daughter appealed quietly to his growing belief that the UMWA owed more to its members than just a paycheck. Charlotte was only twenty-five years old, but the director of West Virginia University's School of Social Work already rated her as one of that program's most creative and accomplished graduates. Her father wanted her to become lawyer or a teacher, but she blossomed when she took a job as a grant writer and a mental health counselor at a coal miners' health clinic after graduating from college.

An intelligent, sensitive young woman with jet-black hair, Charlotte believed that most of the mental health problems she witnessed in the coalfields stemmed from poverty and lack of opportunity. She wanted to change this. Charlotte returned to West Virginia University in 1966 to become a social worker, and while there she became a disciple of community activist Saul Alinsky's theories on grassroots organizing. After she graduated a year later, Charlotte moved to Pittsburgh, where she counseled drug addicts in the city's largely African American Hill District.

She moved back to West Virginia in 1968 and became the director of Monongalia County's Office of Economic Opportunity. Located in the heart of the state's north-central coalfields, the county had one of the highest poverty rates in the nation. It lacked paying jobs, decent housing, adequate medical care, and good schools.

Charlotte was not uninterested in romance—a doctor living in Ohio had asked her to marry him and, until recently, she had dated an amateur actor who performed at the Little Lake Theatre in Canonsburg, Pennsylvania, until he moved to San Francisco—but she focused mostly on her career. When a reporter asked her what she did in her spare time, Charlotte replied, "Tell me what that is," although she admitted she enjoyed "reading and having people over and just sitting and talking." Most of that talk centered around making life better for Monongalia County's poor.

Her vivid descriptions of the human misery she confronted there deeply affected Yablonski. Why, he asked himself, had the UMWA not done anything to address this suffering? Charlotte encouraged him to make the union once again a powerful driver of social and economic justice.

Yablonski's two lawyer sons were more cautious about whether their father should run for the union's presidency, playing the role of devil's advocates. Chip, who was an appeals attorney for the National Labor Relations Board in Washington, D.C., and Ken, who practiced in nearby Washington, Pennsylvania, and represented some of the UMWA's members, handling mostly workman's compensation cases arising from mining accidents, worried about what the campaign would do to their father.

During one discussion, Ken turned to his father and warned him "either you will destroy them or they will destroy you." He would be right about both.

While Yablonski weighed his chances of toppling Boyle, Nader continued his one-man crusade to spark a rank-and-file uprising. On May 22, he publicly appealed to John L. Lewis to lead a revolt to oust the UMWA's current leader. He wrote a four-page letter to the eighty-nine-year-old Lewis—simultaneously sent to the *Washington Post* and the *New York Times*—cataloging Boyle's corruption. While Nader had aired most of these charges in his April letter to Senator Ralph Yarborough, he claimed this time that Boyle was plotting to remove Lewis as a trustee of the union's pension fund and to usurp that position for himself.

Nader recognized that Lewis was the architect of the undemocratic and authoritarian system about which he was complaining, but he knew that the old autocrat remained personally popular in the coalfields. Nader wanted to encourage the widespread, but still disorganized, rank-and-file opposition to Boyle by linking Lewis's name to it. He did not expect nor want Lewis himself to lead a palace coup.

Yablonski tried to enlist Lewis, too. Rumors about his growing dissatisfaction with Boyle trickled out of his inner circle, with Lewis reportedly telling his confidants that appointing Boyle was "the worst mistake I ever made." Yablonski's hopes rose even more when he heard that Lewis had rebuffed Boyle's attempts to enlist him in lashing out at Nader. "They built that cesspool over there," he growled to a fellow union pension fund trustee. "Let them drown in their own slime." Lewis, in an astonishing about face, excused himself and deserted Tony Boyle, the man he brought to Washington in 1948.

Lewis's endorsement would give Yablonski's candidacy a tremendous shot in the arm, boosting its appeal among the union's rank and file. He called Lewis on May 25 to set up a meeting, but the elderly chieftain was too ill. Lewis did not embrace Yablonski's candidacy—perhaps he realized that Yablonski was running against his authoritarian legacy as much as Boyle—but he did not oppose it, either. He, too, was troubled by how far the UMWA had declined.

As he waited for Lewis, Yablonski decided to run for the union's highest office. It had taken nine more meetings with Ralph Nader—after the last one, Yablonski had downed a double Scotch to steady his shaking hands—but he had finally rejected the sycophantic mystique of the labor union to which he had devoted his life. He agreed to run against Tony Boyle.

Yablonski knew he would need the best lawyer he could get once he officially declared his candidacy; Boyle would do whatever he could to sabotage his campaign. Worth Rowley, a partner at the law firm of Rowley and Watts, suggested Yablonski meet with Joseph L. Rauh Jr.

Rauh was one of the country's most skilled and well-known civil rights lawyers. A list of his cases and clients reads like an anthology of American liberalism. He had battled Senator Joseph McCarthy and the House Un-American Activities Committee, laid the foundation for much of the nation's civil rights legislation of the 1960s, and held leadership roles in the progressive organizations Americans for Democratic Action, the National Association for the Advancement for Colored

People, and the Leadership Conference on Civil Rights. His clients included playwrights Lillian Hellman and Arthur Miller, the United Auto Workers, longtime head of the Brotherhood of Sleeping Car Porters A. Philip Randolph, the homeless, and the disenfranchised.

Rauh, who stood just over six feet, two inches—he had played center for Harvard's basketball team—and who always wore stylish bow ties fastened under the collars of his Oxford cloth button-down shirts, towered over the much shorter Yablonski. After he listened to the insurgent's pitch, Rauh peered through his horn-rimmed glasses and told him in his rich baritone voice, "If you had come into my office with a paying case, I wouldn't have taken it. I'm so busy. But this isn't a case. It is a crusade. Just tell me what you want me to do." Rauh agreed to serve as the campaign's chief counsel.

Like Nader, Rauh saw something much bigger in Yablonski's campaign than one election. If Yablonski could win control of one of the most undemocratic unions in the United States, his victory would inspire reformers in other labor unions to challenge their corrupt and ossified leaders. "This will be a hell of a fight," Rauh told reporters prophetically, "and win or lose, the union will be different and better when it's over."

Three years later, the civil rights lawyer vividly recalled that day: "In his straightforward way, Yablonski told me that he had decided to run for the presidency of the UMWA, that he would probably be killed before the fight was over, but that he had to do it." Rauh knew Martin Luther King Jr. and Bobby Kennedy well, but he always said that Jock Yablonski's decision to risk his life for the country's coal miners was the greatest act of courage and moral fiber he ever saw.

Shortly before eleven o'clock in the morning of May 29, 1969, Yablonski walked into the oblong-shaped Pan American Room at the Mayflower Hotel, took a seat at a U-shaped table beside Rauh, and faced the banked microphones and news cameras. The night before, Nader had called several of the city's leading newspapers and television networks in Washington and cryptically told them that a UMWA official

was going to make a major announcement the next morning. Lured by
Nader's flair for the dramatic, reporters, with quizzical looks on their
faces, waited for the stocky, well-dressed man sitting at the table to
begin speaking.

Slowly but deliberately Yablonski read a fourteen-page statement.
It oozed with Nader's influence; the public's watchdog had written it
as a call to arms to revive the country's labor movement. In a voice
made raw by chain-smoking cigarettes and La Corona cigars, he
told the gathered reporters that he was going to oppose Boyle in the
UMWA's December presidential election. He had decided to do this,
he explained, because of "the insufferable gap between the union's
leaders and the working men they were supposed to represent."

Yablonski charged Boyle with "striking ineptitude and passivity" in
not pressing more vigorously for mine safety reforms, and accused him
of adopting an "abject follow-the-leader posture toward the coal industry." He also charged him with running a "dictatorial" and "decaying"
administration that was "riddled with fear."

As he faced the cameras, Yablonski admitted that his own hands
were not clean. He had spent too much time and effort shoring up a
regime that had outlived its time. Haunted by an "increasingly troubled
conscience," Yablonski vowed no longer to be a prisoner of the past.

He spelled out a ten-point platform that Congressman Ken Hechler
would soon trumpet as the coal miners' Magna Carta. It went far
beyond the dollar-and-cents issues that had so long captured the
UMWA's attention. Yablonski promised to greatly expand the union's
one-man safety division, push for federal and state black lung legislation, call a special convention to draft procedures so that miners
could elect their own district officers, run a transparent administration, increase the royalty paid by coal operators into the UMWA's Welfare and Retirement Fund (it still stood at the forty-cents-a-ton rate
Lewis had negotiated in 1952), and maintain an arms-length relationship with the coal industry. He said he would serve for only one term
if elected and would support the mandatory retirement of all union
officials at age sixty-five.

Most radically, he pledged to use the UMWA's vast resources to improve Central Appalachia's woefully inadequate schools, expand its sparse social services, and establish credit unions for its miners. He vowed to force the big coal companies, many of them absentee owners of the region's boundless natural resources, to play a major role in this reformation. Yablonski wanted them to pay their fair share of taxes, something unheard of in state houses gorged with the coal industry's lobbying money.

He also wanted the union to force the coal companies to clean up the region's polluted streams and smoking slag heaps. One burning slag heap in Greenbriar County, West Virginia, was nearly two miles long, one hundred feet deep, and five stories high. Thick yellow smog clung to the county's valleys and hills.

Yablonski cautioned the assembled newsmen that none of this was going be easy; these reforms might cost him his life. "I'm not naïve enough to think that there won't be much difficulty, and I know the lengths they will go."

When a skeptical newsman asked why he had waited so long to tackle the union's corruption and the region's economic problems, Yablonski, who had been waiting for that question, paraphrased the seventeenth-century English poet George Herbert: "When ye be an anvil, lay ye very still. But when ye be a hammer, strike with all thy will." He drew a deep breath and looked at the assembled reporters. He ended with a dramatic flourish: "Today is the day I cease being an anvil!"

He then turned to Rauh and muttered a refrain the veteran civil rights attorney knew well: "Thank God I am free at last."

Yablonski had unshackled himself from his past, but he was about to face a far more dangerous future.

FOUR

Yablonski Ought to Be Killed

Tony Boyle was sitting at his desk only four blocks away when a reporter from *Newsweek* called the union's press office to get his reaction to Jock Yablonski's announcement. When a secretary told him the news, Boyle was incredulous.

He had met with Yablonski for almost four hours the day before to talk about mine safety legislation, and everything had seemed so normal. His old rival had been respectful and, more important, deferential, but Yablonski had fooled him.

Some in the union's hierarchy had thought Yablonski might be planning to topple George Titler, the union's rotund vice-president, but his bid for the top office came as a terrible surprise, especially to Boyle—who had believed all the wonderful things Yablonski said about him while they were traveling together through West Virginia's coalfields. After he recovered from his shock, Boyle screamed at his assistants to comb through the UMWA's cavernous file room and bring him every speck of dirt on Yablonski they could find.

Yablonski expected Boyle to wage a scorched earth campaign. He needed Lewis's endorsement. He called him again on June 1; Lewis was still too sick to meet now, but he suggested the second week of June.

The next morning, Yablonski attended an International Executive Board meeting chaired by Boyle. The atmosphere was icy and neither man spoke to the other. That afternoon, Yablonski conferred

with Rauh, who told him to send a certified letter to Boyle, reminding him of his legal responsibility under federal law to conduct a fair
election.

Under the union's constitution, Yablonski first had to win the nominations of at least fifty of the union's nearly 1,300 locals before his
name could be placed on the December ballot. In his letter, Yablonski
asked Boyle to instruct all paid union staff employees to take a "hands-
off" attitude, to have the union mail out his campaign literature at his
own expense, and to order the *United Mine Workers Journal* to cover
both campaigns fairly and equally.

Boyle's reply came quickly. On June 4, he convened a special meeting of the union's district presidents to discuss how to deal with
Yablonski's treason and insurgency. Its recommendations were dra-
conian, ranging from circulating a recall petition in District 5 to putting him on trial for leaking confidential union information to Ralph
Nader. The district presidents also discussed compiling a dossier on
Yablonski's criminal past that they could send to Nader, Rauh, and
Hechler, and auditing Local 1787, his home chapter in District 5, for
fraud and theft.

Two days later, Boyle fired Yablonski as the acting director of Labor's
Non-Partisan League and ordered him to return to District 5, where
Mike Budzanoski, its president and a Boyle loyalist, would reassign
him. Rauh threatened to sue the union immediately if Boyle did not
reinstate his client, but the union leader did not respond.

Worse news came on June 11: Lewis died that morning of internal
bleeding. This was a crushing blow. His backing of Yablonski's campaign, or even his continued silence, would have greatly raised the
insurgent's chances. Boyle, meanwhile, capitalized on Lewis's death.
In a special tribute issue, the *United Mine Workers Journal* peddled
the fiction that Boyle was Lewis's handpicked protégé, but the two men
were never close. In the 1960s, it was not uncommon at noon to walk
into the opulent dining room of Washington's Carlton Hotel and see
each man eating his lunch alone.

That made no difference to the editors of the tribute issue. There were almost as many photos of Boyle as there were of the late union boss decorating its pages, including one of him on his knees, praying at Lewis's grave.

With Lewis out of the way, Boyle rejected Yablonski's requests to wage a fair campaign. Rauh fought back using the same strategies he used during the civil rights movement, immediately turning to the federal courts and their immense powers to dispense justice. The veteran trial lawyer's strategies paid off: on June 20, United States District Court Judge Howard Corcoran ordered the UMWA to distribute Yablonski's campaign literature.

Unfazed, Boyle convened another meeting of the union's International Executive Board on June 23. He asked the board to name him Lewis's replacement as the union trustee for the Welfare and Retirement Fund, which would give him access to millions more of the UMWA's dollars. After it rubber-stamped Boyle's appointment, the board took up his resolution to fire and reassign Yablonski, which Boyle told his assembled acolytes he had done because the rebel candidate opposed the union's policies. Yablonski was the only member who did not vote in favor of the resolution. He insisted Boyle had fired him because of his candidacy, but most of his stone-faced fellow board members simply stared at him as he and Boyle shouted at one another. Three who did speak accused Yablonski of treason.

Albert Pass, who had provided the storm troopers to police the union's 1964 convention in Bal Harbour, Florida, and who was now the board member from the UMWA's District 20 in Alabama as well as the secretary-treasurer of its District 19, had heard enough.

He rose to his feet and glared at Yablonski through the thick lenses of his black steel-framed glasses. His face knotted in disapproval as his emotions overtook him—as if he were in the throes of one of the Sunday sermons he loved—and he spoke in the coded language of the Kentucky hills to threaten Yablonski's life. "We have a great union and we are going to keep our union. President Boyle!" Pass shouted. "We are not gonna leave you and the other officers sitting out in that field and these damn fellas behind the bushes shooting at you out there by yourself! By God, we will run them out from behind those bushes! We are going to back you! Thank you very much!"

Since Yablonski's shocking announcement, Boyle had mulled over how to punish his longtime rival. As president of the country's wealthiest labor union, he could easily hire battalions of publicists, strategists, and lawyers to guarantee his reelection, but merely defeating Yablonski would not be enough. Yablonski was a traitor and an informant. He had been one of them, a member of the union's inner circle. His treason was as bad as Judas Iscariot's.

Yablonski's treachery violated the unbreakable rules of loyalty and kinship that sustained the union's rigid hierarchy. Equally unforgivable, he had defied Boyle and openly questioned his authority in front of the entire International Executive Board. Taking down Yablonski would send a stark message to anyone else who might be foolish or reckless enough to challenge Tony Boyle—and would also end his threats to expose Boyle's corruption. "I've played every inning of this ballgame," Yablonski had confided to one reporter. "I know what goes on. I know this game from A to Z." He knew where the UMWA's buried bodies were, and understood better than anyone that Boyle held on to his throne by using the UMWA's money to buy loyalty and to spread fear.

After the board meeting ended, Boyle followed Pass and William Turnblazer Jr., the lawyerly, bespectacled president of District 19, into the hallway outside the board's third floor conference room. "We are in a fight," he told them. "Yablonski ought to be killed or done away with." Pass knew an order when he heard one. He stepped forward: District 19 would do it if no other district wanted the honor. "Fine," Boyle replied, as if he had just ordered a sandwich. The conversation took less than a minute.

This was not the first time Pass had stepped forward to deal with someone who challenged the union's authority.

Albert Pass became District 19's secretary-treasurer in 1952, just as mass mechanization began driving its miners out of work. Two years earlier, John L. Lewis had done the unthinkable. He entered into an agreement with the newly formed Bituminous Coal Operators' Association, which owned nearly half the coal mined in the United States. In exchange for higher pay for his miners and increased royalty payments to the union's Welfare and Retirement Fund, he promised peace in the coalfields. He also agreed that coal companies could speed up mechanizing their mines.

Steady production now meant as much to the UMWA as it did to the coal operators, and safety, such as that inside Number 9, took a distant back seat to tons of coal mined. Mechanization cost over 300,000 coal miners their jobs, health insurance, and pensions. Between 1948 and 1964, over one million Appalachians lost their primary means of support. They sank into poverty while long freight trains dragged away the wealth from their mineral-rich mountains, leaving them nothing.

Lewis's bargain also ignited a war. In 1953, big coal operators began openly criticizing the UMWA for not organizing the northern Tennessee and southeastern Kentucky coalfields. Nonunion mines, which took advantage of this vast surplus of out-of-work miners, began to grow rapidly in numbers. By the early 1950s, they accounted for about 20 percent of the working mines in District 19, and they were winning competitive, cut-rate contracts with the government's Tennessee Valley Authority, slicing into the profits of major coal companies, which had labor agreements with the UMWA.

Coal barons urged Lewis to unionize or drive these mines out of business. Lewis ordered Tony Boyle to organize them and "damn the lawsuits." While most of America basked in the "normalcy" of the mid-1950s, his command ignited a guerrilla war in northern Tennessee and eastern Kentucky's hollows and hills. To wage it, Boyle turned to his old staples of beatings, bullets, and dynamite.

He found a willing accomplice in Pass as District 19 descended into a febrile cycle of violence, revenge, and no remorse. Boyle and Pass used the UMWA's money to threaten, brutalize, and kill non-union men. Small coal operators, following the region's Old Testament beliefs, retaliated by assassinating union organizers.

Bloodshed excited Albert Pass as much as a fire-and-brimstone Sunday sermon, and his frequent use of it highlighted his split personality. He was both a cold-blooded killer and a devoted family man. He could order the assassination of the owner of a small "dog hole" mine on a Saturday morning and patiently spoon-feed a daughter who had cerebral palsy that same afternoon. He sprang from an eye-for-an-eye society, which distinguished between a killing, something necessary, and a murder, which was a sin.

Pass commanded a small army of willing henchmen. William Jackson Prater was Pass's field commander in District 19's war against independent coal operators. He was as gifted at buying guns without serial numbers as he was at finding those who could use them. Pass always turned to him when he needed something blown up or someone terrorized. Prater's favorite enforcer was Silous Huddleston, his close friend and a brutal mountain man who once beat a man bloody with a chain after he refused to join the union.

Among Pass's most important duties was the care and feeding of the "Jones Boys," his district's terrorist wing. They were named after the legendary Industrial Workers of the World organizer Mary Harris "Mother" Jones.

The Jones Boys roamed the countryside in packs of cars and pickup trucks, and specialized in intimidation, destruction, and assassination. District 19 became infamous in the UMWA for its shotgun blasts in the night, for baseball bat beatings, and for automobile accidents that were not accidents. Their softer methods ranged from "cowbelling" union foes—locking a cowbell around an offender's neck with a heavy chain and padlock—to "baptizing" recalcitrant operators by holding them face down in rocky creeks, "in the name of John L. Lewis."

On April 11, 1955, the Jones Boys stripped naked John Van Huss, a small nonunion mine owner, and nearly drowned him in a shallow drainage ditch. After they had beaten him senseless, they drove him into the ground like a fence post and forced his miners at gunpoint to curse at him and punch him in the head.

That June, the local prosecutor tried nine UMWA members in the Campbell County, Tennessee, courthouse for Van Huss's attempted murder. Albert Pass, his shirtsleeves rolled up and arms folded, stood in the back of the courtroom, staring at the jury. He was not alone. He had packed the courtroom with his "boys," their coat pockets sagging under the weight of their loaded pistols. It took the jury less than an hour to acquit Van Huss's attackers.

The Kentucky National Guard and federal judges, not intimidated by mountain mores, finally stanched the bloodshed by the end of 1959. Lewis and Boyle never worried about any of this being traced to them; they knew the union's code of silence would shield them from being blamed for causing this death and mayhem.

The UMWA's war against the small operators damaged more than its ethics, however. Lawsuits for property damage cost its treasury millions; by the end of June 1959, small coal operators were asking the United States District Court for the Eastern District of Tennessee alone for more than $15 million in damages. No other labor union in American history has been found liable in so many jury trials for violent conduct. It was all for nothing: the UMWA faced as many nonunion mines in 1959 as it had when its Jones Boys drove Van Huss into the ground in 1955.

Bitter and frustrated, Pass found himself presiding over a district that was losing members and drowning in fear. Nearly 20,000 coal miners had belonged to District 19 in 1947, but by 1964, it had fewer than 5,000. Poverty skyrocketed as union miners lost their pensions and health benefits. District 19's treasury needed constant cash transfusions from the UMWA's Washington headquarters to keep it afloat. Between 1963 and 1968, the union pumped $3,702,159 into District 19, far more money than it sent to any other.

While Pass felt his grip weakening, Theodore Quentin Wilson felt his tightening. Wilson, a lawyer and one of the UMWA's most strident foes, founded the rival Southern Labor Union in 1955 and served as its general counsel. The SLU was friendly to coal companies, tailored its contracts to individual mines, and had no hefty Welfare and Retire Fund to support. By 1966, it was growing in strength in District 19, while the UMWA's continued to fade.

As Pass ruminated over what to do about this threat, one of his two sons was killed in a car wreck. Denny Pass was only eighteen years old. Shattered, Pass withdrew from the world, deep in grief, and threw himself more and more into his union work to escape his sadness. He convinced himself that only the UMWA had treated him fairly in life. He renewed his dedication to ridding it of its enemies.

Pass returned to his old ways. In the spring of 1968, he ordered William Prater and Silous Huddleston to blow up the SLU's headquarters. After that, he compiled a list of its officials to assassinate. Wilson's name was first.

He directed Prater and Huddleston to oversee Wilson's assassination. Huddleston asked Lucy Gilly, his favorite daughter, to help him find a killer. She lived in a tough East Cleveland, Ohio, neighborhood populated by Appalachian refugees, and it did not take her long to find one of them desperate enough to do it.

Robert Gail Tanner was a short-order cook who devoted himself to making chicken-fried steaks by day—he had perfected that skill as a prison-trained cook—and breaking into people's houses at night. An out-of-work coal miner from Clarksburg, West Virginia, with a belly full of bleeding ulcers and pockets stuffed with Rolaids, Tanner had turned to cooking and stealing when he moved to Cleveland. He was chronically short on cash to support his wife and children, and readily agreed to murder Wilson when Lucy offered him $10,000 and the use of a car to do it.

Tanner's appetite for stolen goods derailed his big payday. The police arrested him after he broke into a house in a Cleveland suburb and a housewife came out of the shadows and sprayed him with buckshot from her shotgun. A judge sentenced him to serve two years in prison.

Tanner's arrest and Boyle's request to kill Yablonski sidetracked Pass's plans to kill Wilson. His new plans to assassinate Yablonski were almost scuttled in late June 1969 by another Boyle loyalist who had his own plans to kill the insurgent.

Four days after Boyle gave the order to kill him, Yablonski flew to Springfield, Illinois. His strongest support lay in Pennsylvania and West Virginia, but he knew that nearly 10,000 miners lived in Illinois's southern coalfields. George Morris, a local union president, invited him to meet with a group of union field representatives and miners at the State House Inn. Though he promised Yablonski a friendly audience, it was anything but. What Yablonski did not know was that Morris and four others who attended were on Boyle's personal payroll.

The meeting the next morning attracted only fifteen UMWA members. It lasted for almost an hour in the suite Yablonski had reserved. As it was breaking up, the insurgent candidate was leaning on a table talking to one of the miners about his campaign when a vicious karate chop from behind him landed just below his right ear.

The blow knocked him out for nearly a half hour. When he woke up, his arms were numb. He rolled over on his stomach and crawled to a chair. Morris, who claimed he did not see the attacker, urged Yablonski not to call the police. The bad publicity would hurt his campaign. Yablonski, who wanted out of Springfield as quickly as possible, reluctantly agreed.

When he arrived home in Clarksville, he told one of his brothers what had happened. "They are trying to kill me. They are going to continue trying to kill me," he said as Marg held a bag of ice over his badly bruised neck. The karate chop had smashed into the third and fourth vertebrae of his spinal column; a quarter-inch closer would have killed or paralyzed him from the neck down. Yablonski's doctor concluded that the attack was the handiwork of an expert. The blow had been aimed directly at a major nerve center, causing numbness in Yablonski's right hand and right foot.

Joe Rauh lodged a complaint with the Department of Justice, but the government's lawyers were reluctant to investigate Yablonski's claims. Justice officials told the *New York Times* that they were aware of "the political situation" in the UMWA and were determined "not to be used" to promote any candidate. No one was ever prosecuted for the assault.

When a reporter asked him about Yablonski's injury, George Titler smirked. He derided the attack as a hoax the rebel candidate had staged for political purposes. He said the truth was much less dramatic: Yablonski was drunk and tumbled down a flight of stairs. Boyle echoed his vice-president's snide comments, claiming that one of his foe's own supporters had knocked him unconscious.

Boyle was not done with his strong-arm tactics. The next day, a squadron of his hooligans, each paid $20, stormed into a meeting of Yablonski's supporters in Shenandoah, Pennsylvania, and broke it up. Yablonski, confined to his bed in Clarksville, accused Boyle of employing "fascist tactics."

Yablonski was well enough by July 4 to attend a rally for mine health and safety legislation at the Jefferson Memorial in Washington. There he saw Suzanne Richards, one of Boyle's top aides, standing nearby, and he shouted at her that the union would have to kill him to get him out of the race. Five hundred miles away, Albert Pass was planning to do just that.

FIVE

Loyal Union Men

Tony Boyle and Albert Pass met on July 14 at the UMWA's headquarters. As the two men sat alone in Boyle's cavernous office, the diminutive president told his violent lieutenant not only that Yablonski had to be killed, but that it had to be done as quickly as possible. As the two men sat across from one another, Boyle spun a web of lies that appealed to Pass's conspiratorial mind. Big oil companies, he claimed, were plotting to take over the UMWA. Yablonski was their Trojan horse: he was going to disclose that the union had funneled dues money into the election campaigns of Hubert Humphrey and other friendly politicians, which violated the federal Corrupt Practices Act. Yablonski's admissions could cost Boyle the election and send him to a federal penitentiary.

Pass certainly had no use for the gravelly voiced insurgent. Yablonski had complained to Boyle during the 1964 convention about District 19's heavy-handed storm troopers, and he had offended Pass even more the next year when he came to Knoxville as part of a UMWA fact-finding team. Yablonski, troubled by Pass's failure to add any new members to District 19's dwindling membership rolls, accused him of being lazy and lying to union headquarters about his poor efforts. District 19's strongman was enraged and embarrassed by Yablonski's biting criticisms, and now jumped at the chance to strike back.

Besides, Yablonski was a traitor and a tool of Washington and New

York City outsiders—a greater menace than the SLU's Ted Q. Wilson. Killing him would be an honor and a down payment on the enormous debt District 19 owed the union's headquarters. It would also prove to Tony Boyle that he could always rely on Albert Pass, a loyal union man.

Pass knew the plot to assassinate Yablonski would have to be tightly compartmentalized and ruthlessly executed. He believed there was only one man he could trust to see it through. Pass summoned him as soon as he arrived home in Middlesboro.

William Prater was Pass's right hand, but he never felt comfortable around his mercurial boss. He considered himself better educated—he had attended Purdue University for four months after he got out of the Navy in 1945—more polished, and more businesslike than Pass, who always wore white socks with his dark suits. He also did not like Pass's explosive temper tantrums or his rapid mood swings, which by the summer of 1969, had only gotten worse.

Pass repeatedly berated Prater and his other field representatives for their poor organizing results. He began threatening them with losing their jobs. Only he, Pass warned them, stood between them and poverty. Prater made $10,000 a year as one of District 19's organizers and troubleshooters, which he used to support his wife and seven children. Pass's threats made him a scared and worried man.

His fears and anxieties rose after Pass summoned him in mid-July for a private meeting at District 19's Middlesboro, Kentucky, headquarters. Pass, afraid of being overheard, talked to Prater in his car as the red-faced field representative drove through the district's back roads. Pass told him Yablonski had to be "knocked off." He was in the hands of Big Oil, which wanted to destroy the union. Yablonski also knew too much about the union's corruption. They would both go to jail if he became the union's president.

Pass asked Prater if he knew anyone who would kill Yablonski for $5,000. Prater did not, but he agreed to think it over. He had never questioned Pass, and he was not about to start.

As Prater drove back to his home in LaFollette, Tennessee, he thought about what Pass wanted. While he agreed Yablonski was a treacherous turncoat, murdering a member of his own labor union was something even he had never done. This would require a professional killer, an outsider who could not be traced to the UMWA.

Prater could not go to the Mafia with his problem. The UMWA had no connections to organized crime—it was too xenophobic for that. He could turn to only one man, a retired miner who knew hard men with no ties to the union. Prater had worked with him before to find an assassin willing to murder Wilson. They could work together again to find someone to kill Jock Yablonski.

Silous Huddleston was as rough as the tree-clad hills he came from. He joined the UMWA in 1933 at the age of twenty-five and mastered using dynamite to open up thick, cord-like seams of soft coal. He did not confine his newly learned skills to coal seams, however; he applied his knowledge aboveground to terrorize the union's enemies. He worked at various times as a miner and an organizer; in between, he became one of the UMWA's fiercest advocates and most bloodthirsty enforcers. His organizing philosophy was simple. He once lectured a relative that there were two things that kept a man from working in a nonunion mine: "principle and stark fear." He believed in deploying plenty of the second if the first failed.

Huddleston's zealotry nearly cost him his life. In July 1946, coal company guards tired of his pro-union proselytizing waylaid him, shooting him in the thigh. While he recovered, he bought and ran a small café. Short of money, he robbed one of his own customers that fall. A judge sentenced him to serve three years at the Brushy Mountain State Penitentiary near Petros, Tennessee. He "pulled" twenty-four months of it. (James Earl Ray, the convicted assassin of Martin Luther King Jr., would later serve time at Brushy Mountain.)

Huddleston was released for good behavior in 1948, and returned to the mines until 1963, when his coal dust–coated lungs finally forced him aboveground for good. Prater had helped Huddleston get his pension when he retired, and the two men became close friends and often traveled together across District 19.

While digging coal was behind him, beating up the union's enemies was not. In 1965, Huddleston, now the president of a UMWA local composed solely of retirees, and a pack of union toughs bloodied Steve Kochis in a Wheeling, West Virginia, parking lot. Kochis had run unsuccessfully against Tony Boyle the year before, and he still opposed the union president.

Pass and Prater were disappointed that Robert Gail Tanner had gone to jail before he could kill Ted Q. Wilson, but they were pleased by Huddleston's initiative in finding him. As a reward, Pass sent Huddleston to the UMWA's September 1968 convention in Denver, Colorado, as part of District 19's delegation, and assigned him to "maintain control" of two microphones on the convention's floor.

Huddleston's proudest moment came when he joined a receiving line to meet Boyle, and a union photographer snapped a picture as the beaming hatchet man shook the UMWA president's outstretched hand. He bought three copies and never tired of showing them to his family.

Prater never doubted Huddleston would help him assassinate Yablonski: the old man had a religious faith in his leaders, and he worshiped Boyle. Huddleston carried the ballpoint pen Boyle gave him at the 1968 convention like an amulet. He believed what Pass and Prater told him about Yablonski's conspiring with the big oil companies to destroy the union. The rebel leader threatened Huddleston's way of life. He had to go.

In early August 1969, a stooped, grandfatherly-looking man with a hacking cough boarded a "Hound"—Appalachian shorthand for a Greyhound Bus—for Cleveland. The bus company did not keep passenger manifests; Huddleston wanted to cover his tracks. He was going to see his favorite daughter, Lucy, and talk her husband into finding someone to kill Jock Yablonski.

SIX

Hillbilly Hit Men

Annette "Lucy" Gilly had spent most of her life running from her past. When Huddleston went to prison in 1946, she was only six years old. That same year, she watched her mother die from asphyxiation in a motel room, and her grandmother took her in. Lucy grew up in degrading poverty in the soft coal fields of eastern Tennessee. She was not well educated, but she survived by being cunning. Listening to faraway radio stations at night, she dreamed of living in a big city. She ran away when she was only thirteen years old, married when she was seventeen, and took the "Hillbilly Highway" north to Cleveland.

Lucy was not alone. Nearly 3.3 million Appalachians left their homes between 1950 and 1969 after John L. Lewis's infamous bargain with the big coal companies. Mechanization proved a far more dangerous enemy to their way of life than the company-owned sheriff. Three out of four eastern Kentucky miners were out of work by the mid-1950s. By then, *Look* was calling Central Appalachia America's "underdeveloped country."

Those thrown out of work or forced off their small farms faced two stark choices: they could retreat up the hollows and go on welfare, or leave. For those who decided to flee, their escape valve was the northern city. They flooded into Akron, Detroit, Muncie, Chicago, and Cleveland, where they toiled at unskilled or semiskilled jobs. By 1960, these cities had "little Kentucky" and "little West Virginia" ghettos, where a refugee from the mountains could listen to Hank Williams on the juke box and drink Pabst Blue Ribbon beer. The locals nicknamed them "SAMs"—Southern Appalachian Migrants.

Cleveland, linked to the coalfields by Interstates 71 and 77 and dotted with light and heavy industry, attracted an especially high number of ex-coal miners and their children. Lucy, now divorced, and living on the city's east side, made sandwiches at a kosher delicatessen to support her infant son.

Tall, broad-shouldered, and platinum blonde, with nearly colorless eyes and an expressionless, pale face, Lucy liked to spend her spare time at Cindy's Lounge, a country music bar. She did not drink alcohol anymore, but Cindy's reminded her of her home in Tennessee. She met Paul Eugene Gilly there in 1963. Gaunt and sallow-faced, he owned a small painting company. He seemed to be on the brink of becoming somebody. They married later that November after she became his bookkeeper.

Paul Gilly, the son of a disabled coal miner, was born on March 26, 1933, in Defiance, Kentucky, one of eight children of a coal miner. He spent his childhood moving from coal camp to coal camp along the mountainous Kentucky and Virginia state line. Years later, he was still haunted by the shrill sound of a coal camp's whistle, signaling that another miner had been killed in an underground accident. After the collapse of a mine's roof nearly broke his back, Henry Gilly, Paul's father, bought a small farm, where he struggled to support his family. Even though he had mined coal for thirty-three years, the UMWA told him he did not qualify for a pension. Henry was deeply religious and had been taught never to question God or the union, so he stoically accepted his fate. Paul loved his hard-working, long-suffering father, but he did not want to be like him.

He dropped out of school after the eighth grade, picked tobacco in Kentucky, and then fled, first to Indianapolis and then to Cleveland, where he baked bread, stripped cabinet tops, worked in a metal shop, and put cars together on an assembly line.

Gilly married at nineteen, fathered a child when he was twenty, and divorced his first wife when he was twenty-five. He pulled himself together after his divorce and began working sixteen hours a day. In 1967, Lucy, who always wanted her own business, pestered him into buying the Cozy Corner, a small restaurant. Not satisfied, she prodded him into buying Dalton's, a bigger one, a year later. She always got what she wanted, even though their marriage was falling apart.

Rumors about her, a cot, and men in the restaurant's basement haunted Gilly as he struggled to keep his head above water. Arlin Gibson, Lucy's first husband, had divorced her because she "was running around and drinking." While Lucy had given up alcohol, Gilly was not sure she had given up extramarital affairs. He never completely relaxed when she was with other men.

Too tired most nights to take Lucy out, Gilly watched television while she berated him for being a bore, drinking too much in bars—she refused to let him drink alcohol in their house—and not paying enough attention to her. His poor relations with Ronnie Gibson, Lucy's twelve-year-old son, did not help their marriage. Gilly thought Ronnie was lazy and irresponsible, and he did not mind telling him so, especially after the boy failed to take good care of Peanut, Gilly's pet monkey.

One afternoon, Gilly found Ronnie hiding from him in a closet. He yanked the boy out and beat him with a coat hanger. A doctor sewed up a cut on the boy's left hand and bandaged another one on his shoulder.

Gilly's conflicts with Ronnie were not the only marital problems. Lucy, deprived of her brothers and sisters when she was growing up, regularly invited them and their children to spend weekends with her and Gilly at their Cleveland home. Her relatives emptied Gilly's refrigerator and his bank account. She often gave them money without asking him. This once made him so mad that he left her for ten days, but he could not stay away. He loved Lucy, and her long blonde hair and firm legs could always make him forget their domestic and money problems, if only for a while.

To pick up some much-needed cash, Gilly began spending more and more time in Dalton's basement.

Dalton's—Gilly named it after a friend—was a converted supermarket that seated forty-eight customers and specialized in sandwiches, beef stew, and chili. Gilly was quickly overextended. He could not police the restaurant's staff, who stole from him while he painted houses. One waitress used Dalton's refrigerator and kitchen to feed her family every meal. The restaurant began hemorrhaging money. To make up for the shortages in its cash register, Dalton's began attracting a different sort of clientele.

Its basement became a roosting place for Cleveland's hillbilly underworld whose members were unable or unwilling to adjust to the lake city's industrial rhythms. Nearly everyone in Dalton's basement was guilty of something. The restaurant was soon selling more stolen guns and filched rare coins than bowls of chili and bologna sandwiches, and Gilly began mixing with hardened criminals, like Claude Edward Vealey.

A frequent visitor to Dalton's basement, he was a career petty criminal who believed killing a man was just like shooting a rabbit. Uprooted by mechanization, Vealey's miner father moved his family from West Virginia to Cleveland in 1952, when Claude was nine years old.

Vealey dropped out of school after the ninth grade and drifted from one unskilled job to another. He sold tires, pushed an ice cream cart, and bolted cars together on an assembly line until he realized he could make more money breaking into houses than working. What few attempts he made to go straight, including serving for only two months in the Navy, quickly flipped over in failure.

Vealey was not a reflective man. He did not brood about his failures to keep a steady job or make a right decision. He often froze and retreated into blind drunkenness when he faced a difficult choice. He lived on the razor-thin edge between hard living and self-immolation.

Too drunk to stand and with no moral circuit breakers to override his bad judgment, Vealey once shot his common-law wife in the chest with an M1 carbine. She refused to press charges.

Silous Huddleston knew all about the callous, poorly adjusted men in Dalton's basement who, like Vealey, would do anything for money; Lucy told him. For twenty years, the two had barely spoken. He had walked out of Lucy's life before her mother—Huddleston's second wife—died; he had gone to prison, and remarried for a third time. Lucy was one of his eleven children. But their relationship changed in 1966 after Huddleston's lungs began to fail. He slept sitting in a chair. Fearing her estranged father was dying, she visited him in the hospital. An operation that removed part of one of his lungs saved him. He and Lucy reconciled.

When he visited her in August 1969, Huddleston asked Lucy to talk her husband into finding someone to kill Jock Yablonski. He knew Gilly traded guns in Dalton's basement. "Poor old daddy is about to die," Lucy whined to Gilly. "We have got to do this for him." When that failed, she pouted and sobbed.

Huddleston sensed that his son-in-law was wavering, and applied more pressure. He claimed Yablonski was going to destroy the union, and that Gilly's father, who had never received his union pension, never would if the rebel won the election. Huddleston promised Gilly his father would get his monthly payment if he recruited Yablonski's assassin. His lies did not end there: he said the UMWA would give Gilly a high-paying job and would pay up to a million dollars to get him out of jail if the police arrested him for the murder.

Gilly had never killed anyone. His only brushes with the law were two drunk-in-public charges nearly twenty years before, although he had been shot once in an argument over a woman after a night of antler-rattling in a downtown saloon and robbed at gunpoint one night after leaving a Cleveland bar.

But to save his marriage, to sit one day in what he hoped would be a corner union office, and to get a pension for his father, Paul Gilly agreed to help kill a man he had never seen.

Claude Vealey was doing odd jobs at Nate's Atlantic Service Station on 49th and Superior Avenue in Cleveland in early August 1969 when Gilly approached him while he was having his truck serviced. For Vealey, just released from parole in July, pulling the trigger of a gun would be easier than breaking into houses and changing tires. Gilly chose him because "he was shooting at other people in Cleveland and I heard him bragging about it, so I thought he would be the one to talk to." Vealey seemed to be. His landlady had just evicted him because he had blown out his apartment's windows with a shotgun.

Vealey's only question was how much he would make. Gilly offered him $4,200. Huddleston told Gilly the union would pay $5,000 to kill Yablonski, but he wanted his son-in-law to get an $800 "finder's fee." Forty-two hundred dollars was more money than Vealey had ever seen; if he was lucky, he might clear $200 to $300 for a risky house burglary.

Vealey knew that while he bragged a lot, he had never killed anyone. He would need help carrying out a professional hit. Gilly agreed Vealey could split the money with James Charles Phillips, a thin, worn-looking burglar from Lake City, Tennessee. Vealey first met him in Dalton's basement. Phillips was fascinated with fire, regularly beat his two small children, and walked with a slight limp because he had been shot in his left knee.

Pass was pleased when Prater and Huddleston reported on their progress. In mid-August, he summoned them to his home in Middlesboro, Kentucky, to plan Yablonski's assassination.

He drew a crude street map of Washington, D.C., which showed the UMWA's headquarters building at 900 15th Street, N.W., and nearby McPherson Square, a small park Yablonski walked through every morning on his way to work. Pass told Huddleston that the killers should ambush the insurgent there. Washington had a high crime rate. The police would conclude that Yablonski was just another random victim of a deadly street robbery.

Pass also gave Huddleston Yablonski's photograph, which he tore from a back issue of the *United Mine Workers Journal*. With a pen, he marked it with an arrow and told Huddleston he would pay the assassins $5,000 once he heard about the killing on the evening news.

Huddleston hesitated. What would Pass do if the murder was traced back to him? Huddleston had no desire to return to the Brushy Mountain State Penitentiary. Pass lied to him. "So help me, before God and man," he solemnly swore in his best Sunday school voice, "we'll back you up to a million dollars."

Pass was accustomed to funding the cut-rate Jones Boys. He wanted Yablonski killed for as little money as possible, but even he suspected $5,000 was not enough. Huddleston claimed he had found professional killers; men like that did not come cheaply. When Pass brought his concerns to Tony Boyle, he agreed. They had to come up with a foolproof plan to pay for the assassination. He and Pass talked or met seven times between July 17, 1969, and September 29, 1969.

In the meantime, Gilly wanted to keep Vealey occupied and out of the clutches of the Cleveland Police Department, which kept a thick and growing file on him, so on September 18, at Huddleston's suggestion, Gilly brought Vealey and Aubran Wayne "Buddy" Martin, another career thief from Cleveland, to LaFollette, Tennessee.

Buddy Martin was only twenty-one, but his rap sheet was already two and a half pages long. He was slightly built and wore his wispy blond hair in a ducktail, but what he lacked in size, he made up for in meanness. When he was only eleven, he had grabbed a small boy and threatened to crush his skull with a pool ball after an argument in a bar over a dollar bet with the child's father.

Martin quickly blossomed into a career thief; he was pulling five burglaries a day by the time he was old enough legally to buy a bottle of beer. He sold what he stole in Dalton's basement. He always carried a .25 caliber pistol, had "Little Satan" tattooed on his right forearm, and traveled with a snarling dog he named Big Boy. The dog lapped up bowls of beer in Cleveland's hillbilly bars while his diminutive owner shot pool.

Huddleston proposed burglarizing Ted Q. Wilson's home in nearby Winfield, Tennessee. He told them that Wilson had an arsenal of expensive weapons, and claimed that the SLU leader used them to shoot union pickets.

Huddleston was right about the number of guns: Wilson had twenty-seven rifles, shotguns, pistols, and machine guns scattered throughout his house. The rival union lawyer knew that the UMWA wanted to kill him. While Gilly waited behind the wheel of the getaway car, Vealey and Martin ransacked Wilson's home. They stole all his guns and even the $147 his daughter had saved to buy a horse.

Huddleston and Prater were delighted with the haul, but Pass was not. Burglarizing houses was too risky. He did not want anything to upset his plans to murder Yablonski; he bitterly remembered what had happened to Robert Gail Tanner, the man Huddleston had tapped to murder Wilson a year earlier. He had gone to prison for two years after breaking into a house in Cleveland. But Huddleston argued that the men were restless, and told Pass that the assassins wanted to see the murder money.

Pass redoubled his efforts to raise it. By late September, he and Boyle had constructed an elaborate scheme to use embezzled and laundered union money to pay for Yablonski's assassination. On September 24, Pass wrote directly to Tony Boyle asking for a $10,000 "loan." He claimed District 19 needed the loan to pay for organizing expenses it accumulated between October 1, 1968, and March 31, 1969. He wrote Boyle again on September 30 and requested another loan of $10,000 for "future organizing expenses." Boyle immediately ordered the union's treasurer to deposit $20,000 into District 19's bank account.

After he received the first $10,000 from the union's headquarters in Washington, Pass shepherded his district's six field representatives into his office and told them he needed them to find twenty-three of District 19's most trusted and loyal pensioners. He wanted these men to lie if government auditors later asked them if they had served on a fictitious Research and Information Committee since the fall of 1968. The bogus committee's announced purpose, Pass explained, was to gather information on nonunion activities, to help locate black lung victims who needed compensation, and to "preach the gospel of the union." Its real purpose, he lied, was to launder and kick back money that he could use to defeat the UMWA's political foes in Bell and Harlan counties. Only Boyle, Pass, Prater, and William Turnblazer Jr., District 19's president, knew the money was really going to be used to kill Yablonski.

On September 30 and October 10, the field representatives gave each pensioner a check ranging from $275 to $665 for his committee work "expenses" and took him to a local bank. Each cashed his check and handed the money back.

The pensioners did what they were told. They knew Pass would revoke their pensions and hospital cards if they defied him. The field representatives kicked back $19,695—a picayune amount Boyle and Pass thought would never catch the eye of a prying government auditor looking at all the money the UMWA pumped into District 19—to Prater and Pass.

Turnblazer did not like Boyle's and Pass's scheme. A careful lawyer, he worried that $19,695 was too much money to launder in such a poor area; it would stick out. Pass, as he usually did, overruled him.

"Little Bill" Turnblazer was not going to argue with Pass. He tried to do that after Pass resorted to violence to solve even District 19's routine negotiating problems, but the strongman just stared at him. Turnblazer wanted to use reason and logic in his dealings with the coal companies instead of bullets and dynamite, but he never had the courage to reel in Pass, even when Pass's thuggish tactics disturbed his lawyerly sensibilities and challenged his religious beliefs.

And Turnblazer knew he could not appeal to the UMWA's high command in Washington. William Sr., his late father, whom John L. Lewis had appointed to serve as District 19 president in 1922, had always taught him never to question an order handed down by the union's masters. Tony Boyle had made it clear what he wanted. He had visited Middlesboro on July 18 and stopped by Turnblazer's house. As he sat in the back seat of his chauffeured Cadillac driven by Pass, Boyle complimented him on his house and warned him not to let Yablonski take it from him. Turnblazer felt a chill creep down his spine. He knew if he did not do what Boyle and Pass wanted, he would lose his home, the means to educate his three sons, and possibly a lot more.

On October 3, 1969, Pass gave Prater a manila envelope stuffed with $10,000. He also gave him a pair of green rubber gloves, and ordered him to wipe off any fingerprints on the money, which Silous Huddleston helped him do the next night.

Nine days later, Gilly and Lucy visited Huddleston in LaFollette. Restless, they burglarized the house of Norval Dippel in nearby Jellico, Tennessee. Dippel owned and operated the Four Leaf Coal Company, and he opposed the UMWA's organizing drives in District 19. That night, as Lucy tried on Mrs. Dippel's fur coat and some of her jewelry, Gilly met with Prater and Huddleston. The two District 19 men warned him that the union had no patience for failure. It would hire other killers if Vealey and Phillips did not murder Yablonski soon. Gilly pushed back: his two accomplices wanted to see the murder money first.

On October 13, Pass met Prater in Harrogate, Tennessee, a short distance across the Cumberland Gap from Middlesboro, Kentucky. He told Prater to give Gilly $6,000, but to hold on to the other $4,000. He wanted Yablonski killed as cheaply as possible.

Huddleston boarded another Greyhound bus to bring the $6,000 to Cleveland. Gilly needed it: Vealey and Phillips were arrested the next day in Youngstown, Ohio, for breaking into a house. Phillips's stepfather posted his bail on October 21, and Lucy and Gilly posted $750 to free Vealey the next day.

That evening, Gilly sat at his dining room table in front of his gun cabinet and methodically wiped off any fingerprints on the bullets lined up in front of him. Just before midnight on October 22, he put on a suit and picked up Vealey and Phillips at the Family Tavern, a badly misnamed hillbilly bar in East Cleveland. Both men lived in tiny walk-ups above the bar.

In a small briefcase on the floor of the front seat rested two Browning automatics and a .38 Smith & Wesson revolver. Gilly reached into the briefcase and pulled out a faded clipping from the *United Mine Workers Journal* that Huddleston had mailed to him, showing three men. An arrow pointed to the man in the middle.

"That is Yablonski," Gilly told Vealey and Phillips, "the guy you are supposed to kill." He explained to them in a way they could easily understand why they had to shoot him. "Tony," a Cleveland paving contractor, wanted Yablonski murdered because he was sleeping with his wife. With that simple lie, Gilly pulled Lucy's maroon Chevrolet on to the entrance ramp of Interstate 76 and pointed it towards Washington, D.C.

SEVEN

Whatever the Sacrifice May Be

By the time Jock Yablonski's assassins left Cleveland, his campaign was in full swing. Nothing about it had been easy. The karate chop that slammed into the back of his neck in Springfield had done more than almost kill him: it had underscored, in the most brutal way, that Tony Boyle and the union's old guard intended to stay where they were.

To round out his 1969 ticket, Boyle selected George Titler, the UMWA's rotund vice-president, and John Owens, who had been its secretary-treasurer since 1948. Owens now sported a poorly fitting silvery-blue hairpiece on his once shiny head, which made him all but unrecognizable to miners who knew what he looked like only because of old union photographs hanging in their districts' headquarters. Boyle knew neither man would question his reelection tactics, no matter how corrupt or thuggish.

It was David versus Goliath from the start. The UMWA's constitution required Yablonski and Boyle to win the nominations of at least fifty locals to have their names placed on the December 9 ballot. A UMWA presidential candidate had needed the nominations of just five locals before Boyle's handpicked reform committee amended the union's constitution in September 1964 after Steve Kochis got on the ballot that summer. In 1969, the nomination period lasted from July 9 to August 9.

Yablonski faced enormous hurdles. His war chest contained only $60,000, nearly half of which came from his own bank account. Most of the rest came from his two brothers. His campaign—Miners for Yablonski—worked out of a small rented office on Connecticut Avenue in Washington, D.C. Fred Barnes, a former reporter for the *Washington Star*, staffed its one-man press office. Chip Yablonski, Jock's younger son, ran the campaign.

Chip was only twenty-eight, but he had finished near the top of his class at the University of Pittsburgh Law School, and had won a highly coveted clerkship with the United States Court of Appeals for the Third Circuit. He practiced as an appellate lawyer with the National Labor Relations Board while he worked on his days off for his father's campaign. Yablonski trusted his son's judgment. He knew Chip could implement his and Rauh's campaign strategies.

Ralph Nader supplied two "Nader's raiders," both law students, to help him. Yablonski tapped Harry Elmer Brown, a fifty-two-year-old local union officer and a member of the Black Lung Association from Delbarton, West Virginia, to be his vice-president. He asked Richard Weaver, a union dissident from Maidsville, West Virginia, to run against John Owens, but he never campaigned.

The UMWA's size and structure also worked against Yablonski. The union had approximately 193,000 members—even the union's secretary-treasurer did not know exactly how many members it had because he did not keep a membership roll—scattered across twenty-five districts in twenty-seven states and four Canadian provinces. They lived and worked in an estimated 1,297 locals, depending on who was counting. Yablonski's campaign had no list of local officers, members, polling stations, or even mining sites.

Two blocks away from his opponent's one-room headquarters, Boyle presided over a reelection machine that had net assets close to $100 million and a Welfare and Retirement Fund worth $180 million more. Boyle, thanks to his unlimited power to appoint, fire, and erase pension and health benefits with the stroke of his pen, controlled his coal miners' money and their votes by fear and intimidation.

This was especially true for the union's 70,000 bituminous mining pensioners. Unlike most American unions, the UMWA forced its
retirees to pay monthly membership dues. These dues allowed them
to collect their monthly pensions and vote in union elections. Their
payments added another $1 million a year to the union's already
bulging coffers.

The UMWA's constitution required a local to have at least ten working members. Boyle largely overlooked this legal requirement—the
only "bogus" locals he disbanded were pro-Yablonski ones in District
5, the insurgent's power base—because it was easier for him to manipulate the union's retirees if they remained in their own voting blocs.

On June 24, 1969, he did exactly that. Boyle used deceit—he lied
to one of the two other trustees and failed to seek the agreement of
the third who was in the hospital—to ramrod through a $35-a-month
boost to the retirees' pensions. The UMWA's letter trumpeting this
raise from $115 to $150 a month gave Boyle sole credit, even though
previous notices of pension increases had been signed "U.M.W.A.
Welfare and Retirement Fund." Congress's General Accounting
Office reported sixteen months later that the monthly increase would
bankrupt the union's pension fund by 1975 unless the coal operators
increased their contributions to it. These had been stuck at forty cents
a ton since 1952.

Manipulating the union's retirees was only the beginning. Boyle
looted barrels of cash from the UMWA's treasury to bankroll his
reelection. He did this under the guise of "organizing expenses" and
purportedly monitoring dust conditions in the mines. Instead of
recruiting more coal miners into the union's ranks, he padded the
UMWA's payroll with extra workers whose only jobs were to campaign
for him; Yablonski later claimed that the UMWA put more men on its
payroll in the last half of 1969 than it had in the twenty years before
that. Boyle bribed others with lavish vacations, disguised as union fact-
finding missions.

He also forced district presidents and field organizers to contrib-
ute portions of their salaries to pay for his campaign. He got rid of

those who refused. More high-ranking district officials were replaced in 1969 than in any other year in the UMWA's history.

Boyle extorted over $142,000 from the union's staff. Those who were too strapped to donate were offered generous loans from the UMWA-controlled National Bank of Washington. He promised his loyalists hefty salary boosts after he defeated Yablonski.

He pumped over a million dollars into UMWA districts in Pennsylvania, West Virginia, and Ohio, where his opponent's insurgency was the strongest. Three hundred and sixty thousand dollars were funneled into District 5, Yablonski's home ground. This money was used to buy votes and pay the salaries of Boyle's campaign workers, who were given jobs as "dust committeemen and temporary organizers." In those districts where he expected the hardest-fought contests, Boyle increased the payroll by $748,000 over what the union paid in salaries in 1968.

Bribery was not the only election fraud he practiced. To prevent Yablonski's nomination, Boyle's followers refused to tell reform-minded miners when and where they could vote. When that failed, they threatened to shoot or fire those who backed Yablonski. They also stuffed ballot boxes, destroyed anti-Boyle ballots, and moved clocks ahead to end voting. One local even struck Yablonski's name from the ballot after a Boyle supporter told its members he was dead.

Boyle converted the *United Mine Workers Journal* into an arm of his reelection campaign. While the *New York Times* and the *Washington Post* covered Yablonski's May 29 press conference announcing his run, the *Journal* did not even mention it. It did mention Boyle, though; between June 1 and August 15, 1969, his name appeared 166 times in boldface type in 120 pages of the *Journal*. Yablonski's name appeared once.

Its editor did not completely ignore him. Justin McCarthy, who was also the UMWA's publicity director, assembled an eight-page scandal sheet in late June entitled *Election Bulletin*, and dispatched it at union expense across the coalfields. Its pages excoriated Yablonski for being an "ex-convict, thief, deserter of his family, shakedown artist, and informer on his brother union members."

Yablonski rebutted these charges in "Jock Yablonski is Fighting Mad," his own newsletter drafted by his wife. "I cannot stand silent," Yablonski told its readers, but the damage had already been done. He believed the *Election Bulletin*'s greatest impact was on Nader. By mid-July, Nader appeared to have all but deserted him.

The seeds for this distancing were sown before Nader read McCarthy's scandal sheet. He wanted Yablonski to spend more of his own money to fund his election bid and to campaign more vigorously. He did not realize how badly hurt Yablonski had been in Springfield.

Yablonski had his own expectations for Nader. He wanted him to raise money and help him more than donating the services of two law students. Nader refused; he did not raise money for anyone. Since Yablonski's May 29 news conference, he kept insisting to the press that he was not going to play any role in the campaign. The UMWA was not Nader's only focus. He was spread too thinly as it was.

Boyle worked very hard to cut Nader's ties to Yablonski. Boyle hated the consumer champion, but he was afraid of him. He knew the media attention Nader could attract to cover the rebellion. After he met with his closest aides, Boyle decided to show Nader that his own credibility could be badly tarnished if he continued backing Yablonski.

Boyle dispatched two aides to show Nader a copy of the *Election Bulletin* and some of its underlying sources. Nader later denied that he believed any of the hateful material they showed him, but Yablonski was convinced he did. Whatever the truth, the public's ombudsman became increasingly unavailable when Yablonski sought his counsel. The rebel leader felt seduced and abandoned.

To compensate, Yablonski began feeding more and more off the energy, passion, and courage of those who came to hear him speak. The union's betrayal of them pushed and pulled him forward. At rally after rally, he watched as Boyle's henchmen wrote down his supporters' license plate numbers and recorded their names. Friendly coal operators, who enjoyed their cozy relations with Boyle, threatened to fire miners who supported the rebellion. They still came to his rallies.

The stakes could not have been higher. "You know," Yablonski confided to his West Virginia campaign secretary in between speeches, "this damn union is in danger of being destroyed. If something doesn't change, there won't even be a union in 10 years."

On July 13, Yablonski spoke to a small cluster of miners gathered in the bleachers of a rundown and weedy athletic field in Matewan, West Virginia, a mountain hamlet that had seen more than its share of labor violence in the early 1920s. It was a blistering hot day. Yablonski peeled off his suit jacket, loosened his tie, and rolled up his sleeves. He gave a speech focused on Boyle's neglect of coal miners' health and safety and his rampant corruption.

"When I see my union moving in a direction of unconcern for men who have to engage in the dangerous conditions of coal mining," he shouted in his gravelly voice, "then it's time somebody speaks up, regardless of what the sacrifice may be!" Warming up to the crowd, Yablonski blasted Boyle's "Gestapo" tactics, and his "reign of tyranny." Yablonski closed his speech with a threat to Boyle. After accusing him and his closest associates of embezzling hundreds of thousands of dollars from the union's treasury, Yablonski predicted that "the spotlight of truth is going to be shined on them . . . and they are going to have to answer!"

Miners were listening to Yablonski; so were others. That same day, local newspapers published a notice from the UMWA's District 30 warning him to stay out of northeastern Kentucky, or else. But on July 31, the Physicians' Committee for Miners' Health and Safety, who had helped lead the West Virginia black lung revolt, endorsed him.

Three days later, a group of seventy-eight miners, widows, and pensioners from the Association of Disabled Miners and Widows—a number chosen symbolically to honor the seventy-eight miners who had died inside Consol Number 9—sued the UMWA in federal court, asking for $75 million in damages. They charged the UMWA with conspiring with its Welfare and Retirement Fund, the National Bank of Washington, and the Bituminous Coal Operators' Association to defraud them of their pensions.

Yablonski's revolt had emboldened those left behind by the union to fight back.

While Yablonski attacked Boyle in the coalfields, Joe Rauh went after him in the courtroom. His skillful legal assault on Boyle gave the rebel's campaign momentum and publicly highlighted Boyle's strong-arm tactics. On June 27, Rauh sued to force the UMWA to have Yablonski reinstated as the acting director of its Labor's Non-Partisan League, a post Boyle had fired him from on June 6. A federal judge enjoined the UMWA on July 16 and ruled in Yablonski's favor six days later. This victory, coupled with Rauh's earlier triumph forcing the union to mail his client's campaign literature, kept the rebellion alive and in the pages of the country's major newspapers.

Rauh had far more success in the courts than he did with President Richard Nixon's Department of Labor. Desperate to protect his client's life and to give the union's coal miners their first free election in more than fifty years, Rauh turned to the Department of Labor and its powers to investigate and overturn corrupt union elections. These powers were spelled out in various provisions of the Landrum-Griffin Act.

Five of the 1959 act's seven titles were devoted to how labor unions should be governed. These titles gave union members a "Bill of Rights," made unions report on their finances, established fair election procedures, and empowered the Secretary of Labor to ask a federal judge to overturn tainted elections and order new ones. Congress gave the Secretary these powers, but its overarching hope was that unions, given more democracy, would reform themselves without federal intervention.

Rauh was not that optimistic: he had too much experience dealing with labor unions. Still, he knew that Section 601 of the

Landrum-Griffin Act gave the Secretary of Labor the right to investigate election irregularities at any time, and he wanted the Department of Labor to step in during the monthlong nomination phase to deter any more violence and record any violations it could later use to ask a federal court to set aside the election if Yablonski lost. Rauh began inundating Secretary of Labor George Shultz with long letters detailing Boyle's election abuses. His first two letters cited over thirty infractions of the Act.

Shultz, a former dean of the University of Chicago's Booth School of Business, responded on July 23, 1969. He admitted he had the power under Section 601 to look into campaign abuses, but he wrote that it was the Department of Labor's longtime policy not to investigate allegations of misconduct until after an election was over. Shultz did not want to be accused of favoring one side over the other until all the votes were counted.

Shultz's narrow construction of his department's powers appalled Rauh, but he was the sixth Secretary of Labor since 1959 who had interpreted them that way. No secretary since the act had been passed had used it to foster an adversarial relationship between the Department of Labor and organized labor.

Shultz had another incentive to do nothing: President Nixon was no supporter of Big Labor, or it of him. The country's unions had lined up solidly behind Hubert Humphrey in 1968. Nixon's "law and order" administration stopped at Big Labor's doors. At most, his Department of Labor practiced a policy of benign neglect when it came to unions. Rauh always believed that Shultz's inaction cost Yablonski a lot more than the election.

While the federal government declined to act, Big Labor deserted Yablonski. George Meany, the conservative head of the AFL-CIO, wanted the Department of Labor to stay on the sidelines. He did not want federal investigators sticking their noses into internal union matters, nor did he want Yablonski's uprising to spread among his own ranks.

Meany signaled this to Nixon and Shultz during an interview he gave to reporters when he dismissed Yablonski's campaign to oust Boyle as nothing more than a naked power grab. "This is one of those boys from the kitchen," he chided, "who has decided he wants to live in the living room." Meany had a low opinion of Boyle, but he had an even lower one of federal meddling.

None of this stopped Yablonski. He barnstormed across the coalfields of Pennsylvania, Ohio, and West Virginia. Chip Yablonski spent countless hours poring over the UMWA's semiannual audit reports, to find the addresses of the union's locals, and the *Keystone Coal Industry Manual*, a trade publication, which listed the locations of the UMWA's organized mines. By August 11, Yablonski had captured the nominations of ninety-six locals. Boyle won the endorsements of 1,056 locals, but Yablonski had clawed his way onto the December 9 ballot.

In an accusation-studded press conference the next day, Yablonski called his nomination victory a "great day" for American labor. "Even Tony Boyle's violence and corruption and fraud," he told reporters, "couldn't keep me off the ballot." He renewed his claims that Boyle had embezzled "huge sums" from the union's treasury and given several coal companies a free pass to skimp on their payments to the UMWA's Welfare and Retirement Fund.

Edward Carey, the UMWA's bombastic general counsel, dismissed Yablonski's allegations as vicious lies. When a reporter asked him if he expected violence during the campaign, Carey scoffed. "Violence? No," he said. "Coal miners are sweet and gentle people."

Hawey Wells knew better. The black lung doctor and rebellion supporter often flew his own airplane to Yablonski's campaign rallies, and discovered before flying to one rally in West Virginia that someone had stuffed his plane's gas tank with pinecones and dead leaves. If he had not checked, the flight would have been his last. A week later, unknown burglars ransacked his house. Wells found his wife's underwear impaled on a souvenir spear in his living room.

Yablonski knew better, too. Eddie Yablonski, his nephew and a burly ex-Marine, began traveling with him. Yet danger continued to loom over his campaign. The threats against his life came so regularly that he stopped counting them, much less reporting them.

They were not going to end. Tony Boyle was going to make sure of that.

EIGHT

The Hunt

On October 23, 1969, Paul Gilly's Chevrolet nosed into downtown Washington, D.C., just after sunrise. He got lost immediately; he could not find the UMWA's headquarters. After he, Vealey, and Phillips drove for nearly an hour through the capital's gridded streets, he pulled over, found a phone booth, and called Lucy in Cleveland. She dug out Albert Pass's hand-drawn map and told him the building was on 15th Street.

The three men were exhausted after their all-night drive. They ate breakfast in Sholl's Cafeteria next to the union's headquarters. As they swilled cups of coffee and munched on donuts, Gilly thought he saw Yablonski leaving the restaurant. He trailed the man out onto the sidewalk. Luckily, the light was brighter outside than it was in the dimly lit restaurant. Within seconds, Gilly realized he was stalking the wrong target.

He found another phone booth and called the union's headquarters to ask where he could find Yablonski. The receptionist told him Yablonski was on the "Hill." Gilly, who had never been to Washington or followed the nation's politics, did not know what she meant.

The receptionist also told him that Yablonski often stayed with his younger son during the week. After a federal judge reinstated him to his job as the acting director of Labor's Non-Partisan League, Yablonski worked in Washington and returned to Clarksville on weekends.

Gilly found Chip Yablonski's address in the phone book. He and his wife lived in Bethesda, Maryland, only seven miles from downtown Washington.

Without a street map, Gilly spent hours threading his way through the Maryland suburb's tree-lined streets. He finally found the house, but his car developed brake trouble. He rented a jack from a gas station attendant, and Phillips repaired the car's brakes. Nearing midnight, it was too late to go back to the house. They slept in Gilly's car in the gas station's parking lot.

At eight o'clock the next morning, Gilly parked near Chip Yablonski's house. Phillips wanted to firebomb it with a rag stuffed in a lighted gas can, but Gilly vetoed that. He was not yet desperate enough to murder innocent bystanders. Gilly waited in the car while Phillips and Vealey rang the doorbell, each armed with a .25 pistol. They were going to shoot Jock Yablonski when he came to the door.

Shirley Yablonski, the rebel leader's daughter-in-law, answered the door. Vealey asked her if "Jack or John Yabliski" was there. She strained to understand what they were asking because of their thick mountain accents. They claimed they were looking for work and that Yablonski had promised to help them find some, but she was wary of the two rough-looking, unshaved men at her door so early in the morning on her dead-end street. She called for her husband.

Chip Yablonski did not like what he saw any more than his wife. He told Phillips and Vealey that his father was in Scranton, Pennsylvania, about 250 miles away. His lie—Yablonski was showering upstairs and driving to Scranton later that morning—extended his father's life.

Vealey and Phillips walked back to the car. They told Gilly that Yablonski was in Scranton. The unexpected news of the insurgent's campaign swing into northeastern Pennsylvania forced Gilly to improvise. His instructions from his handlers did not go beyond killing Yablonski in Washington or Bethesda, but Gilly decided to go to Scranton. He was too far in to quit now.

The three would-be killers arrived that afternoon. Gilly looked for

Yablonski's address in the local phone book. He thought Yablonski lived on a farm in Scranton—he did not know the man he was hunting was just beginning to campaign in the state's anthracite coalfields.

The anthracite coal miners were particularly bitter. Boyle had stripped two of their districts of the right to elect their own senior representatives and merged them with a third, ending democratic rule. The miners' grievances ran even deeper than that. Their pensions, $100 a month in 1949, had shrunk to $30 by 1961. Boarded-up storefront windows were just as common in Carbondale and Wilkes-Barre, Pennsylvania, as they were in the soft coal towns of Nitro and Farmington, West Virginia.

Thumbing through the Scranton phone book, Gilly found a phone number and address for a Joseph Yablonsky whose last name ended with a "y" instead of an "i." He called him anyway and learned that he worked for a wire frame company and had nothing to do with the UMWA. Gilly did not believe him, and drove by Yablonsky's home. He finally gave up when he saw he lived in a neighborhood instead of on a farm.

Frustrated, Gilly called Lucy from a local bar and asked her where Jock Yablonski lived. She called back a half hour later, after she telephoned her father. Huddleston told her he lived in Clarksville, a tiny coal mining town in the grimy Monongahela Valley, several hours away in the heart of southwestern Pennsylvania's black and scarred soft coal country.

The three men arrived in Clarksville at 5:30 a.m. on October 25. The lights were already on in many of the borough's small clapboard-and-brick houses as the miners who lived in them returned home from another cat-eye shift or readied themselves for another day's work in the sprawling mining complexes that lined the banks of the Monongahela River, only three miles away. The men again slept in Gilly's car, this time parked beside a smoldering slag pile. After they woke up, Gilly stole the phone book from a public booth next to the fire station and found Yablonski's phone number. Marg told him that her husband was still in Scranton and planned to return to Washington, D.C. that night. Gilly wanted to drive back to Washington, but Vealey and Phillips refused. They had had enough. They wanted to go back to Cleveland.

It was not a completely wasted trip: they found Yablonski's nearly invisible fir-lined driveway, and memorized Clarksville's simple layout, dotted with bars such as Wapinski's and Kormuth's, which reflected the town's deep Eastern European roots, where its miners threw down bullshots—whiskey with beer chasers—and argued about the approaching UMWA presidential election. They drove up and down the heavily forested hills that surrounded it, scouting the best vantage points from which to watch the secluded farmhouse. Gilly pointed out that they could toss their murder weapons and gloves into the Monongahela River, whose dark waters ran beside the road that led out of the borough toward Cleveland.

Gilly was exasperated when he returned home. He complained to Lucy about how bad Vealey smelled, how they had slept in the cold car, and how they could not find Yablonski. The union had to do more to help if it wanted him killed.

On October 27, Huddleston and Prater met with Pass and relayed Gilly's complaint about Yablonski's schedule. Pass told Prater and Huddleston to drive downtown and come back in two hours. When they left, he called Boyle in Washington.

After the phone call, Pass slipped Prater an envelope filled with another $5,000, but he told him not to tell Huddleston, who was waiting in the car. He still wanted Yablonski killed for a rock-bottom price, and he hoped it would be for a lot less than the $6,000 Huddleston had given to Gilly and the $9,000 Prater now held.

Pass met with Boyle a few days later, during a campaign swing in Big Stone Gap, Virginia. He told the union leader that he had given Prater $15,000 to assassinate his foe. Boyle cut the conversation short when a group of miners walked toward the two men, but he told Pass he expected regular updates on the plot.

Gilly, Phillips, and Vealey remained determined to get paid. They returned to Clarksville on Halloween. On the way, they stopped at a picnic site and took turns shooting at a trash barrel for target practice. As they watched from one of the two vantage points they had found six days before, they saw Marg and Charlotte drive away from the house.

Gilly drove down the hillside and left Phillips and Vealey in the Yablonskis' driveway. They found an unlocked door in the rear of the house, and, inside, a small Bedlington terrier about six months old. The puppy did not bark. The two men stayed in the house for almost half an hour, exploring its layout. Career thieves, they could not resist stealing a handful of silver dollars and some foreign coins Yablonski had brought back from a union-sponsored trip to Turkey. They also raided the family's refrigerator and made themselves sandwiches. Huddleston later scolded them for having something to eat, but they assured him they put everything back.

On November 7, the three men met at Gilly's house in East Cleveland, no closer to killing Yablonski than they had been when they first set out to assassinate him in Washington. Phillips wanted them to think more creatively. He suggested jabbing Yablonski with a needle dabbed in arsenic while he was making his way through a crowd after giving a campaign speech. After Lucy called a local drug store, she told him that they needed a prescription to get arsenic. Phillips recommended using off-the-shelf rat poison instead.

Phillips proposed breaking into the farmhouse again, dousing the family's food with the poison, and leaving the can in Yablonski's bedroom closet. The police would conclude the insurgent had killed himself and his family. As a back-up plan, the small-time thief said he could inject the poison into Yablonski's La Corona cigars. Huddleston later dismissed this idea after he and Lucy experimented with a needle used to vaccinate hogs to pump water into a cigar; it became soggy and fell apart.

Phillips was not done: he had three more ideas. They could kidnap Charlotte and shoot Yablonski when he came to rescue her. If that failed, they could detonate a sack of dynamite underneath Yablonski's second-floor bedroom window, or toss firebombs through the farmhouse's first-floor windows, burning to death everyone inside.

Two days later, Gilly called Yablonski's house early in the morning and learned that Yablonski was going to speak that afternoon in Pineville, West Virginia. He could not find Phillips on such short notice, but he found Vealey hunkered over a beer at the Family Tavern. Gilly told him they could shoot their elusive quarry on the highway after his speech and speed back to Cleveland.

Yablonski's campaign appearance on November 9 at Pineville High School drew a large crowd. The morning's clouds had lifted to bring a cold, crisp, sunshine-filled Sunday afternoon to southern West Virginia. He was in an upbeat mood. Congressman Ken Hechler, as well as Hawey Wells and Don Rasmussen, two of the black-lung doctors, joined him on the stage.

Hechler felt uneasy. The crowd was heavily sprinkled with Boyle supporters, who kept arriving by the carload. Many of them just sat in the grass, drinking whiskey out of glass bottles and staring at Yablonski.

Levi Daniel, an African American miner who was the chairman of Yablonski's campaign in Raleigh County, West Virginia, introduced the candidate to the crowd. Daniel praised Yablonski for promising to reverse the UMWA's steep decline and courageously telling the truth about the union, no matter the consequences.

When he rose to speak, Yablonski seized upon Daniel's themes. He called his campaign a "cause for the people" and a "crusade." Only the miners, he told the crowd, could pry their union from Boyle's clutches and restore its proud heritage as one of the country's most important engines for social change and economic justice. The UMWA's greatest strength, Yablonski reminded them, was the bravery of its rank-and-file members.

Yablonski pointed to a young UMWA member who had just returned from Vietnam. He told the crowd that Boyle's goons had pulled a knife on this veteran because he spoke out against the union's corruption. "Is this America?" Yablonski bellowed. "I don't believe it is, and I don't believe West Virginia wants this kind of America!"

Gilly and Vealey stood in the crowd, watching their quarry's every move. They had never seen him in person. Gilly was unmoved. He thought about what Huddleston had told him: Yablonski was "Satan's cousin" because he wanted to destroy the union. He had to be killed.

As the rally broke up, Yablonski climbed into an open convertible and sat in the back seat. Gilly and Vealey planned to pass his car on the road leading out of Pineville and shoot him in the head, but their plan quickly went awry. Hechler joined the rebel candidate in the back seat, as three other cars pulled in behind the convertible and followed it to a nearby airport.

Vealey was apoplectic. He shouted to Gilly that he wanted to kill everyone in the caravan, but the winding mountain road made any clear shots impossible. When the four cars finally turned off at the airport exit, the two men continued on to Cleveland.

Lucy coldly reminded Gilly what he had promised her and her father when he told her about his latest failure. On November 12, she and Huddleston went to see William Prater. Lucy did her best to convince Prater that her husband and his men were doing the best they could. They had broken into Yablonski's farmhouse—she showed Prater the stolen coins from the home and some campaign literature from Pineville—and discussed poisoning and firebombing him.

She and Huddleston asked Prater if the union would still pay if innocent people were killed. Huddleston said he did not want the killers coming after him if the union did not pay them. Prater was under mounting pressure from Albert Pass to finish the assassination, and told them that he did not care if they slaughtered Yablonski's entire family or everyone in Clarksville. Gilly and his boys could run down Yablonski with an airplane if they had to.

Satisfied, Huddleston told Gilly to do whatever he had to do to finish the job. To earn some quick money, Gilly, Vealey, and Phillips burglarized the home of Dr. Lee Sergeant in LaFollette, Tennessee. Huddleston was upset over the way Sergeant had treated his wife's broken hip; he pointed out the doctor's house to them. They stole jewelry and guns from the house, taking a chrome-plated .38 Smith & Wesson pistol with a white pearl handle from a closet shelf on the second floor. Gilly kept it. It might make a good murder weapon.

Albert Pass was not happy. He wondered why his trio of hit men was burglarizing a house in Tennessee instead of assassinating the man who was blowing the whistle on the union's leaders. He would have been even unhappier if he had known that Gilly had almost killed Phillips during the same break-in.

Phillips had smelled perfume in one of the house's bathrooms and become sexually aroused. He wanted to rape the doctor's daughter, but she was not home. Phillips's lewd remarks deeply offended Gilly. He called Phillips a "no good son of a bitch" and threatened to blow off his head. Stealing a pistol that could be used to assassinate the man who wanted to destroy the union was one thing, but raping a teenage girl was something else.

Pass did not know about the confrontation in the house, but he did know that Jock Yablonski was still alive. On November 20, he summoned Prater and Huddleston to a meet him at the Knoxville airport.

He harshly questioned them for twenty minutes on their attempts to kill Yablonski. "You have fooled around long enough!" he rebuked them. "We have got to call this thing off for awhile." It was too close to December 9's voting. "If Yablonski is killed now," he berated Prater and Huddleston, "people will think the union killed him to keep him from winning the election." Yablonski was not going to win the election; Pass already knew the final vote count in District 19.

If Pass knew the election's final results already, Yablonski did not. He kept up a relentless pace, often pushing himself for twenty-two straight hours before gulping down a double Scotch and switching off his motel room light for a couple hours of sleep. Since winning a place on the

December 9 ballot, he had focused most of his attention on West Virginia and Pennsylvania, where half the union's members lived. Miners for Yablonski offices sprouted up in Ohio, Indiana, Virginia, Illinois, and western Kentucky, too.

Eastern Kentucky and Tennessee were different matters. Yablonski stayed out of District 19. He was no coward, but he was also no fool; there were already enough death threats. He confided to Ken Hechler that if he were assassinated, bitter men from the hills of eastern Kentucky would likely be the ones behind it. When Hechler pressed him, Yablonski presciently named Albert Pass as the most likely architect of his murder.

None of his fears kept him from pushing for union democracy, better mine safety, rank-and-file say in contract ratifications, UMWA-established credit unions, $200-a-month pensions, and fifteen days of paid sick leave. He did not stop there. In his speeches, he slammed Boyle for refusing to debate him and demanded an end to Central Appalachia's environmental mayhem.

Yablonski scored his biggest points by harping on how far the UMWA had fallen since Lewis stepped down. In a fiery mid-November address inside the John L. Lewis Building in Oakwood, Virginia, he promised to lead the union's miners to a safer, cleaner life. He blamed Boyle for allowing the once great union to languish in the backwaters of organized labor.

"Coal miners in this country, as members of the UMWA, used to be trailblazers in the labor movement!" he shouted, his tie askew, his voice hoarse. "Lo and behold, we've become the trailers! Men working in steel mills, automobile plants, rubber plants, and other diversified industries have got better pay, better working conditions, better pensions, better sick leave, better considerations than coal miners have and by God, I don't like it!"

Yablonski's attack on the union's decline resonated with more and more coal miners. In 1969, the highest-paid machine operator in the UMWA made $4.38 an hour, while a machine operator in the building-and-construction trades made as much a $7 an hour. Lewis had made his miners the highest-paid industrial workers in the United States, but they were now struggling to stay in the middle of the pack.

While Yablonski picked up support in the coalfields, Joe Rauh added to his campaign's momentum in the courtroom. During the last week of October, he asked a federal court to force the UMWA to follow fair voting procedures. John Owens, the union's secretary-treasurer, admitted during Rauh's cross-examination that the union had printed 82,000 extra ballots.

After he observed that the officers of the UMWA "pay attention to the [union's] Constitution when they want to and when they don't they don't," United States District Court Judge George Hart admitted that he could do little to guarantee that the election would be honest or fair—that was up to Richard Nixon's Department of Labor. With Boyle already well ahead according to his internal polls, Owens agreed to make some concessions. He promised to return the extra ballots to the printer, prepare an accurate membership list, and send letters to each UMWA local, reminding them that they were legally required to follow the fair-election procedures spelled out in the Landrum-Griffin Act.

By then, Yablonski's entire family had joined him in his effort to topple Boyle. Chip resigned from his job at the National Labor Relations Board and was working full time at his father's campaign headquarters in Washington, while Ken worked at getting out the vote in southwestern Pennsylvania's District 5. Charlotte left her job as the head of the Office of Economic Opportunity in Monongalia County, West Virginia, to work on her father's campaign in Pittsburgh and then in Washington.

She was especially excited about translating into action his ideas to make the UMWA a major player in overhauling Central Appalachia's decaying economy. On November 2, 1969, she attended a pro-Boyle rally in Uniontown, Pennsylvania. An irate miner grabbed her "This is Yablonski Country" sign and tore it up.

While Charlotte crisscrossed the coalfields, her mother savaged Boyle with her caustic pen. In October, Marg published "A Test for Coal Miners" and "Another Test for Coal Miners," which Yablonski mailed to thousands of miners. These pamphlets contained twenty-one questions with multiple-choice answers. "Why," one question asked, "have Boyle and Owens allowed $67 million of your money to lie around in a vault not collecting a penny's worth of interest?" Two of the possible answers were "Boyle thinks it's all his and likes to have it handy to count" and "Boyle and Owens are plain stupid." She encouraged test-takers to mail their responses to Boyle's home address in Washington, D.C.

On November 26, Yablonski got help from a completely unexpected quarter. The Department of Labor's Office of Labor-Management and Welfare-Pension Reports released a five-page summary of its investigation into the UMWA's finances. The probe, which had started on March 4, 1969, vindicated Ralph Nader's earlier claims that Boyle and Owens were the beneficiaries of a now $1.5 million off-the-books pension plan, that the union's leaders practiced rampant nepotism, and that they permitted and took advantage of lavish expense accounts that required no receipts or accounting. Some UMWA officials claimed hotel and travel expenses for every day of the year. Leonard J. Lurie, the report's principal author, referred his findings to the Internal Revenue Service and to the Department of Justice's Organized Crime and Racketeering Section.

The report generated a firestorm. Nader demanded Boyle's resignation. Congressman Hechler criticized the UMWA's president on the floor of the House of Representatives and accused him of plundering his members' dues. Boyle belittled the report's findings, telling his followers it was a "smear job" and "union busting."

Yablonski tried to capitalize on the news. He publicly began predicting that Boyle would soon be "a cellmate of Jimmy Hoffa," the International Brotherhood of Teamsters' president who had gone to prison in 1967 for jury tampering and fraud. At the same time, he and

Rauh, with eleven union members, began drafting their own twenty-five-page lawsuit accusing Boyle, Owens, and Titler of embezzling $18 million of the UMWA's funds. Over $3 million of it, they claimed, had found its way into District 19's coffers.

The next day was Thanksgiving. Gilly picked up Vealey that morning at the Family Tavern. They could eat turkey and pumpkin pie later; they had to kill Jock Yablonski first.

NINE

The Most Dishonest Election in American Labor History

They arrived in Clarksville that afternoon. Gilly was on edge. He had exploded in anger after Huddleston told him that Yablonski's murder had to be delayed. He was worried that Pass might want his $6,000 back. He had already spent over $1,000 of it to free Vealey from a jail in Youngstown, Ohio, and for travel expenses.

Huddleston had assured Gilly that Pass did not expect the money to be returned, but Gilly did not believe him. Terrified that the union would want its money back, he asked Huddleston if they could shoot Ted Q. Wilson, the Southern Labor Union's general counsel, instead. The old terrorist told Gilly to forget about Wilson and to be patient.

Gilly could see the assassination plot unraveling. James Charles Phillips was already gone—he had dropped out after Vealey accused him of not sharing some rings he had taken while burglarizing Dr. Lee Sergeant's house. Concealing stolen loot from his fellow burglars was the least of Phillips's problems. Three days after the break-in, the Cleveland police arrested him for carrying a concealed weapon and raping his girlfriend's four-year-old daughter.

Gilly suspected that Vealey was not far behind Phillips. The surly West Virginian complained incessantly about not making any money. Desperate, Gilly decided to defy his father-in-law and the union's bosses. No one would care about the timing once they killed Yablonski.

Gilly and Vealey drove to the vantage point overlooking the back of the farmhouse. It was a holiday; there were too many people visiting to try anything during the day. The two men waited for several hours until, finally, the last guest left. Gilly drove down the hill and parked beside the fir trees that blocked the farmhouse from the main road.

Vealey, carrying an M1 carbine semiautomatic rifle, crept on to the porch and peered through the window. He saw Yablonski sitting alone, watching television. All he had to do was jam the rifle's barrel through the glass and squeeze the trigger.

Vealey stood there for nearly ten minutes, staring at the man he had come to kill. He never raised his rifle. Fear and the enormity of what he was about to do quickly erased what little nerve he had mustered. Despite all his boasting in Cleveland's hillbilly bars, Vealey had never shot anyone except his common-law wife after a night of binge drinking. Unsure of who else might be in the house and what it would feel like to actually kill someone, he talked himself into believing he could not get away safely after he shot Yablonski. He slinked back slowly to the car.

Gilly was enraged. He scolded Vealey for being a coward. How, he yelled, were they going to pay back the blood money they had already spent? He and Vealey would be next on the union's murder list if they did not kill Yablonski soon; the UMWA had plenty of other hard men on its payroll. Vealey did not say a word. He stared ahead in silence.

Two days later, before Boyle spoke to a crowd of miners at a campaign rally, he summoned Pass to a meeting in Madisonville, Kentucky, and instructed him to halt his plans to assassinate Yablonski until after the election. Pass had done that already on November 20 in Knoxville when he told Prater and Huddleston to rein in their hit men, but he did not know that Huddleston could no longer control Gilly. Only the house painter's breathtaking incompetence, Vealey's lack of nerve, and bad luck had kept the killers in check. Huddleston had not had the courage to tell Pass about Gilly and Vealey's Thanksgiving Day trip to Clarksville.

Huddleston was in the crowd at Madisonville when Boyle told his audience that Yablonski was "unfit" to lead the UMWA and guilty of "lies, defamation of John L. Lewis, conflicts of interest and anti-union acts." He listened intently as Boyle spoke about his opponent's plot to hand over the union to outsiders and deny 70,000 UMWA retirees their pensions. Boyle's words only confirmed what he already believed: Yablonski had to be killed to save the UMWA and its pensioners.

Huddleston called Lucy that night after he learned what Boyle told Pass and asked her to pass a coded message to her husband: "Tell Paul not to go hunting, there is a game warden behind every tree." Gilly was in no mood to listen. He was tired of Lucy's relentless badgering and tearful pouting because he had failed to kill Jock Yablonski "for her daddy." He would show her and the men who had hired him that he was not a fumbling loser. Gilly was also tired of spending endless hours in a cramped car with Vealey, who reeked of body odor so badly he often had to roll the down his car's windows, no matter how cold it was outside.

On December 2, he and Vealey set out for the fifth time to kill Yablonski. While barreling down Interstate 77 two hours from Cleveland, one of the rear tires on Gilly's car rolled off. A tow truck brought them to Dick's Phillips 66 Station, on the outskirts of Cambridge, Ohio. Gilly tried to conceal their trip's true purpose by telling the gas station attendant, "This shoots down our hunting trip to West Virginia."

They had to catch a bus back to Cleveland. By the time Lucy and Gilly retrieved the car on December 4, the election was only five days away. Gilly was no longer willing to defy Huddleston this close to the voting. He reluctantly decided not to return to Clarksville until after the election.

Boyle was not worried about beating Yablonski. He presided over the UMWA's vast system of rewards and punishments, controlled its gorged treasury, and commanded its 70,000 voting retirees. They depended on him for their pensions and hospital cards. He had cemented their allegiance by boosting their pensions from $115 a month to $150.

Boyle was also running an effective race. At first, he was a reluctant campaigner; he had defeated Steve Kochis in 1964 without leaving his Washington headquarters. This time was different. Boyle's handlers understood that Yablonski was a much more formidable opponent than Kochis, and they knew that the press, including the big city dailies, were going to devote a lot of ink and space to covering something most people in the coalfields had never seen—a hotly contested UMWA presidential election.

To combat Yablonski's threat, Boyle hired Oscar Jager, a long-time public relations man who specialized in representing labor unions, and Alex Bilanow, a veteran Washington journalist, to oversee his campaign's messaging. Bilanow charged $750 a week—over $5,000 in today's dollars—for his services, while Jager charged twice as much.

They were worth every penny. Jager and Bilanow methodically cranked out campaign flyers entitled "Boyle Leadership Brings Pork Chops," "Your Program for UMW Progress," and "Straight Ahead with Tony Boyle." These leaflets trumpeted Boyle's successes since 1964: he had won the union's miners a $10-a-day pay increase, eight paid holidays, time and one-half for working on Saturdays, and double time for working on Sundays.

They recruited Roy Lee Harmon, the poet laureate of West Virginia, to burnish their client's image. Harmon composed "W. A. 'Tony' Boyle," a thirty-six-line verse that extolled him as a "Modern Moses who was born to lead, who knew a miner's life . . . a miner's need."

They also stole Yablonski's platform. Boyle rolled out their handiwork in his Labor Day speeches in Logan, West Virginia, and Elkhorn, Kentucky. It was the first time in twenty-five years that the union's top officer appeared on a stage in Central Appalachia. Many miners had never seen a hotly contested UMWA presidential election, much less voted in one. Many others thought only one man could run for office.

In between sets of bluegrass music and bouts of professional wrestling, Boyle confessed that his union had "tremendous catching up to do." He, too, wanted $200-a-month pensions, greater mine safety, a cleaner Appalachia, and a more adversarial relationship with the coal industry, he claimed. The only plank of the rebel's platform he did not steal was the one that gave miners the right to elect their district officers—he was not ready to go that far. Boyle personally selected all the senior officers and approved the staff in nineteen of the UMWA's twenty-three American districts.

Though he was temperamentally incapable of giving up control of the union's internal election machinery, he promised to establish a commission to study "structural changes." To blunt any criticism, Boyle vowed to fight for a daily wage of $50, something most of the country's major labor leaders sought as fervently as Perceval looked for the Holy Grail.

Yablonski called Boyle's Labor Day speech a "major moral victory" for rank-and-file coal miners. He had forced Boyle to leave his remote Washington headquarters, travel to the coalfields, and admit that what had once been the country's greatest union had slipped badly under his rule.

Nowhere were Boyle's failings more glaring than in mine safety, but thanks to Yablonski, he now embraced Congress's attempts to pass a federal safety act that made black lung a compensable work-related illness and set strict dust-control standards underground. He even supported abolishing the Coal Mine Safety Board of Review, an industry-dominated panel created in 1952 that often reversed the Department of Interior's few decisions to close dangerous mines.

Yablonski's satisfaction was short-lived.

Boyle was a born alley fighter who could not resist hitting him below the belt. He revived his earlier charges that Yablonski was a pawn of oil and gas companies, a tool of Washington outsiders, a blasphemer of John L. Lewis, and a "Brutus who stabbed Caesar." His toadies on the campaign trail said even worse things about him.

In their narratives, Yablonski was the member of a childhood gang who had gunned down a fellow thirteen-year-old in a fight over tobacco in discarded cigarette butts, the plunderer of a can of pennies meant for orphans, and an Army deserter in World War II. Yablonski had not served in World War II because he had only one kidney; he was medically ineligible.

Boyle also railed against Yablonski's use of the courts. He complained that big oil companies were secretly funding Rauh's lawsuits and that these legal challenges drained the UMWA's treasury and contributed to union busting.

The most devastating broadsides Boyle fired at Yablonski came from his opponent's own mouth. In rally after rally, he played five excerpts from four speeches Yablonski had given between April 1 and May 4, 1969. Each praised Boyle's bold leadership and revolutionary accomplishments. By late November, Boyle had spent $18,000 of the union's money blanketing the coalfields with thousands of 45rpms blaring out Yablonski's laudatory speeches.

He complemented these records with a handbill called "The Two Faces of Joseph Yablonski," which made the insurgent look duplicitous. The handbill pointed out that Yablonski, who now condemned Boyle as a corrupt thief, had said only eight months before, "There is no man, there is no man anywhere in this country, with a greater dedication to the well-being of the UMWA than your distinguished president, W. A. Tony Boyle." When newsmen questioned him about his unctuous words, Yablonski replied lamely that the union wrote those speeches for him. "I did not know they were taping those speeches. Somebody was writing them for me, and I just did what I was told."

His defense got little sympathy. Some miners believed he was a power-hungry traitor, one who had turned against Boyle solely for personal gain. Others bought Boyle's charge that Yablonski was a malevolent puppet controlled by big-city outsiders who wanted to seize control of the UMWA and abolish it.

Another vocal segment argued that John L. Lewis had anointed Boyle to be his rightful heir, and that it was a sin to question their dead patron saint's judgment. Still more swallowed Boyle's lie that Yablonski was planning to strip the union's 70,000 pensioners of their right to vote in the union's elections. Oscar Jager spent over $50,000 on television and radio spots trumpeting Boyle's leadership and blasting Yablonski's treachery.

Yablonski fought back as best he could. On December 4, he spoke in a cramped Summerville, West Virginia, high school auditorium. "Coal miners tell me, you will have no problem winning at our mine, but they are going to steal it from you. Well, I don't know if any of these fellows want to go to jail for Tony Boyle. You know," he said prophetically, "the net is around him already. I guess Tony Boyle must see me behind every post and every tree and under every bed. My shadow follows him wherever he goes!"

Three days before, Joe Rauh had made another attempt to wake up the slumbering Department of Labor. He had warned Secretary George Shultz that only an investigation could prevent the "ugly violence" that was sure to follow if the government did not monitor the election.

The *Washington Post* agreed with Rauh. Its editorial board observed that only a strong federal presence could guarantee honest voting.

Shultz responded with a letter on December 6, in which he stuck to his earlier position. There would be no investigation until after he received "a valid post-election complaint" under Section 402(a) of the Landrum-Griffin Act. Until then, the UMWA had to police itself. With that, Shultz drew the blinds and left Yablonski alone in the street with his enemies.

The next day, Yablonski drove to Man, West Virginia, for his last campaign rally. Fittingly, he talked about mine safety and the union's duty to protect the lives and limbs of its members.

He appeared on December 8 on WOAY-TV, an ABC affiliate that covered southern West Virginia. Yablonski lamented that so much mudslinging had marred his contest with Boyle. He had wanted the race to focus on substantive issues, but his opponent had succeeded in dragging it into the gutter. Yablonski closed the interview by predicting that the voting on December 9 would bring about a democratic and responsive union.

The election's outcome was never in question. On October 30, Chip Yablonski had sent out requests with self-addressed postcards with prepaid postage to the UMWA's estimated 1,297 locals asking when and where they planned to hold their voting. He received only 345 replies. The campaign was able to dispatch election observers—some recruited by Ralph Nader and many sporting official-looking observer's certificates that the Miners for Yablonski manufactured—to just 400 locals. Boyle relied again on widespread fraud.

Yablonski's polling-place observers saw one UMWA official voting for thirty men. Another union local received only ninety-five ballots, yet Boyle won by 145 votes to 5. In still another, working miners were paid $50 a carload to bring pro-Boyle pensioners to the polls.

Boyle won by 80,577 votes to 46,073. He got only 52 percent of the working miners' vote, but 87 percent of the pensioners' ballots. Yablonski could not overcome the UMWA's baked-in culture of dependency and retribution.

He expected to lose by large margins in such Boyle strongholds as Kentucky, Tennessee, and Alabama, and he was right, but even he was staggered by some of the returns. In District 19, the vote was 3,723 for Boyle and only 87 for Yablonski, exactly as Pass had predicted over a month before.

William Prater, as Pass's right-hand man, had a ready explanation for Yablonski's crushing defeat in District 19. "The reason Mr. Yablonski did so badly in our district," he told reporters, "was that he was not known. Over 75 percent of our people could not even pronounce his name."

Yablonski lost 4,651 to 391 in Alabama's District 20, where Pass served as its International Executive Board member. The rebel candidate won in District 6, which covered the West Virginia panhandle and southern Ohio, District 17 in central West Virginia, and District 25 in northeastern Pennsylvania's anthracite region, but he lost in all the others, including District 5, his home base.

Yablonski watched the returns in his Clarksville living room with Marg and Morton Dean, a veteran CBS newsman, and his initially upbeat mood grew darker and darker as the vote counts rolled across the bottom of his television screen. Unable to watch anymore, he told Dean that Boyle had stolen the election. It made no difference to him that this was the first UMWA election since 1920 in which the incumbent's share of the vote was not 80 percent or better.

Boyle greeted news reporters in the predawn hours of December 10. He characterized his victory as one over outside interests who wanted to control the union. When reporters asked him who these outside parties were, he was ecumenical. They consisted of "crusaders, do-gooders, doctors, lawyers, politicians and the federal government."

Justin McCarthy, the editor of the union's newspaper and the union's chief spokesman, admitted he had heard of some "election irregularities," but none of these troubled him. "Nobody got his head broken open," McCarthy joked to the press. "I'd say it was a real honest, clean election."

Yablonski refused to concede, but Boyle's supporters flooded West Virginia's radio and television stations with the lie that he had. He fought back by issuing a statement that called his defeat "a transitory setback" and the election the "most dishonest in the history of the American Labor movement." Boyle's victory, he wrote in a statement to the press, was directly attributable to his embezzling millions of dollars from the union's treasury.

He also blamed the departments of Labor and Justice for his defeat, claiming their idleness paved the way for Boyle's theft. He promised he would "see Boyle in court" and vowed to continue fighting.

On December 11, he sent a telegram to Secretary George Shultz, demanding that the Department of Labor impound the ballot boxes and investigate the election's irregularities. Shultz was very reluctant to take such extraordinary measures, but he invited Yablonski and Rauh to come on December 15 to the Department of Labor to talk about their demands.

The day before he left for Washington, Yablonski drove to Sophia, West Virginia, to address three hundred of his staunchest supporters. Arnold Miller, a gaunt retired miner who suffered from black lung and who had managed his campaign in Districts 17 and 29, organized the rally. Yablonski held nothing back. He accused Boyle of stealing the election—and he had plenty of proof.

Chip Yablonski and Clarice Feldman, who had worked together at the National Labor Relations Board, immediately after the union announced the results, began assembling first-hand accounts of voting fraud. By the time they were done, they had collected over one hundred instances. These included union officials announcing the results before votes were counted, refusing miners' their right to a secret ballot, excluding election observers, filling out ballots on behalf of pensioners, and threatening to kill anyone who voted for Yablonski.

That Sunday afternoon brought snow and sleet, but Sophia's high school gymnasium was packed to its rafters. Dozens of Boyle's thugs, guzzling whiskey, milled around outside or loomed in the doorways.

Elmer Brown, Yablonski's vice-presidential running mate, urged him to be careful, but Yablonski refused to back down. "Well, maybe we lost the skirmish," he croaked in his hoarse voice, "but we are still going to win the war!" After he finished his speech, Yablonski told his son Ken that he had accomplished more in the last seven months than he had in thirty-five years in the union.

When reporters interviewed him after he spoke, Yablonski remained defiant, and said he would never again knuckle under to Boyle and his sycophants. "They think they can make some kind of deal and I'll agree to it," he rasped. "Well, there is only one thing I'm going to agree to do. I'm going to agree to have a complete, comprehensive audit of the United Mine Workers of America and turn the results of that audit over to the Justice Department and let Tony Boyle go to the penitentiary, where the hell he belongs!" This was the last time many of Yablonski's supporters would see him alive.

Yablonski's meeting at eleven o'clock the next morning with the

Department of Labor's lawyers went predictably. Rauh recounted how Boyle had stolen the election and why the Department's investigators had to intervene before the union's thugs destroyed all the evidence that proved as much.

When the government lawyers had been listening, stone-faced, for almost an hour and a half, Rauh misstepped. He told them that the Department of Labor's intervention would give "momentum" to Yablonski's efforts to oust Tony Boyle, and he pleaded with Laurence Silberman, the Department's solicitor, to enter the fight against "the enemy." The government's lawyers were strongly disinclined to get involved anyway, but they jumped on Rauh's plea as proof that Yablonski wanted to draw the Department of Labor into an internal union shootout. The civil rights lawyer's emotional appeal went nowhere.

While Yablonski was engaged in his quixotic struggle to enlist the Department of Labor, Boyle was outwardly conciliatory. He promised to heal the wounds the election had inflicted on the UMWA. He even claimed he had no plans to fire Yablonski as acting director of the union's Non-Partisan League.

That was true—but he still planned to kill him. Boyle's election victory had done nothing to temper his hatred for Yablonski. He called Pass on December 16 and ordered him to jumpstart his foe's assassination. He was tired of Yablonski's threats. Boyle suggested killing him inside his Clarksville farmhouse.

Pass met with William Prater the next night at a roadside pull-off in Harrogate, Tennessee. He authorized Prater to pay the killers $15,000 if they could assassinate Yablonski by January 1. Prater relayed Pass's message to Huddleston. "Call your boys," he said. "Tell them to move ahead with the plan."

Huddleston telephoned Gilly in Cleveland and told him the assassination was back on, and for more money. The house painter could show his gratitude to the union by killing Chip Yablonski too, but Huddleston ended their conversation with a warning: if Gilly could not shoot Jock Yablonski by New Year's Day, Tony Boyle was going to take the job away from District 19 and give it to a district in Pennsylvania. Huddleston reminded his son-in-law that District 19 had never failed the UMWA and was not going to start now. Gilly and his boys had to kill Yablonski.

Boyle flew to Billings, Montana, on December 18. He was not going to come back to Washington, D.C., until January 3. He wanted to be far away when his enemy was assassinated.

TEN

I Shall Die an Honest Man

Gilly did not waste a moment: time was running out. Huddleston had given him a deadline. He had only two weeks left to kill Yablonski, and if he failed, the union would find someone else to do what he had already failed five times to do.

He called Yablonski on December 17, claiming he was a laid-off miner looking for work. Could Yablonski help him if he stopped by his house? Yablonski told him that the mines around Clarksville were hiring—all Gilly had to do was fill out a job application and show up for work.

Gilly, desperate, refused to be put off. He called again, and told Yablonski he was coming to Clarksville the next day.

He picked up Vealey from the Family Tavern at 9:00 a.m. on December 18. He did not tell him that the union had raised the contract to kill Yablonski to $15,000; Vealey believed the union was willing to pay only $4,200 to rid itself of its most vocal critic. Gilly wanted to pocket the extra money—he could use it to pay off his debts from Dalton's. Vealey would never know the difference.

They arrived in Clarksville a little after 12:00 p.m. Following their set routine, Gilly's Chevrolet climbed up the Clarksville-Marianna Road overlooking the rear of Yablonski's farmhouse. They saw two familiar cars in the driveway, Yablonski's and Charlotte's. Late that afternoon, Marg and Charlotte drove away in a dark blue Ford Mustang.

Gilly and Vealey followed them to Pearl's Beauty Salon in neighboring Fredericktown. Certain that the two women would be there for a couple hours, they raced back to Clarksville.

Gilly pulled into the farmhouse's long driveway. He carried a .25 pistol in his jacket pocket, and Vealey jammed the .38 revolver they had stolen in November from Dr. Sergeant's house into his own. When Yablonski came to the screen door, Gilly introduced himself as the out-of-work coal miner from West Virginia who had called the night before. He then introduced Vealey, whom he called Charles Johnson, as a fellow miner who was also looking for work.

Yablonski studied his two visitors closely, and did not like what he saw. Neither man looked like a coal miner—their hands were too clean. Coal dust worked its way into a miner's skin until its blackness became a part of him; no soap, no matter how potent, could ever wash it all out.

Something else bothered him about the two men: Gilly said they were from West Virginia, but their car's license plate said Ohio. Yablonski did not invite the two men inside. He suggested they apply for work at the Blacksville Coal Mine.

As they stood in front of their target, Vealey began to worry. Gilly had parked his car near Yablonski's front porch. They were too visible, especially from the two vantage points they used to spy down on the farmhouse. Anyone looking down on the house could see them. As he nervously fingered the gun in his pocket, he expected Gilly to give him the signal to shoot.

It never came. Finally, Gilly mumbled "Thanks," and he and Vealey got back into the car. Each blamed the other for not shooting first. They drove to Kormuth's Tavern on Main Street and bought a six-pack of Iron City beer, which was brewed in nearby Pittsburgh, for the long drive back to Cleveland.

Marg and Charlotte soon returned from the beauty parlor, and a few minutes later, Ken Yablonski and Karl Kafton, a long-time friend, also arrived. Yablonski told them about his strange visitors. Suddenly, he blurted out, "I think there are two men here in town who want to kill me!"

The three men climbed into Ken's car and drove into Clarksville. Yablonski saw Gilly's car parked in front of Kormuth's Tavern; they eased in behind it. It was too dark to see the features of the two men sitting in the car, but Kafton wrote down Gilly's license plate number on a small notepad he always carried in his shirt pocket.

Kafton was not the only person interested in the Chevrolet. John Price, the bartender at Kormuth's, was worried about the car idling in front of the bar, and even more worried about the rough-looking man with a receding hairline and long sideburns staring at him across the bar. A robber had emptied Kormuth's cash register less than a year before and gotten away. Price was not going to let that happen again. After Vealey left the bar, the bartender asked one of his regular customers to follow him out. He circled behind the car and wrote down "Ohio CX-457."

After Yablonski, Ken, and Kafton returned to Yablonski's house, Kafton contacted Russel Whitlatch, a retired miner who now worked as a dispatcher for the Shadyside, Ohio, police department. He told Kafton that the car was registered to Annette Gilly.

Kafton called Lucy, claiming to be a Pennsylvania state trooper. He told her the driver of her car might have witnessed a hit-and-run accident on the Pennsylvania Turnpike. She admitted that her husband had driven her car to Pennsylvania to find work. When Kafton quizzed her about what her husband did, she said he was a house painter.

Shortly after he left Clarksville, Gilly stopped in California, Pennsylvania, and called Lucy. Her news about the phone call from the Pennsylvania State Police bothered Gilly. He had not witnessed any accident on the Pennsylvania Turnpike. He had not driven on it to get to Clarksville—he was too cheap to pay its tolls. The call must have come from Yablonski, who now had Lucy's license plate number and name.

Gilly knew he had to be more careful; he needed a different car.

Yablonski wondered why a painter from Ohio was claiming to be an unemployed coal miner from West Virginia. None of Gilly's story made sense. He called the Pennsylvania State Police. One of its troopers confirmed Whitlatch's information, and later told the FBI that Yablonski seemed surprised a woman owned the car.

Whatever his suspicions were, Yablonski did not let them stop him from continuing his battle with Boyle. Section 402 of the Landrum-Griffin Act required that he had to exhaust all his internal remedies in the union first before he could file a formal complaint with the Department of Labor asking that the election be overturned. As a first step, he planned to present his case at the International Executive Board's January meeting.

He sat down in his study that night and wrote two letters. He addressed the first to Boyle; George Titler, the union's vice-president; and John Owens, its secretary-treasurer. Yablonski told them that he was formally challenging the election's results.

He addressed his second letter to the union's tellers, elected union officers entrusted with tabulating the election's official results. He attached eight appendices to his letter that documented how Boyle had stolen the election by practicing rampant voting fraud and looting the union's treasury. He concluded it with a bold exhortation and a chilling prophecy: "Tellers," he wrote, "stand up before it is too late. I, too, once submitted to the discipline of Tony Boyle. But I shall die an honest man because I finally rejected that discipline."

Gilly did not know what was worse: Lucy's hectoring followed by her icy silences, or his father-in-law's barrage of phone calls asking why Yablonski was not in the ground. Gilly had had enough. He had wanted to quit after his and Vealey's latest fiasco in Clarksville, and he even had summoned the courage to tell Lucy that he was "out." She had responded by icily reminding him that he had promised to kill Yablonski. What little resolve he had managed to muster dissolved. He promised her that he would see the murder plot through to its end.

On December 21, he and Lucy drove to Tennessee to meet with Huddleston. Gilly knew his father-in-law was a trusted union foot soldier who would rather die than fail his District 19 masters. Huddleston would come up with something.

After Gilly described his and Vealey's latest failure—he claimed that Marg and Charlotte had returned to the farmhouse unexpectedly—Huddleston stared at the ground for a long time. "Dynamite," he finally answered. Sticks of dynamite were staples of union violence, especially in Kentucky and Tennessee.

Gilly liked the idea. It was clean and impersonal. A lit stick of dynamite was a lot more reliable than Claude Vealey. It was also more useful: if he could not use it on Yablonski, he could always sell it for $12 a stick in East Cleveland's hillbilly ghetto.

Huddleston's long-standing ties to the "Jones Boys" gave him a large network of violent contacts to draw on. On December 21, he introduced Gilly to George Smith Jr., one of the terrorist group's most proficient and enthusiastic users of dynamite.

"Tennessee" Smith, as he was known locally, had joined the union in 1959, at the height of District 19's war with the small coal operators. He had honed his destructive skills by blowing up nonunion trucks, bulldozers, augurs, and tipples, and had forged a close working relationship with William Prater, who selected and approved all his targets.

Three stretches in the penitentiary—two at Brushy Mountain for stealing and one in the Florida for contributing to the delinquency of a minor—only added to his reputation as one of the UMWA's toughest strong-arm enforcers. At nearly six feet tall and weighing over two hundred pounds, Smith looked the part. The only things more striking than his bushy mountain-man beard were his tattoos: a dagger that snaked down his left arm, and "1948" stamped on his right forearm, memorializing the date of his first stay at Brushy Mountain.

Huddleston and Gilly met with Smith at the small farm where he lived with his common-law wife and six children. Mechanization had closed most of the mines around Jellico, Tennessee, and Smith now struggled to make ends meet. Huddleston came right to the point. He would pay Smith $2,100, plus expenses, to stuff a burlap feed sack with one hundred pounds of dynamite, tie it to a pole, lean it against Jock Yablonski's second-story bedroom window in Clarksville, and detonate it using cords and fuses.

Huddleston assured Smith that his son-in-law, who stood at his side, was a "good fellow you could trust." Gilly offered to drive him to Clarksville. Smith was tempted, and listened intently as Huddleston described the thickness of the stone walls of Yablonski's farmhouse. He could use the money, and he liked the professional challenge.

His wife had other ideas. She did not want her husband mixed up in a murder—her family could not survive another of his stays in prison. He was in legal trouble enough as it was: the Campbell County sheriff had arrested him barely a month before for stealing tools from a local mechanic, and this latest run-in with the criminal justice system had already cost her $1,000 in bail. Smith feared his wife's wrath more than the union's. He backed away from the plot.

Albert Pass vetoed the dynamite idea, anyway. He met the next day with Prater and Huddleston at District 19's headquarters. When Huddleston told him about the plan to blow up Yablonski's house, Pass said no. Any Tennessee or Kentucky lawman, he lectured with the crisp logic of his business-school-trained mind, knew that dynamite was District 19's favorite way to erase a foe. Pass did not want Yablonski's assassination traced to his Middlesboro doorstep.

The only sure way to get rid of him was to gun him down. Huddleston told Gilly to forget about blowing up Yablonski. He had to shoot him.

That same day, Yablonski drove to Washington from Clarksville to meet with Joe Rauh. The civil rights lawyer gave his client some bad news: federal grand juries in Pennsylvania and Virginia had decided not to indict any UMWA officials for embezzling union funds to pay for Boyle's reelection. Equally depressing, the Department of Justice was closing its investigation into the savage karate blow that had almost killed Yablonski in Springfield, Illinois.

Yablonski was shocked. How, he asked, could an administration that had campaigned on law and order not punish such naked criminal behavior? Rauh tried to buoy Yablonski's flagging spirits by reminding him that the Department of Labor had yet to rule on his requests to impound the election's ballots and investigate its outcome.

Rauh should have saved his breath. William Usery, an assistant secretary of labor, mailed a letter to Yablonski that same morning that said the government was not going to seize any of the election's ballots. Usery did not even bother to address Yablonski's request for an investigation.

Yablonski fired off a blistering telegram to Secretary George Shultz the following day. He called Usery's evasion a "cheap trick unworthy of a government agency." He ended his reply with one last broadside into the Department of Labor: "This is a bad day for those Americans who believe in clean, democratic unions."

Yablonski's biting words fell on deaf ears in Washington. "The Boyle faction is lower than whale shit at the bottom of the Pacific as far as we're concerned," one high-ranking government official colorfully confided to a reporter, but the Department of Labor was not going to budge until Yablonski produced more evidence that Boyle had stolen the election.

While Yablonski was brooding over his latest setbacks, Gilly revived his feckless partnership with Claude Vealey. On Christmas morning, he drove in a car he had borrowed from his brother to the Family Tavern. Vealey, smelling of alcohol and reeking of body odor, staggered down the stairs of his apartment above the tavern.

By late afternoon, they were at their familiar perch overlooking the back of Yablonski's farmhouse. Their seventh attempt to kill him was no more successful than their other six: too many holiday visitors

streamed in and out of the house. They waited in vain for an opportunity to follow Yablonski's car onto the main road, shoot him, and
dump his car and body into the swirling Monongahela River.

They finally gave up at 1:30 a.m. on December 27 and paid four dollars to rent a filthy room with paper-thin walls at the West Brownsville
Motel. Gilly tossed and turned in the bed, and Vealey dozed fitfully
on a mattress sprawled on the floor while "Bobby," one of the seedy
motel's down-and-out permanent residents, talked and moaned in his
sleep in a neighboring room. The next morning, after they both shaved
with Bobby's razor, they left for Cleveland.

They needed more than a shave. They needed a third man who
would not hesitate to kill.

ELEVEN

Leave No Witnesses Behind

P aul Gilly first tried to re-enlist James Charles Phillips, but the rangy hoodlum wanted nothing more to do with him. He was still bitter over Gilly's threat to kill him inside Dr. Sergeant's house. He was also too busy meeting with his lawyer. He and Vealey were scheduled to stand trial on January 5, 1970, in Youngstown, Ohio, for breaking and entering.

Gilly next offered a share of the blood money to two other men in Dalton's basement. Neither was interested in killing a man he did not know.

Out of options, he asked Aubran Wayne "Buddy" Martin to meet him on December 29 in the Family Tavern's backroom. Vealey came, too. Gilly told them that the union was now willing to pay $5,200 to kill Yablonski, and he promised Martin $2,000 if he would join them. It was almost New Year's Eve. Martin was broke. He could use the money to celebrate. He nodded his head and ordered a bag of potato chips.

Martin's hair-trigger temper was well known in East Cleveland's honky-tonks. Fueled by alcohol, he often lashed out in dangerously unpredictable ways. In early 1969, bouncers threw him out of Cindy's Lounge on Lorraine Avenue for fighting. One of them, amused by his fair features and ducktail haircut, called him a "sissy." Martin returned with a machine gun. He shot out the tavern's windows, raked its bar with gunfire, and wounded one of its patrons in the buttocks.

Vealey admired Martin's volatility. He never blinked. Martin was a loaded weapon filled with natural-born meanness. Vealey was sure the pint-sized West Virginian would kill Jock Yablonski and anyone else who got in his way while he was doing it.

Six months before, Martin had offered Vealey fifty dollars to help him murder a black nationalist in Cleveland. Vealey began drinking heavily the night before—he always got nervous before a big job—and didn't hear Martin honking his horn and pounding on his door the next afternoon.

Martin went by himself. He crept up to his target's front porch and hurled a lit bottle of gasoline through the front window. The bomb exploded in the living room, badly burning the black nationalist and killing a nine-year-old African American girl. Martin taunted Vealey the next time he saw him, telling him he had missed out on making an easy fifty dollars.

Gilly had purposely kept Martin out of his plot to assassinate Yablonski. He did not like him: he had a loud mouth and was too hard to control. He had let Martin take part in the September burglary of Southern Labor Union leader Ted Q. Wilson's house in Winfield, Tennessee, only because he could not find Phillips.

Gilly was too desperate now to worry about Buddy Martin's mouth or temper. This was going to be his eighth attempt to kill Yablonski. If he failed this time, Martin was going to be the least of his problems.

Three days earlier, four local high school students interviewed Yablonski at his Clarksville home. He did not dwell on his defeat. He spoke about the poverty and hopelessness he had witnessed in Central Appalachia. He condemned the region's lack of economic diversification and its residents' two choices of coal mining or welfare.

Yablonski ridiculed Boyle's campaign promises to revive its sagging economy and clean up its polluted air. "They have heard political promises before," he cautioned the students, "but these mean nothing." As the videotape trailed off, he was already thinking about what lay ahead. His moods alternated between steely determination and nagging self-doubt.

"Maybe I made a fool of myself," he mused on December 27 during a family dinner at his son Ken's house. "Maybe it was all a mistake." As Yablonski brooded over his defeat, he was especially agitated with Ralph Nader. He felt used and abandoned.

Yet Yablonski knew he had come a long way in seven months. Moral outrage had formed only part of his decision to run for the union's presidency, and he had wanted to become the UMWA's leader for personal, more selfish reasons. Campaigning had changed all that. His outrage had become real and all-consuming as he criss-crossed the coalfields. He had seen with his own eyes how the union had turned its back on men who had given it everything they had. Yablonski had played no small part in allowing this to happen as a powerful district leader and as a member of the union's International Executive Board.

He wanted to atone for that, and he had. He had told one of his sons that he had done more for the union's rank and file during his run for the presidency than he had in his entire career as a top UMWA official, but there were still so many things to do.

Yablonski first had to be reelected as District 5's International Executive Board member. This was not going to be easy. Boyle had beaten him in his home district on December 9, and his hatchet men now occupied the district's highest offices. They would stop at nothing to oust Yablonski from his board seat.

He also had to keep ratcheting up the pressure on the Department of Labor. Joe Rauh was confident that he could force Secretary Shultz to overturn the election now that it was over. Boyle had violated the Landrum-Griffin Act too many times, and Yablonski had won too many lawsuits for the Secretary to ignore, but all this was going to take time, and it would be an uphill battle.

One way to jolt the Department of Labor into action was for Yablonski to testify in front of a federal grand jury investigating the UMWA finances, which he was scheduled to do in January in Washington, D.C. He was not going to hold anything back, even if his testimony called into question some of his own actions.

Tomorrow would be a new day. All he needed was some rest and time to reflect. Recharged and refocused, he could once again begin his dangerous gambit to drive Boyle from the union forever and return it to the men it was supposed to protect and serve.

Chip Yablonski, his wife, Shirley, and their young son, Jeffrey, drove through a snowstorm on December 27 to attend dinner at Ken's house and visit his family for the holidays. When they went to his parents' house the next day, Chip was shocked to see a Parker Brothers' 12-gauge double-barrel shotgun lying on a windowsill in the master bedroom, and a Winchester .22 caliber long rifle leaning against the far wall. Chip knew his father hated guns. He was also surprised to see the dawn-to-dusk floodlights on the corners of the old farmhouse's roof. Yablonski's two brothers, who lived close by, insisted he arm himself and illuminate the outside of his home at night.

Yablonski worried about his own safety, but he never believed his enemies would harm his family. Even the American Mafia drew the line at murdering a target's family. Still, the thought may have haunted him.

Yablonski had begun reading in his downstairs study Arthur Lewis's *Lament of the Molly Maguires.* The book told the bloody story of a secret society of Irish miners that waged a no-holds-barred war between 1850 and 1877 against mine owners in northeastern Pennsylvania's hard coal fields. During these last few days in December, he opened the book to a chapter about the killings of a coal operator and his wife.

Marg never worried about her own safety, but she did worry about her husband's. She confided in a close friend that she thought Boyle was "a nut" who might do anything. On December 28, Chip took Charlotte and her to the Coyle Theater, an art deco movie house in nearby Charleroi, to see *Butch Cassidy and the Sundance Kid*, which had been released late that October. Marg loved the playful banter between Paul Newman's Butch Cassidy and Robert Redford's Sundance Kid.

Charlotte had been waiting for a phone call from Joe Rauh about a job in Washington, D.C. She was bored in Clarksville, and she did not want to go back to West Virginia or Pittsburgh.

She had resigned from her job as the director of Monongalia County's Office of Economic Opportunity after the Morgantown newspaper accused her of using her position to campaign for her father. She was drawn inexorably into her father's cause. Its goals invigorated her. Charlotte was outraged by the poverty she saw in the coalfields. After the election, she turned down an offer to work at one of Pittsburgh's largest hospitals. She wanted to go to Washington and learn how to craft public policy. Rauh, with his many contacts inside the government, was going to help her do that.

Chip and his family returned to Bethesda on December 30 with plans to attend a New Year's Eve party in Northern Virginia. Before they left, Yablonski gave his son a letter addressed to Rauh about the Department of Labor's refusal to impound the December 9 ballots. He was not giving up.

Gilly picked up Vealey and Martin late that same morning. He drove his accomplices to an empty house he was remodeling on Cleveland's west side, where he was planning on moving with Lucy and Ronnie, her son. Gilly believed too many African Americans were overrunning his old neighborhood; the thief and would-be murderer was worried about crime.

Gilly handed Vealey and Martin a .38 revolver with pearl handle grips—the pistol stolen from Dr. Sergeant's house in Tennessee—and a brown M1 carbine, for which his father had traded another pistol during an October gun show in Mount Sterling, Kentucky. Its original owner had bought it from a mail-order catalog. The M1 was a short semiautomatic rifle used by the military. Surplus M1s flooded the firearms markets after World War II.

As he sat at his dining room table in front of his well-stocked gun cabinet the night before, Gilly had thought carefully about what guns to bring. He did not want to take any chances. The six-shot .38 caliber revolver provided plenty of close-up killing power, and a competent marksman could hit a target two hundred yards away with the M1. They could use it to shoot Yablonski in the head while he was driving his car.

Gilly led Vealey and Martin past a jukebox and into the basement; he wanted them to practice firing both weapons before they left for Clarksville. He pumped some dimes into the jukebox to drown out the cracks of gunfire coming from below. As Hank Williams sang "Your Cheatin' Heart" and Johnny Cash lamented being caught in a burning "Ring of Fire," Vealey and Martin blasted away at wooden blocks Gilly had set up as targets.

At around 1:00 p.m., after Gilly was satisfied that Vealey and Martin were familiar enough with the guns to kill Yablonski, the three men climbed into a light blue Chevrolet Impala with a black vinyl top belonging to William Gilly, Paul's brother. Lucy had borrowed the car that morning, telling William's wife that she needed it to visit her sister in Akron, Ohio.

Gilly steered the Impala towards Clarksville. This was his and Vealey's eighth attempt to kill Yablonski. The three men barely talked. "There was not much discussed," Vealey later explained. "We was [sic] just going down there to kill him [Yablonski], that was it."

They stopped in Wheeling, West Virginia, for gas. Gilly used the service station's telephone to call Yablonski's farmhouse. When Marg answered, he pretended to be Steve "Cadillac" Kochis, who had run unsuccessfully against Tony Boyle in 1964. She said Yablonski would be home by 8:00 p.m.

They stopped again in Fredericktown, about five miles outside Clarksville. They ate sandwiches and bought a pint of Seagram's Seven Crown whiskey in a paper carton and a six-pack of Stroh's beer to chase it. Vealey and Martin were drinkers seven days a week.

They drove five miles south on Route 88 and pulled over just before entering Clarksville. They planned on following Yablonski when he drove by and shooting him with the M1 carbine, but they never saw him.

After it became too dark for them to see any of the cars driving by on Route 88, Gilly drove to the cleft in the hill overlooking the rear of Yablonski's farmhouse. He started drinking, too. Prater and Huddleston had made it clear to him that he could not afford any more botched attempts. He tried to block out their threats by focusing on the twinkling lights in the farmhouse below.

Yablonski had been busy with union politics. After Chip left, he had lunch with Lou Antal, the president of one of District 5's locals and one of his most trusted lieutenants. He asked Antal to oppose Mike Budzanoski, a long-time Boyle loyalist, for the presidency of the district. Boyle had handpicked Budzanoski to replace Yablonski after he forced him to resign as District 5's president in 1966.

Antal agreed to do it. As the two men parted, Yablonski warned him to be careful. He predicted Boyle's goons would come after Antal once he announced he was challenging Budzanoski. Antal cautioned Yablonski to be careful, too: he was the one Boyle really wanted to hurt.

That night, Yablonski drove to Fredericktown to attend the wake for the mother of one of his campaign workers. While he was at the funeral home, Jean Slosarik, Shirley Yablonski's sister, who often stayed with Marg while Yablonski was away, visited with Charlotte and Marg at the farmhouse. Marg invited her to come over for a holiday drink and to see the family's huge Christmas tree.

The women talked about family matters and presents. Charlotte, who had her hair in rollers, proudly showed off a new black handbag and a copy of *The French Lieutenant's Woman*, John Fowles's historical novel. Marg chided her for staying up until 3:00 a.m. to read it.

Charlotte drank one glass of Scotch and mixed two glasses of whiskey and ginger for Marg and Slosarik. Neither she nor her parents had any New Year's Eve plans. Yablonski returned home from the wake a little after 9:00 p.m., downed one Scotch, and went upstairs.

Two hours earlier, President Richard Nixon had signed the Federal Coal Mine Health and Safety Act of 1969, fearing a nationwide coal strike if he were to veto it. This landmark legislation created what became the Mine Safety and Health Administration, and provided for federal payments to miners who were permanently disabled by black lung. Yablonski had advocated for its passage while campaigning.

Jean Slosarik left the farmhouse at 10:00 p.m. It was raining hard and beginning to sleet.

Gilly drove down the hill to Wapinski's, another bar on Clarksville's Main Street, after the men ran out of Stroh's beer to chase their Seagram's whiskey. Vealey bought a six-pack of Iron City beer. They returned to their hillside lookout. As they drank, they tossed their empty bottles out the car window and decided to kill everyone in the house.

Meanwhile, before turning in, Yablonski read Alex Hailey's *Airport*, a 1968 best-selling novel about a large metropolitan airport trying to operate during a massive snowstorm. He snapped off his bedside lamp around 11:30 p.m. Marg sometimes enjoyed a late movie or Johnny Carson's *The Tonight Show*, but not this time. Her husband was still tired from campaigning.

Charlotte was asleep in the bedroom next door. She was curled up under a blue-and-white bedspread and a multicolored wool blanket. She lay on her right side, her jet-black hair in rollers. Her right arm was tucked underneath her face.

Gilly, Vealey, and Martin waited for nearly an hour and a half after the farmhouse's lights went out. It was now or never. The weather was getting worse. With beer and whiskey coursing through his veins, Gilly snaked the car down the winding hill, crossed a narrow bridge over a small creek, and rolled to a stop near Yablonski's tree-lined driveway.

Vealey and Martin pulled on dark gloves. They wore no masks and carried no rope. They were not going to leave anyone alive who could identify them. They grabbed the .38 revolver and M1 carbine and walked up the driveway. Gilly wanted to stay in the car, but they told him they would not go inside unless he did, too. The three men peered through the farmhouse's Christmas-card-lined windows. No one was up.

Vealey cut the telephone wires, and he and Martin flattened the tires on Charlotte's Ford Mustang. Martin disabled Yablonski's maroon Chevrolet Caprice by ripping out its ignition wires. No one in the farmhouse was going to be able to call for help or drive away.

They stepped onto the back porch, where they confronted three locked storm doors. They concentrated on the one on the far left, which stood in front of a wooden door that led down a short hallway into the living room. Martin unscrewed the door's aluminum molding and laid it against the outside wall. Rascal, the small Bedlington terrier puppy Vealey had first seen when he and Phillips had broken into the farmhouse on Halloween, wagged his tail. He slept between the storm door and the propped-open wooden door. Vealey let the puppy out into the yard. Rascal never barked.

Vealy knew the farmhouse's layout. He searched its downstairs while Martin and Gilly waited at the foot of the wide staircase. He walked past the family's Christmas tree, with opened presents still underneath it. A holiday wreath hung over the living room's fireplace mantel.

The dusk-to-dawn floodlights meant to protect the house's exterior bathed its interior with enough light for the men to see where they were going. The three assassins removed their shoes and tiptoed up the staircase. Martin whispered that he would kill Charlotte. He told Vealey to shoot Yablonski and Marg.

An empty bedroom stood at the top of the stairs to the second floor. To its right lay a short hallway with two bedrooms at its end. The door to the left was open. Inside, Yablonski and Marg were asleep. Charlotte's door, to the right, was closed.

Martin had not come all the way from Cleveland to fail. Two thousand dollars was a lot of money, and he wanted it. He slowly pushed open her door, and leaned over her bed. He lowered the pistol about four inches from her head and squeezed the trigger twice. Both bullets entered the top of her skull. One tore through Charlotte's brain, collapsed her right eye, and lodged on the right side of her upper lip. The other also sliced through her brain, went into her right arm just above the elbow, and exited into her mattress.

Vealey, who was standing in front of the master bedroom's open door, heard the two whip-like cracks coming from Charlotte's bedroom. He was supposed to shoot Marg and Yablonski as soon as Martin fired. He stepped inside the bedroom. This time, he told himself, this time. By himself or with Paul Gilly, Vealey was just a small-time hood, not capable of killing anyone. Acting now as part of a murderous team with Martin, he did the inevitable.

He raised the MI carbine and pointed its stubby barrel at Yablonski and Marg. He pulled its trigger. Nothing happened—the semiautomatic rifle was jammed. Fumbling with it, he pushed the button that released its magazine, and its 15-round clip bounced off the floor. Marg, jarred awake by the shots from Charlotte's room, began to scream.

The gunshots from Charlotte's bedroom and his wife's screams shook Yablonski violently from his sleep. He began groping for the box of shotgun shells he kept beside the unloaded double-barrel shotgun on the windowsill. Gilly, who was standing behind Vealey, grabbed the rifle from his accomplice's shaking hands and snapped back in its ammunition clip. He aimed it at the Yablonskis. He shot Marg, who had pulled a lavender bedspread and a blue blanket over her head, in her left shoulder before the carbine jammed again.

Martin, as if on cue, stepped into their bedroom and emptied his .38 at close range into the startled couple. Marg died almost instantly after one of Martin's bullets slammed into her right shoulder, deflected downward after hitting her right collarbone, and lacerated the main artery to her left lung.

Yablonski had had enough time to grasp that his daughter was probably dead and that his wife was motionless on their bed. He reached for the empty shotgun. By then, Martin's first shot had shattered his right wrist, cut his radial artery, and climbed up his forearm. Martin fired two more times at Yablonski, who crumpled to the floor.

Vealey heard Yablonski gurgling, choking on his own blood. Set loose now by Martin's savagery and juiced up on whiskey and beer, he took the pistol from Martin's hand and shoved five bullets into its chamber. He stepped around the bed and fired four times at his helpless target.

Yablonski was in a kneeling position between his bed and a knocked-over bedside lamp, now sprayed crimson at its base. Dark red stains fanned out across the front and back of his white T-shirt. His killers' bullets had ripped through his aorta, lodged deep in the upper part of his stomach, pierced his esophagus, severed his jugular vein, and plowed through the back of his head—the coup de grace. Through the acrid smoke and eerie light, Martin found $240 in a money clip on top of the dead man's dresser and shoved it into his pocket, while Gilly tried to pick up all the killers' spent shell casings.

Vealey retraced Martin's footsteps and walked into Charlotte's room. He wanted to make sure she was dead and to see if she had any cash lying around he could steal. Her shattered head and a quick search of the top of her dresser answered his questions. He stepped back into the dimly lit hallway, clutching only his pistol.

Their grisly job done, the three killers walked down the staircase. Gilly stole three canisters of film from a desk on the stair's landing, matter-of-factly reasoning that their theft would help make the police believe that the killings were no more than a house burglary gone horribly wrong.

They put on their shoes, let the puppy back into the house but not before Martin threatened to kill it, and climbed back into their car. It was sleeting hard and starting to snow. They tossed their murder weapons and wire cutters into the Monongahela River just past

Fredericktown and headed for Cleveland. It had taken them just ten minutes to break into the house and slaughter the family.

We finally got Yablonski, Gilly thought, as he drove through the blowing snow back to Cleveland. No more wasted trips with the foul-smelling Vealey, no more sitting for hours in a parked car on a chilly hillside watching the old farmhouse, and no more hounding from Lucy and Silous. All he had to worry about now was staying out of jail.

That was not going to be as easy as he thought.

TWELVE

The Work of a Maniac

They arrived in Cleveland at 7:30 that same morning, after they crossed the ice-clogged Cuyahoga River. Six months before, an oil slick on the river had burst into flames, ushering in the nation's first Earth Day. A freezing wind filled with snowflakes blew across it now.

Gilly left Vealey and Martin at Rabbit's Café on East 7th Street, promising to return with the money he owed them for killing Yablonski. Vealey, still on edge, wandered across the street. Tomorrow would be the first day of a new year and a new decade. He wanted to look his best to ring in both.

He got his hair cut and bought some wash-and-wear slacks, socks, and a pair of $14 leather shoes before rejoining Martin inside the café. They shot pool and drank several red and black cans of Black Label beer, a Cleveland specialty, while they waited for the biggest payday of their lives.

Lucy woke up when she heard Gilly unlock the door. She plugged in the coffee pot and braced herself for another of his endless excuses about why Yablonski was still alive. Instead, she found him sitting morosely on the edge of the bathtub. Whatever relief he had first felt about killing his elusive target had faded. In a low voice, he told her they had killed everyone in the house.

Lucy stared at him, but she did not make a sound. One of her brothers and his wife lay sleeping in the next room, and she did not want them to hear her interrogating her husband. Gilly did not seem to want to talk about what had happened inside the farmhouse anyway. He asked her to unlock the small safe they kept in the house. She opened it and took out $2,750.

Gilly showered and changed into the clothes he wore when he was painting houses. He needed an alibi. He wanted his neighbors to believe he had been painting earlier that morning. As he drove away in his work truck to pay Vealey and Martin, Gilly told Lucy to return the getaway car to his brother.

His brother's wife almost gagged when she opened the driver's side door. The car smelled of the sweet-sour mixture of an open whiskey bottle mixed with Coca-Cola and Vealey's rancid body odor. Six Payday candy bars, shards of soggy French fries, and a 1970 calendar from a gas station in Cambridge, Ohio, lay scattered on its wet and muddy floor.

Gilly found Vealey and Martin shooting pool in Rabbit's back room and handed each man an envelope. Vealey's contained only $1,000. Gilly, a prudent small business owner, had deducted the $750 he had spent in October to free his accomplice from the Youngstown, Ohio, jail cell. Martin's held $1,720. Gilly promised to give him another $280 in a couple days.

Vealey's and Martin's pockets were stuffed with more money than they had ever seen. They were determined to spend it as fast as they could. Vealey handed his common-law wife $30 to buy a new dress and some shoes for New Year's Eve, and spent the rest on a 1963 Oldsmobile 88. Martin followed in Vealey's unsteady footsteps, spending over $900 on a 1964 Ford Thunderbird. They drank away the remainder. They had snuffed out three lives for two used cars and some cheap booze.

By Monday, January 5, Ken Yablonski was worried. He had not seen his father in a week. He had called him on New Year's Day, but could not get through. Ken assumed his father, mother, and sister were in Bethesda, Maryland, visiting his brother.

Still, he could not escape a gnawing feeling of dread. His worry ballooned when a friend stopped by his law office in Washington, Pennsylvania, and told him that he had not seen his father that morning. January 5 was Inauguration Day all across Pennsylvania for mayors, judges, and other state and local officials who had been elected that November. Yablonski, a powerful fixture in Washington County's Democratic Party, had not shown up at the local courthouse for the swearing-in ceremonies.

Alarmed, Ken asked William Stewart, a longtime friend, to drive with him to his parents' farmhouse in Clarksville. Ken pulled into his father's driveway at 12:45 p.m. Bottles of milk and a stack of newspapers lay on the icy steps. The family's mailbox was gorged with letters and magazines. Rascal, Marg's puppy, and an awful smell greeted them when they unlocked the kitchen door. The odor, which the deputy county coroner later described as the "smell of rotting meat," got stronger as they moved through the dining room and living room. Both men knew something was horribly wrong.

They quickly climbed the stairs and turned right toward the two bedrooms at the end of the short second-floor hallway. They walked into the master bedroom and spotted a large bloated clump lying on its back. A blood-spattered lavender bedspread covered it. All Ken could see when he peeled the bedspread back was a black face. He did not recognize his mother until he saw her long raven hair.

"My God!" he yelled. "What have they done to her face! Where is my dad!" He staggered into the smaller bedroom to his right and saw Charlotte, face down on her bed, curlers in her jet-black hair. Dried blood, seemingly everywhere, caked her white pillowcases and blue and white bedspread. Her legs were black and green.

Desperate to find his father, Ken ran back into the master bedroom. He found Yablonski's body, slumped and twisted to the right, wedged in between the bed and a nightstand. A crimson-spattered reading light lay across the right side of his lower back. A large brown spot covered the back of his T-shirt, and dried pools of darkened blood

stained the floor where his body lay. Stewart heard anguished cries of
"Oh my God!" and "What are we going to do!" coming from the master bedroom.

Ken ran down the steps. He tried to call the nearby Pennsylvania
State Police barracks in Waynesburg, but the kitchen phone was dead.
The two men drove to a Sunoco service station on Clarksville's main
street. "They murdered my family!" Ken told the state police dispatcher
on the other line.

He and Stewart drove back to the farmhouse and waited for the
police. In shock, Ken ate handfuls of snow. "My God," he moaned.
"Who could have done such a thing?"

Huddleston was anxious. New Year's Day had come and gone, and he
had heard nothing from Gilly or Lucy. Worse, he had heard nothing on
the radio or seen anything on television about Yablonski's death. He
wondered if Gilly had failed again.

Unable to contain his curiosity any longer, he called his son-in-law
on January 3. Gilly sounded strange and distant. He finally mumbled
cryptically about having finished the "big paint job." Huddleston did
not know what he was talking about. He chatted briefly with Lucy and
hung up.

Huddleston was not the only one wondering what was going on.
That night, Pass called Prater, ordering him and Huddleston to meet
him the next day in his office in Middlesboro after he taught his Sunday morning Bible study class.

When they arrived, Pass berated his two underlings. Why, he asked,
had he heard nothing about Yablonski's murder? Huddleston meekly
suggested that his "boys" might be having trouble finding him. Pass
brushed aside another of the old man's seemingly endless excuses. He
had had enough. He ordered Huddleston to rein in Gilly and his accomplices. He needed time to come up with a better way to kill Yablonski.

Pass did not have to think about this for long. On January 5, he sat
in his living room watching the local six o'clock news on WBIR-TV

in Knoxville, Tennessee. Ten minutes into the broadcast, Pass finally heard what he had waited nearly six months to hear: "The unsuccessful candidate for the President of the United Mine Workers recently [*sic*], Joseph Yablonski, has been found dead along with two women at his home in Clarksville, Pennsylvania. State police say Yablonski was murdered."

Pass's telephone rang five minutes later. Prater had watched the same broadcast. He asked Pass if he could give Huddleston the $9,000 he was holding for the killers. Pass told him to do it.

Huddleston was also watching the six o'clock news. What Gilly said about the "big paint job" finally made sense. He drove immediately to Prater's house and rapped on his basement door.

The field representative pretended to be shocked that Marg and Charlotte were also dead. "What did they do!" he lashed out at Huddleston, as he handed him a large manila envelope stuffed with $9,000. Huddleston was too relieved to be done with Yablonski's assassination to remind Prater that he was the one who had told Lucy and him that he did not care if the killers slaughtered everyone in Clarksville.

Trooper Elmer Schifko was on routine patrol on January 5, 1970. A former military policeman, he had joined the Pennsylvania State Police in 1958 after answering a job advertisement in the local newspaper. His colleagues in the state police liked working with him because he had a no-nonsense attitude and paid close attention to detail. He was just finishing his lunch that Monday when his police radio crackled with an urgent message ordering him to go to the Yablonskis' farmhouse in Clarksville because "something was going on."

Schifko arrived at 12:45 p.m. Ken Yablonski and William Stewart were waiting on the farmhouse's back porch. Schifko's suspicions that the worst had happened were aroused by what he saw on the outside. Cut telephone wires dangled in the air, and both the Yablonskis' cars, one with two tires flattened and the other with its hood ajar, sat disabled in the long, winding driveway. Two half gallons of milk stood near the kitchen door beside six newspapers. Two of them, a *Browns-ville Telegraph* and a *Pittsburgh Press*, were dated December 31, 1969.

Two other state policemen soon joined Schifko. They entered the farmhouse and began making their way up the circular staircase. The odor of decomposing bodies was so overpowering that one of the policemen vomited on the stairs and turned back.

Farrell Jackson, the Washington County coroner, followed them. He had known Jock Yablonski well; in 1958, Yablonski had persuaded George Leader, then Pennsylvania's governor, to appoint him to his position. As he examined the body of his dead friend, Jackson noticed that shotgun shells were lying underneath it. Yablonski must have frantically groped for the shotgun resting on the windowsill, the coro-ner thought, before he was so brutally cut down. The gun's breech was cracked open.

As he waited for Dr. Ernest Abernathy, the Washington County chief pathologist, to determine exactly how the family had been killed, Jackson told a gaggle of local reporters that he was sure the killings were "the work of a maniac." His fear seemed well-founded: almost five months before, the Manson family had butchered actress Sharon Tate and four of her friends in her isolated house in the Hollywood Hills.

Joseph Snyder, a captain in the Pennsylvania State Police and a stu-dent of violence in the coalfields, offered his own theory on why the family had been killed. As he watched ambulance crews pack their bloated bodies into plastic containers, Snyder said he was sure their murders were an "act of vengeance."

The phone rang in Chip Yablonski's Washington, D.C., law office just after he returned from walking across L Street to get a sandwich. A family friend told him that his father, mother, and sister had been mur-dered. Within hours he, along with his wife, son, and Joe Rauh, began boarding a flight from National Airport to Pittsburgh.

Chip saw a reporter waiting near the gate. "You guys just didn't believe how rotten this union was," he scolded the newsman. When the reporter asked him if he believed the UMWA had anything to do with his family's murders, he wheeled around and said, "I'm convinced of it without even knowing it."

The news of the triple murders broke over Washington like a thunderclap. Ralph Nader excoriated the departments of Labor and Justice for their failures to act while Yablonski was still alive. "Mr. Yablonski's struggle to rally coal miners against corruption and violence," he told reporters, "was against overwhelming odds and the indifference of government enforcement agencies to his charges."

George Shultz called the killings "a shocking event" and a tragedy. Congressman Ken Hechler sent a telegram to Boyle, imploring him to post a sizable reward for the arrest of the killers.

The coal miners who had voted for Yablonski spoke even louder. Twenty thousand of them in Pennsylvania, Ohio, and West Virginia threw down their tools and walked out of the mines.

Boyle's response was much less emotional. He claimed he learned about the killings on January 5 when the editor of the union's bimonthly newspaper called him with the news that Yablonski had murdered his family and shot himself. Senie Gibson, one of his secretaries, believed she knew who killed Yablonski, and told Boyle's personal assistant that it sounded like something Albert Pass would do. The assistant told her to be quiet.

Boyle told an ABC newsman there was no link between the bitterly fought election and the murders. "The election is over. Why would anyone want to kill Yablonski and his wife and daughter?"

To outside observers, he seemed genuinely baffled and hurt. "People say I run a corrupt union. I took over what John L. Lewis built up and it is no better or no worse that it was then," he said as he stared into the camera.

Boyle claimed he did not know what caused this "terrible tragedy." After he said how much he respected Yablonski, he offered the union's full cooperation in catching his killers.

Rauh, who had been around labor unions most of his professional life, did not believe a word Boyle said. He boarded a flight back to Washington the next morning for an appointment with John Mitchell, the attorney general of the United States. Rauh wanted the FBI to enter the case.

Rauh thought Director J. Edgar Hoover was a fascist, but he respected the FBI's legendary ability to track and capture criminals. The bureau's network of field offices in all fifty states gave its agents a national presence, something the Pennsylvania State Police lacked. Hoover's G-men also had a cutting-edge crime laboratory, vast networks of informants, and deep reservoirs of cross-indexed investigation files and fingerprint cards.

Mitchell, a former municipal bond lawyer who directed Richard Nixon's presidential campaign in 1968 and who later went to prison because of the role he played in covering up the Watergate break-in, was the public face of the administration's "law and order" platform. In their thirty-minute meeting, Rauh argued that the murders were connected to the election and that their planning likely extended far beyond the borders of Pennsylvania. He pointed out that only the Department of Justice and FBI had the reach and the resources to bring the killers and whoever hired them to justice.

Mitchell first had to convince Hoover. The FBI director worried about the lack of federal jurisdiction. From what he read, the murders had all the hallmarks of crazed killers such as the Manson family or of hardened thieves such as the two drifters in Truman Capote's *In Cold Blood* who had massacred the defenseless Clutter family ten years before in Holcomb, Kansas, stubbing out Americans' illusions of small-town serenity and security.

Hoover argued that local and state lawmen usually handled murder cases and that his agents had better things to do than get ensnared in an internecine labor union war. What was to become known as the Weather Underground organization, a radical leftist group founded in 1969 in Ann Arbor, Michigan, was just beginning its bombing campaign to overthrow the United States government.

While Mitchell tried to cajole Hoover, Rauh held a press conference outside the Department of Justice's headquarters on Pennsylvania Avenue. He condemned the Justice and Labor Departments for their "icy indifference."

Mitchell was a wily politician in his own right, and knew the murders were going to be front-page news for a long time. He did not want the Nixon administration looking soft on crime.

He short-circuited Hoover's concerns by asking Raymond P. Shafer, the governor of Pennsylvania, to request the Department of Justice's help in solving the vicious murders. The Yablonski family had already lobbied the governor to ask for federal help. Shafer agreed to do it after he consulted with the head of the Pennsylvania State Police.

At 6:30 p.m., the attorney general ordered Hoover to comply with the governor's request. Mitchell based the FBI's jurisdiction on the federal law that prohibited Yablonski's killers from interfering with his rights as a labor union member. And they did—by killing him.

The FBI director complained privately that Mitchell was playing politics, but he complied with the attorney general's order. He instructed Cartha "Deke" DeLoach, his second in command, to "press vigorously." DeLoach designated the murders "a Special," or a major case, which meant that all the Bureau's vast resources could be drawn upon to solve them. That night, the teletypes in seventeen FBI field offices, from Montana to New York, rattled into action with a terse message from DeLoach, ordering their Special Agents in Charge to run down all leads in the Yablonskis' murders.

They were going to find the first of these in tiny Clarksville.

PART II

THE WALLS OF JUSTICE

THIRTEEN

YABMUR

Ian MacLennan was not the type of lawman who waited for orders. His twenty-seven years in the FBI, including three as a deep undercover operative during World War II in South America, had baked into him an intuition that allowed him to predict what he was about to be ordered to do long before his distant Washington commanders told him to do it. In January 1970, MacLennan was the head of the FBI's Pittsburgh field office. He immediately dispatched one of his agents to the tiny borough fifty-five miles to the southwest after the teletype machine in his office clattered with the news of the triple murders in Clarksville. He instructed him to begin working with the Pennsylvania State Police and exploring what federal laws the killers might have broken.

MacLennan was certain his field office would soon be playing a key role in the hunt for the Yablonskis' killers. He later told a reporter that he could "smell it coming." He was right. Deke DeLoach, the FBI's deputy director, designated Pittsburgh as the investigation's "office of origin." The Pittsburgh field office was soon coordinating the work of sixteen other FBI field offices assigned to run down leads in the murders.

DeLoach appointed Joseph Sullivan, the Special Agent in Charge of the New York field office, to be the case's overall supervisor. Sullivan, with his balding head and bifocals, looked more like the methodically trained lawyer he was than one of the FBI's top field men. He had honed his skills in other high-profile killings, including the murders of three civil rights workers in 1963 in Philadelphia, Mississippi— Goodman, Schwerner, and Chaney—and bombings committed by the Ku Klux Klan in North Carolina. His experience in overseeing cases in rural areas, where all outsiders were suspect, made him an ideal choice to lead a triple murder investigation centered in the remote Central Appalachian coalfields.

State troopers and detectives were already collecting evidence and interviewing Clarksville's residents by the time the FBI entered the case. On January 6, they commandeered the Clarksville Volunteer Fire Department's building and converted it into their investigation's hub. Twelve officers manned its telephones around the clock.

Wild rumors and far-fetched theories about who killed the family flowed through the fire station. These ranged from the United Auto Workers, who some claimed wanted to take over the UMWA by framing Tony Boyle for murder, to Mafia bosses who coveted the union's wealthy pension fund. Even one of Charlotte's former boyfriends, now living in San Francisco, was briefly a suspect.

State police detectives interviewed Ken and Chip Yablonski. They asked both men to provide timelines of their whereabouts from December 30, 1969, until the earliest days of January 1970. The detectives ruled out the grieving sons as suspects after they passed polygraph tests.

Time seemed to blame Yablonski himself. One of its writers observed that Yablonski, "who had kind of a wild glint in his eyes, was haunted by many demons. It is not surprising he died violently, reaching for his gun. He was in and around violence most of his life."

Others pointed out that it could not have been the union. Its killers favored blowing up its foes with dynamite or erasing them with shotgun blasts. Such speculations did nothing to help investigators.

While scores of policemen and agents fanned out across Clarksville, others scoured the Yablonski's farmhouse for physical evidence.

By nightfall on January 5, the state police had recovered two .38 slugs from the family's mattresses, one from underneath the nightstand near Yablonski's corpse, and another, which cut a deep gouge into the floor, under his body. They also found an empty .30 shell casing lying in the second-floor hallway. This meant there were at least two killers.

Dr. Ernest Abernathy, the pathologist, added to the bullet count that night. His autopsies of the three bodies yielded five more slugs: one in Charlotte's lip and four more in Yablonski's forehead, chest, hip, and forearm. Abernathy found no evidence that the two women had been sexually assaulted.

Later that morning, the state police found another .38 slug under the radiator in Yablonski's bedroom and a .30 copper-jacketed bullet in the mattress where Ken had found his mother's swollen body. The killers had fired eleven bullets in all at the sleeping family, striking their three victims nine times.

Troopers Glen Werking and Elmer Schifko searched Yablonski's downstairs den while investigators combed through the two bedrooms. They found a lined yellow legal pad lying on a desk. Someone had written on it a name, a license number, and a Cleveland, Ohio, address.

The "YABMUR" investigation—for reasons of economy on its telex machines, the FBI assigned abbreviated names to its cases—was about to wash up on Lucy Gilly's front steps.

Lucy did not flinch when two FBI agents knocked on her front door on January 8, just three days after the Yablonskis' bodies were found; she knew Yablonski had her name and license plate number. Coolly, she admitted that she was the owner of a maroon Chevrolet described in the December 18, 1969 teletype the two agents showed her, but she denied that either she or her husband had used it to drive to Pennsylvania in mid-December.

The FBI agents interviewed Paul Gilly later that afternoon at the house he was remodeling on Cleveland's west side. He confessed he had traveled to Pennsylvania, but he lied about why. The house painter told the agents that he had borrowed Lucy's car to take a woman he met in Fay's Bar in East Cleveland to West Virginia and Pennsylvania. Gilly sheepishly admitted he had not told his wife about this because he had sex with this woman on Lucy's back seat. He claimed the woman's name was "Jeanne" and that she was a country-western singer.

Gilly's story bothered the two agents. It was too glib, too rehearsed, and too fantastic. They began searching for Jeanne with little hope of finding her.

That same afternoon, two FBI agents from the Washington field office questioned Boyle inside his cavernous office at the UMWA headquarters building. He was smug. The day before, he had offered a $50,000 reward to anybody who could bring the killers to justice.

He claimed he could not think of anyone who would commit such an "atrocity," but he gave the agents a laundry list of possible motives. He pointed out that the union's retirees were furious with Yablonski because he planned to take away their right to vote in the UMWA's elections. Perhaps one of the old timers had snapped. He also speculated that his dead foe had run afoul of someone in the harness racing business or shaken down the wrong man in Washington County for a political contribution.

Boyle was sure the murders had been committed to cast the UMWA in a "bad light." When his questioning ended, he promised to contact the agents if he remembered anything else about Yablonski's unsavory past.

Down the hall, Edward Carey, the union's florid-faced general counsel, held a press conference. He invited the Department of Labor to investigate the election, and announced in a letter to Secretary Shultz that the UMWA was waiving all its rights under the Landrum-Griffin Act to delay a government probe until Yablonski's successors exhausted all their internal appeals. He believed Shultz would quickly uphold the election's results. The Secretary accepted Carey's invitation and began dispatching teams of investigators and auditors into the coalfields. It had taken Yablonski's murder to finally prod the Department of Labor into action.

Carey insisted that the election had been held with the "highest degree of integrity and honesty." He wanted the waiver and the union's $50,000 reward to end any speculation that the UMWA had played a role in the deaths. The union's lawyer ended his press conference with some ill-chosen words: "I bet my very life that this [the murders] is not connected with the union."

So, seemingly, was an arrest the Cleveland Police Department had carried out earlier that morning. Buddy Martin, badly hung over from another night of heavy drinking, had fired a sawed-off shotgun into the air and threatened to kill his landlady after she complained that the car he had just bought was blocking her driveway. She called the police. They found him passed out, but he fought furiously when they tried to handcuff him. They subdued him by knocking out his front teeth with a blackjack—a heavy leather pouch filled with lead—arrested him, and charged him with assaulting a police officer. Edward Carey had never heard of Buddy Martin, but he was about to.

The coal tipples that lined the rolling snow-covered countryside formed a silent honor guard for the Yablonskis as their funeral cortege weaved its way from the funeral home in Millsboro, fifteen miles to the north, to the Church of the Immaculate Conception in Washington, Pennsylvania. Over a thousand mourners waited to greet the three oak coffins.

The night before, many of the same mourners had filed by the closed brown caskets at the Burkus Funeral Home in nearby Millsboro. One sentiment was heard over and over as they passed by: "It's a shame— what a shame—a damn shame."

Joe Rauh stood in the white Gothic church's vestibule waiting for the bodies to arrive. He clutched a sheet of paper with the names of eleven coal miners who were Yablonski's coplaintiffs in the lawsuit he had filed on December 4, 1969. The lawsuit charged Boyle and his cronies with embezzling millions of dollars from the UMWA's treasury.

He talked quietly to each of the eleven men, one at time. Did they want to continue with the lawsuit? Many of these men had wives and daughters. Their faces were stamped with grief and fear.

None of them had expected taking on Boyle and his goons to be easy, but neither had they expected their challenge to end with three bodies—two of them innocent women. Elmer Brown, who had run as Yablonski's vice-president, hesitated. On January 3, two days before the Yablonskis were found, an anonymous caller told him he was next. He stared at the floor a long time before he answered Rauh. He slowly nodded his head. He owed that much to Jock. Only two plaintiffs refused to go on with the lawsuit.

Monsignor Charles Owen Rice, the priest who had married Jock and Marg thirty years before, officiated at the funerals. He wore white vestments, the symbol of hope in death. Rice stood before the three coffins arranged in the shape of a cross, as he struggled to make sense of the murders. He urged the coal miners in the audience, many of whose massive shoulders and big bellies strained against their white shirts and Sunday suits, to carry on the "great cause" of ousting Tony Boyle from their union and restoring democracy to the UMWA.

An activist priest, Rice had taken part in the civil rights movement and the 1967 antiwar march on the Pentagon. As he looked down at the mourners, he spoke about the blood-drenched decade of the 1960s and compared Jock Yablonski's assassination to that of the Kennedy brothers and Martin Luther King Jr. The Yablonskis' murders, he observed, were "a deed of infamy that had in it much of all that sickened us in the decade that just finished." Many miners, their coal-darkened calloused hands clasped in prayer, nodded in agreement.

No representatives of the country's largest labor unions came to the funerals or sent flowers. Only Walter Reuther, the president of the United Auto Workers and the target himself of at least three failed assassination attempts, including one that shredded his right arm, denounced the murders and called for an immediate federal investigation.

It was one degree above zero when the three hearses, their tires spewing smoke, finally ground to a halt near the highest hilltop in the Washington Cemetery. Six coal miners carried Yablonski to his grave. Subzero twenty-mile-an-hour gusts of wind cut through the mourners' coats and numbed their faces. The funeral tent's persistent snapping made it impossible to hear the priest's final words as the coffins were lowered into the frozen ground.

After the graveside service was over, many of the funeral-goers returned to the church's basement for hot coffee and lunch. More than seventy of Yablonski's followers joined Mike Trbovich, who had served as one of the rebel's campaign managers, and Joe Rauh in a school that stood next to the church. Some squeezed into children's desks while others lined the classroom's white walls.

Rauh stepped in front of them and gazed at the floor. He knew that if he looked into their faces, he would burst into tears. In his baritone voice, he explained to them how they could force a new election and continue their battle to clean up their union. He pledged to stand by them if they wanted to continue fighting. He asked them to raise their hands if they wanted to keep Yablonski's rebellion alive.

When he lifted his eyes, he saw that every hand in the room was raised. No one spoke for surrender. He was jubilant. After the meeting, he shouted to waiting reporters, "The rebellion against Boyle goes on!"

Before the funerals, a reporter asked Mike Trbovich who was behind Yablonski's assassination. He answered without blinking. "You better ask Albert Pass."

Two FBI agents did so on January 9, just as the Yablonskis' funerals were wrapping up. The FBI had not ruled out that burglars had surprised and murdered the sleeping family, but it seemed unlikely. Agents in its Kentucky and Tennessee field offices knew all about

District 19's violent history of providing muscle whenever the union wanted to teach somebody a lesson.

The FBI also knew that Yablonski had alleged that Boyle had illegally loaned District 19 more than $3,500,000, and had been set to testify before a federal grand jury sitting in Washington, D.C. If the UMWA was behind Yablonski's assassination, its killers were probably from the Kentucky or Tennessee hills.

Pass told the two agents who had come to interview him that he had known Yablonski since 1943, but he denied knowing anyone who could have killed him. William Turnblazer Jr., District 19's president and one of Pass's co-conspirators, was more circumspect. He told the agents he was not going to talk to them without his lawyer.

Pass knew the agents would be back. He ordered his secretary to begin preparing phony worksheets for his mythical Research and Information Committee. These fake time sheets showed the amount of money each of its twenty-three members had earned from October 1968 until the end of September 1969.

Lucy went to LaFollette, Tennessee, two days later. Her father had $9,000 in murder money he wanted to get rid of. She took only $1,000 because she was afraid the FBI was watching her. Huddleston promised he would hold on to the rest. He put $8,000 into a plastic coleslaw container and hid it in a storage cellar behind his house.

On January 13, two FBI agents knocked on his front door. They had no reason to suspect he played any role in the Yablonskis' killings, but they knew about his bloody past and his time at Brushy Mountain. Huddleston admitted he knew who Yablonski was but little else. He told the agents he did not know anyone who wanted to harm him.

Huddleston's interview worried Pass. The day before, the Department of Labor had notified him it was sending a team of auditors to District 19's headquarters in Middlesboro. Secretary of Labor Shultz was dispatching audit teams to most of the UMWA's districts. They wanted to know if Boyle and his cronies had siphoned off any of the union's money to pay for his reelection.

Pass was taking no chances. He established a legitimate Research and Information Committee. He also summoned his six field representatives and warned them that the auditors were probably going to question the twenty-three members of the original, bogus committee.

Pass wanted the field representatives to remind their members that they had received $19,695 for organizing expenses and spent it all on themselves. None of them had kicked back any money. To reinforce their silence and their lies, Pass ordered them to tell the old men they would die in the electric chair if they broke ranks and told the auditors the truth.

James Charles Phillips was jealous and suspicious. Claude Vealey and Buddy Martin were driving new cars, when both men had been broke just two days before. Vealey's live-in girlfriend had burst into tears when he left town with Paul Gilly on December 30 because she did not have enough money even to buy groceries—Phillips fed her. Now, Vealey was driving a sporty-looking Oldsmobile. Phillips questioned his neighbor about his new wealth. Vealey lied. He claimed he, Gilly, and Martin had robbed a bar in West Virginia.

Phillips was not the only one who doubted Vealey's story. On January 3, two men from the Tennessee hills overheard Martin in the Family Tavern bragging about how he "made it big the other night," and had earned "blood money" doing it. One of the men was Cleve Byrge, Phillips's stepuncle.

How Martin made his "blood money" became clearer on January 5, the day Phillips heard on the radio that the Yablonskis had been murdered. He asked Vealey if he knew anything about the killings. The West Virginian giggled and said he would never do anything like that.

Phillips did not believe him. On January 12, he told his stepuncle that Gilly had tried to recruit him to kill Jock Yablonksi. He feared the three killers were going to murder him next because he knew too much.

Byrge saw Vealey the next day. Vealey told him about Buddy Martin's arrest. He seemed worried and distracted. He mumbled to Byrge
that he was going to West Virginia.

Byrge had heard enough. On January 15, he and James Haynes, who
had also heard Martin boasting about blood money, went to the FBI's
Cleveland field office and asked to speak to the FBI agent in charge of
the Yablonski case. They were eager to collect Boyle's $50,000 reward
and save Phillips's life. The two men told an agent investigating the
murders that he should be looking for Buddy Martin, and two other
men named Paul and Claude. They said Martin was in the city jail.

Joseph "Joe" Masterson, an agent assigned to the murders, called
the city jail and learned that a prisoner named Aubran "Buddy" Martin
was serving fifty-five days in the House of Correction in nearby War-
rensville for assaulting a police officer a week before. Martin was about
to meet an FBI agent a lot more streetwise than he was.

FOURTEEN

We Got Lucky

Joe Masterson was sure he was going to die. A speeding car packed with marijuana was about to cut him in two. The Federal Bureau of Narcotics agent had two choices: he could jump out of the way, or draw his pistol. Masterson drew his service revolver and aimed it at the center of the driver's forehead.

Crippled Louie, a drug smuggler who had earned his nickname the hard way after Canadian police shredded one of his legs in a gunfight, blinked first. He slammed on the brakes of the speeding car within a few feet of Masterson, threw it into reverse, and backed it into a sea of oncoming traffic, which crushed the car's frame.

Louie was trapped in his badly damaged car. He offered rolled-up wads of cash to any passerby who could free him. Masterson and two officers from the New York City Police Department pried Louie loose and stuffed him into a squad car before a growing crowd of excited onlookers could rescue him. Tired of working endless drug stakeouts and worrying that his luck was going to run out, Masterson joined the FBI a month later, in June 1965.

The FBI paid more than the narcotics bureau, and it provided its agents with a much richer diet of cases. Masterson began chasing bank robbers and hijackers instead of drug dealers and their red-eyed customers. His first two postings were Louisville and Newark. In late 1967, the FBI sent him to its Cleveland field office.

Masterson's experience as a narcotics agent working the streets gave him an edge over many of his new colleagues. Hoover had never wanted anything to do with drug cases because of the temptations they dangled in front of his men, but Masterson believed narcotics cases offered some of the best training a young agent could get.

He developed a sixth sense in the seamy world of high-stakes illicit sales, unscrupulous informants, and heart-stopping undercover drug buys. He learned to read faces and body language as well as he could a banker's ledger or an accountant's spreadsheet.

Masterson needed all his street smarts when Buddy Martin came sauntering out of his jail cell the afternoon of January 15, 1970. With a cigarette loosely hanging from his lips, Martin looked cocky and self-assured as he took a seat in the jail's visitor's room. Masterson sized him up instantly as a "hard ass, cold-nosed punk."

He started with a broad question. He asked Martin where he was on December 31. Martin claimed he had spent the day and night with his wife. He could not remember where he was the two days before that.

The FBI agent changed direction. Did Martin buy a 1964 Ford Thunderbird on New Year's Eve? Martin said he did not. His wife bought the car. He would never buy a car for her with his own money, he added dismissively.

Masterson pretended to be satisfied with Martin's answers. He snapped his notebook shut, thanked him for his time, and got up to leave. As he neared the door, he wheeled around and stared into Martin's expressionless face. "Why," he asked, "did you murder the whole family?"

Masterson's question slammed into Martin like a hard punch. He turned pale and started shaking. His cigarette hit the floor. Masterson continued to bore into him. "Did Claude and Paul join you in slaughtering the Yablonskis?"

Still trembling, Martin denied killing the family or knowing anyone named Claude or Paul. Masterson smirked at him and asked the jail's warden if he could search the prisoner's wallet. It contained a slip of paper with phone numbers for both names. Masterson knew then that Martin was one of the killers; he found the same two names and numbers in Martin's address book the next day when he searched his apartment. "We got lucky," he later admitted.

Masterson was not the only one who got lucky. On January 16, 1970, three auditors from the Department of Labor began raking through District 19's financial records. They were looking for any clues that showed Tony Boyle had used the union's money to defeat Jock Yablonski.

The auditors were puzzled by $19,970 connected to a mysterious Research and Information Committee composed of twenty-three retired coal miners. Two loans from the UMWA's headquarters in Washington, D.C.—one for $10,000 in September and another for the same amount in October 1969—had paid for its activities. Albert Pass had written directly to Boyle when he requested the loans. Each committee member had received a check for his expenses on September 30 and on October 10. The committee's disbursement journal showed payments of $12,315 to the twenty-three men in September and $7,650 in October.

The auditors questioned Pass about the committee. He claimed it had played a key role in District 19's campaign to organize nonunion coal miners in southeastern Kentucky and Tennessee. The members had secretly collected information on mine openings and closings.

Pass said their services had been invaluable: the coal operators knew all the UMWA's field representatives by sight, but they did not know the pensioners. The retirees were able to travel around the coalfields, collecting priceless intelligence. He said the committee's work started on October 1, 1968. He could not answer why none of the twenty-three men had submitted any receipts or itemized expense records.

More troubling, none of the committee members could give the auditors the names of any mines they had visited, or explain how they had spent the money the union had paid them. Even their wives did not know about the two checks the union gave to each member.

None of this made any sense to the auditors. How, they wondered, could old men living on $150-a-month pensions and social security conceal such bonanzas from their wives? The payments to each committee member ranged from $400 to $650 in September and from $300 to $350 in October—fortunes in the southern Appalachian coalfields. Mysteriously, none of the members had deposited any of this money into their tiny bank accounts.

On January 29, 1970, the chief of the audit team sent its findings back to headquarters in Silver Spring, Maryland. He characterized the nearly $20,000 paid to the committee's members as "unusual" and pointed out all the discrepancies in the pensioners' statements. He recommended that his report, especially its appendix prepared by Gene Confer, who had broken out the amounts each of the twenty-three pensioners had received, be forwarded to Hollis Bowers, who ran the Department of Labor's Special Investigations Branch. Perhaps Bowers could figure out what the committee's true purpose was.

Phillips did not like going to the FBI, but he liked dying a lot less. While Masterson questioned Martin, Phillips drove to Paul Gilly's house. He was scared. He had heard a rumor while drinking in the Family Tavern that detectives wanted to question him about the murders.

Their meeting was tense. Each man threatened the other: Phillips told Gilly he would tell the police everything if the killers tried to pin the triple murders on him, while Gilly warned Phillips to keep his mouth shut if he knew what was good for him. Their confrontation only heightened Phillips's growing fears that he was going to become the next murder victim.

Phillips weighed his options as he brooded over Gilly's threat. If he went to the FBI, he knew he would have to confess his own role in stalking Yablonksi, but he decided going to jail was better than going to the cemetery. On January 17, Phillips walked into the FBI's Cleveland field office and began talking.

He told the FBI about the contract on Yablonski's life and how Gilly and Vealey had offered him some "easy money" if he helped them kill him. Phillips also described an elderly white male whom he had met during a trip to LaFollette, Tennessee. He believed this man gave Gilly at least $4,000.

That same day, agents questioned Adelheid "Vicki" Farthing, Phillips's girlfriend. She said she heard Vealey shout on December 29 that he was "going to Pennsylvania with Paul." The FBI began casting a wide net for Vealey and preparing search warrants for Gilly's two houses in Cleveland.

They tracked Vealey to Marmet, West Virginia, where his mother lived, and then back to Cleveland. Phillips told Masterson that Vealey had a new girlfriend, Diane Cook, whom he had met during a New Year's Day drinking spree. She worked as a checker at Whitman's Market, a few blocks from the Family Tavern.

Masterson had a hunch. Vealey would not flee the city for good without saying goodbye to her. He and other agents staked out the market.

While they waited for Vealey, other agents searched Gilly's houses. They carted away an arsenal of weapons, some blocks of wood that had been used for target practice, and a highway map of the northeastern United States with Clarksville circled.

Masterson was right: they did not have to wait long for Vealey to appear at Whitman's. The FBI arrested him on January 20, while he was in a parked car outside the market. Agents charged him with bail jumping: he had failed to appear on January 5 in Youngstown for his burglary trial. Vealey staunchly maintained his innocence. He did not kill anyone. Masterson and another agent questioned him for two hours. They were almost sickened by Vealey's pungent smell. The sullen West Virginian, Masterson later recalled, "stunk to high heaven."

Masterson decided to play on Vealey's greed and his fears. He told Vealey about the $50,000 reward for the capture and conviction of the Yablonskis' killers, but he pointed out to him that he probably would not live long enough to collect it.

He warned Vealey that some very angry Pennsylvania State policemen were coming to get him, policemen who loved Yablonski. He
doubted Vealey would live long enough to cross the Pennsylvania state
line unless he cooperated with the FBI. Masterson's story terrified
Vealey. He agreed during the early morning hours of January 21 to tell
him everything he knew about the killings.

Vealey's confession covered twenty single-spaced pages, accompanied by five crudely drawn diagrams of the house, the killers' overlook, and their escape route. On its blue-lined pages, Vealey coldly and
methodically described what happened in the early morning hours of
December 31, 1969, inside the Yablonskis' farmhouse:

> I aimed the carbine at the Yablonskis, who had awakened. Mrs.
> Yablonski laid in the bed and was screaming . . . Paul Gilly . . .
> fired one time at the Yablonskis . . . Buddy Martin came over,
> stepped just inside the door and fired four times . . . After
> Buddy fired the woman made no further sounds and I could
> hear Yablonski gurgling. I took the weapon from Buddy . . . and
> fired two shots at Yablonski. (The FBI later determined that he
> fired four shots at him) . . . When I fired, Yablonski had fallen
> into a sitting position on the floor . . . We went downstairs, put
> our shoes back on in the hallway, went out the same way we
> came in.

The FBI arrested Gilly and Martin later that day. First-degree
murder was a state crime, but that did not stop Robert Krupansky,
the United States Attorney for the Northern District of Ohio, from
detaining the three killers. He charged them with conspiring to interfere with, and actual interference with, Yablonski's rights as a union
member by force and violence. These federal charges would hold the
murderers in Cleveland jails while local prosecutors in Pennsylvania
collected enough evidence to indict them for first-degree murder in
Washington County.

JOSEPH ANDREW "CHIP" YABLONSKI
A lawyer who campaigned with his father in 1969 and who backed Arnold Miller in 1972, he slept with a loaded pistol under his pillow after his family was murdered. (© DON STILLMAN)

ARNOLD RAY MILLER
Photographed here with Chip Yablonski at his December 15, 1972, news conference after his election victory over Tony Boyle, Miller brought democracy back to the UMWA.

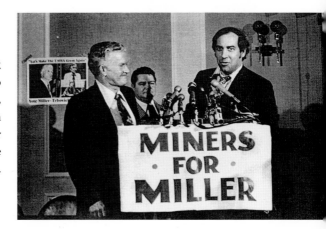

RALPH NADER
The public's watchdog against corporate greed and corruption, he believed that safety in the coal mines was impossible without a democratic UMWA that was not in the coal industry's hip pocket. (LIBRARY OF CONGRESS, PRINTS & PHOTOGRAPHS DIVISION, PHOTOGRAPH BY THOMAS J. O'HALLORAN [LC-DIG-DS-01260])

KEN YABLONSKI
Pictured at the May 1972 Miners for Democracy Convention, he warned his father, "Either you will destroy them or they will destroy you," after Yablonski decided to run against Boyle. (LANA REEVES)

CHARLOTTE YABLONSKI
A social worker, she was staying at her parents' farmhouse when one of her father's assassins crept into her bedroom during the early morning hours of New Year's Eve 1969. (TERRY DEGLAU)

MARGARET "MARG" YABLONSKI
Marg was Jock Yablonski's playwright wife. She believed Tony Boyle was a "nut," but she never dreamed her husband's decision to run against him would cost her so much.
(JOSEPH A. YABLONSKI)

JOSEPH "JOCK" YABLONSKI
A longtime union insider and a fiery orator, Yablonski predicted his own assassination when he ran against Boyle for the UMWA's presidency.
(© DON STILLMAN)

AUBRAN WAYNE "BUDDY" MARTIN
Dubbed the "baby-faced killer" by the Special Prosecutor, Buddy Martin was only twenty-one years old when he emptied his pistol into the sleeping family. (FBI / U.S. GOVERNMENT)

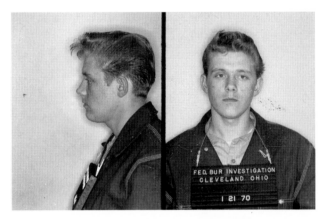

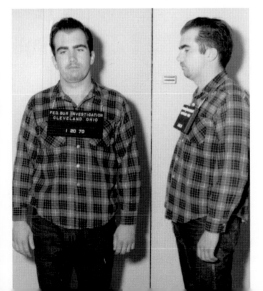

CLAUDE EDWARD VEALEY
A small-time thief who was highly skilled at failing, Vealey confessed to the three murders within hours of his arrest and testified against both his co-conspirators. (FBI / U.S. GOVERNMENT)

PAUL EUGENE GILLY
Shown here after his arrest, Gilly was a Cleveland house painter whose wife and father-in-law hounded him into recruiting Jock Yablonski's killers from the hillbilly underworld. (FBI / U.S. GOVERNMENT)

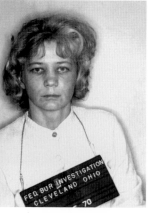

ANNETTE "LUCY" GILLY
A master manipulator with a cold-blooded instinct for survival, Lucy was willing to do whatever it took to save herself from the electric chair after the Yablonskis were murdered.
(FBI / U.S. GOVERNMENT)

SILOUS HUDDLESTON
Photographed after he was sentenced to the penitentiary in 1946 for grand larceny, Huddleston was one of the UMWA's most brutal enforcers. He was the middleman in the assassination plot.
(FBI / U.S. GOVERNMENT)

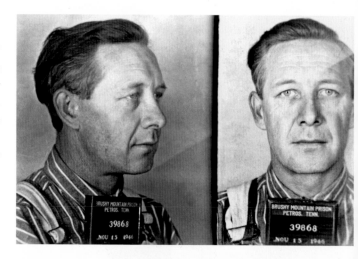

ALBERT EDWARD PASS AND WILLIAM JENKINS TURNBLAZER JR.
Shown here while holding court in District 19, Pass (center) and Turnblazer (right) presided over the union's most violent precinct. Boyle tapped them to oversee Yablonski's assassination.
(FBI / U.S. GOVERNMENT)

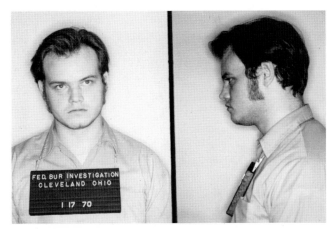

JAMES CHARLES PHILLIPS
Afraid that Yablonski's killers were coming after him next because he knew too much, Phillips walked into the FBI's Cleveland field office on January 17, 1970, and started talking. (FBI / U.S. GOVERNMENT)

JOSEPH MASTERSON
Pictured here (second from the left) standing beside Paul Gilly (third from left, with pocket handkerchief) in a police lineup, the wily FBI agent applied his street smarts to solving the murders. (FBI / U.S. GOVERNMENT)

RICHARD AUREL SPRAGUE
The best prosecutor in Pennsylvania if not the country, Sprague, pictured here in his Philadelphia office, staged the killers' trials with a master show-man's sense of drama, order, and pitch.
(COURTESY OF RICHARD SPRAGUE)

JOHN L. LEWIS
Coal miners worshipped the larger-than-life Lewis, pictured here lecturing a congressio-nal committee, but he built the sycophantic and undemocratic system that Tony Boyle exploited so ruthlessly.
(LIBRARY OF CONGRESS, PRINTS & PHOTO-GRAPHS DIVISION, PHOTOGRAPH BY HARRIS & EWING [LC-DIG-HEC-29156])

MURDER WEAPON
Stolen during a house burglary in Tennessee, this pistol was used by the killers to murder all three Yablonskis. A U.S. Navy diver fished it out of the icy Monongahela River.
(FBI / U.S. GOVERNMENT)

**YABLONSKIS'
FARMHOUSE IN
CLARKSVILLE,
PENNSYLVANIA**
Built in the eighteenth-
century, this is the stone
farmhouse where Jock,
Marg, and Charlotte
Yablonski were cut down
during the early morning
hours of December 31, 1969.
(JOSEPH A. YABLONSKI)

JOSEPH RAUH JR.
Photographed at the Mayflower Hotel with Jock Yablonski during the insurgent's
May 29, 1969, campaign kickoff, the civil rights lawyer believed he was joining a
crusade against union corruption. (ASSOCIATED PRESS / HENRY BURROUGHS)

WILLIAM JACKSON PRATER

Prater, pictured here in a white coat surrounded by lawmen while on his way to the Erie County Courthouse, turned on his union bosses after he was convicted.

(BETTMANN / CONTRIBUTOR VIA GETTY IMAGES)

WILLIAM A. "TONY" BOYLE
Shown here on the campaign trail ranting against those who threatened his control of the UMWA, Boyle believed Yablonski committed treason by challenging him for the union's presidency.

Krupansky also charged the three men with obstructing justice, given that Yablonski was supposed to testify in January before a newly impaneled federal grand jury in Washington, D.C., about his claims that Boyle and his inner circle had embezzled money from the union's pension and retirement funds. Krupansky believed the killers assassinated Yablonski to keep him from testifying.

Vealey's mother was shocked by her son's arrest. Claude, she insisted, was not that "kind of person." Carol Richardson, Vealey's common-law wife, was also taken aback by the three arrests—but for different reasons. She told the FBI that Vealey did not have the nerve to kill anyone, Gilly was not the type, and Martin was too dumb to be involved in a planned murder.

On January 22, the district attorney's office in Washington County, Pennsylvania, issued arrest warrants, accusing the men of three counts of premeditated murder. Justin McCarthy was overjoyed by the news. The UMWA's spokesman told reporters the union was "delighted" there had been a break in the case, and crowed that the arrests vindicated the UMWA. None of the accused killers had any ties to the union.

Tony Boyle and Albert Pass were determined to keep it that way.

Boyle and Pass met in Washington, D.C., the day before the arrests. Pass had come to attend the International Executive Board's January 22 meeting. The two men had not seen one another since the murders.

Both were delighted that Yablonski was dead—he could no longer threaten them. In a rare display of conscience, however, Pass confessed to Boyle that he hated that Marg and Charlotte had been killed, too. Boyle nodded his head. He didn't mention that he had suggested assassinating Yablonski in his Clarksville home.

Their mourning for the two innocent women quickly over, Pass told Boyle about the Department of Labor's audit of District 19's records. He assured him everything was in order and that the auditors seemed satisfied with what he had told them about the Research and Information Committee's work. Boyle was not so sure. He wanted a thicker file on the committee's work. He instructed Pass to give a formal presentation about the committee to the union's executive board; when he did, he was met with a standing ovation.

While Pass was basking in undeserved praise, Masterson, with two other FBI agents and a deputy United States marshal, whisked Vealey to Clarksville, where he retraced the killers' bloody footsteps. By that evening, he had led the lawmen to where he and Martin had thrown the murder weapons into the Monongahela River, to the assassins' two vantage points overlooking the farmhouse, to the various bars he and Gilly had been in, and to the West Brownsville Motel, where he and Gilly had slept on December 27. Teams of evidence technicians, other FBI agents, and state policemen trailed behind them, searching for hard proof that Vealey was telling the truth.

They were not disappointed. Digging through nearly a foot of snow, they recovered the beer cans and the whiskey carton the assassins had tossed out of their car's windows while they were waiting for the lights to go out in the farmhouse. Forensic experts at the FBI's laboratory in Washington found the fingerprints of all three men on several of the cans, and Vealey's on the carton. They located another of Gilly's fingerprints on a bottle of Sprite that still sat on a table in the yet-to-be cleaned West Brownsville motel room he and Vealey had rented nearly a month before. Investigators also found maroon paint scrapings from Lucy's Chevrolet on a guardrail Gilly had hit while sliding down a hill at one of the vantage points.

The same day the FBI took Vealey to Clarksville, Phillips told other agents in Cleveland about his October 1969 trips to Washington, D.C., Scranton, and Clarksville with Vealey and Gilly to kill Yablonski. He said Gilly had called Lucy from Scranton and Clarksville to get information on Yablonski's whereabouts, which phone call records verified. He also told the agents about how he and Vealey had broken into Yablonski's house on Halloween and studied its layout.

While Phillips continued to supply the FBI's Cleveland agents with incriminating information, other agents found Jeanne Seely, the country-and-western singer Gilly claimed to have taken to West Virginia and Pennsylvania on December 18. Seely was a well-known vocalist with Jack and the Jolly Green Giants band who won a Grammy Award in 1966 for "Don't Touch Me." FBI agents located her on January 22 after calling scores of Central Appalachian country music recording studios and radio stations. Seely told the agents she had never heard of Paul Gilly and certainly had never had sex with him, much less in the back seat of a car. The band's calendar showed she was not even in Ohio, Pennsylvania, or West Virginia on December 18.

The FBI's most remarkable finds came after Clarksville's residents noticed a coal barge on the Monongahela River anchored near a small hole the FBI had cut through the icy crust coating the river's surface. Agents had swung fire axes to make a circle wide enough for a man's body to slide through six inches of ice. On January 24, the thermometer registered three degrees above zero in Clarksville. A bone-chilling wind made it even colder on the river.

None of this stopped Kenneth Russell from jumping off the barge and plunging through the small hole into twenty feet of swirling water. The FBI agent struggled against a strong current as he searched the riverbed littered with old tires, beer cans, tree limbs, and pieces of cable from a vanished footbridge. Late that afternoon, he wrestled free the killers' M1 carbine from thick mud and brought it to the surface. Agents wrapped it in plastic and sent it to the FBI's laboratory in Washington.

Within hours, the FBI traced its serial number to its original owner in Dayton, Ohio. Luther Anderson had ordered the rifle on October 10, 1965, from a Spiegel mail-order catalog for $63, to hunt deer. He sold the rifle once and bought it back. Then, on October 20, 1969, Anderson took it to a gun show in Mt. Sterling, Kentucky, where he traded it for a .38 caliber Smith & Wesson pistol and some whiskey. Henry Gilly, the man he traded guns with, had arrived in a maroon Chevrolet with Ohio license plates driven by his son, Paul.

Fred Schunk, a stockily built United States Navy master diver, found the .38 chrome-plated pistol on January 27 after spending three days crawling on his stomach on the riverbed. Phillips and Vealey identified it as one of the weapons they stole on November 14, 1969 from Dr. Sergeant's home in LaFollette, Tennessee. They told agents Gilly kept the pistol for himself.

That same day, the FBI got another break. Richard Baron, a small-time thief just released from the city jail, hitchhiked to the federal building. He told agents he had shared a jail cell with Martin for almost a month, and said the killer often had trouble sleeping because he was haunted by what he had done: he confessed to Baron that he could still see the Yablonskis' facial expressions and could not get them out of his mind.

Meanwhile, Phillips kept talking. The FBI showed him a photograph of Silous Huddleston. Phillips identified him as the elderly man in LaFollette who gave Paul Gilly $4,200. Vealey corroborated Phillips's statements. He said Gilly told him that Huddleston was the "go-between" between them and the man funding the murders.

While the agents in Cleveland built their cases against Lucy and Huddleston, others in Clarksville continued to gather evidence against the three killers. Their pictures in the local and Pittsburgh newspapers prompted several Clarksville residents to call the FBI. These eyewitnesses included bartenders, their customers, and liquor store cashiers who saw the three men drinking and eating in local taverns or sold them cartons of whiskey and six-packs of beer. Others said they had seen the killers' car, with out-of-state plates, lurking near the Yablonskis' farmhouse.

Trooper Elmer Schifko made a house-to-house sweep of residences near the Yablonskis' home. He asked their neighbors if they had seen anything suspicious during the last two months near the old farmhouse. The policeman found Kathy Rygle, a fourteen-year-old girl who showed him a sheet of paper she had saved from Thanksgiving when she and her cousin had played a game they had invented.

As the two girls sat by the Rygles' living room window a block away from Yablonski's farmhouse, Kathy had written down the state and license plate numbers of passing cars, while her cousin called out their makes and models. The fifth car they had seen that aftenoon was a maroon Caprice with Ohio license plate number CX-457.

United States Attorney Robert Krupansky had heard enough. On January 29, a federal grand jury sitting in Cleveland indicted Gilly, Vealey, and Martin with conspiracy and with violating Yablonski's rights as a union member by killing him.

A week later, the same grand jury indicted Lucy for conspiring with the three killers to murder Yablonski. When a team of FBI agents searched the Gillys' house again, they found a thick stack of newspaper clippings about the Yablonski murders.

Lucy appeared in court handcuffed to a chain around her waist. She pleaded innocent. After her husband was arrested, she knew she was going to be next. Her father suspected that too. Huddleston told Lucy the union would never abandon her unless she deserted it. If she did, its goons would kill her. Huddleston told her they were already plotting to silence Phillips because he had talked to the FBI.

Huddleston had his own problems. His immediate one was to hide the $8,000 he was still holding for Yablonski's killers. He knew the FBI was watching him. He persuaded seventy-two-year-old Dave Brandenburg, one of the twenty-three members of the phony Research and Information Committee and a self-ordained preacher with a third-grade education and a wife almost fifty years younger than he was, to hide it for him. Huddleston overcame the reverend's moral scruples about hiding "blood money" when he told him he could keep $500 for himself and another $500 if he had to hold on to it longer than three months.

Huddleston was right about the FBI's growing interest in him—Vealey's and Phillips's statements made sure of that. From the beginning, he maintained he knew nothing about the murders. When two agents interviewed him on January 22, they confronted a talented liar.

Huddleston praised Yablonski. His death had deprived the UMWA of a great leader. He did tell the truth about one thing: he told the agents about his deep love for the union. He admitted it was even deeper than his love for God.

Six days later, he told two FBI agents that he believed Ted Q. Wilson and the rival Southern Labor Union murdered Yablonski and his family. The agents were dumbfounded by Huddleston's lies.

The day before, George Smith Jr., had exposed Huddleston's attempt to recruit him to swing a lit hundred-pound sack of dynamite against Yablonski's bedroom window in Clarksville. Smith had told a friend about Huddleston's pitch. The friend had read about the murders in the newspaper and gone to the FBI. Smith then gave the FBI a nine-and-a-half-page statement admitting that Huddleston had offered him $2,100 and expenses to travel to Clarksville with Paul Gilly. He told the agents his life was not worth a "plug nickel" now because he had "talked."

Once he learned that the FBI was focusing on District 19, Hollis Bowers read the Department of Labor's audit report on the Research and Information Committee. Bowers ran the Department's Special Investigations' branch. He wondered why Albert Pass had written directly to Boyle to ask for the $20,000. All Pass's other requests for money had gone to John Owens, the UMWA's secretary-treasurer.

Bowers, a former FBI agent, believed he was staring at the fund that paid for Jock Yablonski's assassination. On February 17, he called Robert Krupansky, who immediately asked to see the report. Bowers flew to Cleveland the next afternoon. The United States Attorney agreed with Bowers's conclusions once he had read it.

Krupansky subpoenaed Huddleston to testify before the Cleveland grand jury. Huddleston refused to answer any questions, only giving the jurors his name, address, and former occupation. They indicted him on February 25, 1970.

The next day, Krupansky summoned Pass, Prater, and Turnblazer to appear before the same grand jury. He kept Prater on the witness stand for most of the day. After he finished testifying, Prater denounced the government's investigation. "Throughout our entire history," he brazenly lectured a television news crew, "people are always trying to pin things on the union and this is no exception."

Other labor bosses felt the same way. *American Labor*, one of organized labor's biggest trade magazines, ran an article in its February issue entitled "Equal Time for Tony Boyle." It circled the wagons around the embattled UMWA president and assailed his attackers, especially Yablonski's two sons and Joe Rauh, and claimed that any attack on Boyle was an attack on all labor unions. Not all the article's points were wrong, however: its anonymous author noted that "who ever paid the bill [for these bargain-basement assassins] had even less sense than the killers."

Union vice-president George Titler continued the attacks, telling the *Charleston Gazette* that Yablonski was a "thief." Titler bemoaned his transformation into a martyr. He suggested that Yablonski, who was "so crooked he could hide behind a corkscrew," had ties to the Mafia. "It is probably something like this," Titler confided to the reporter, "that got him killed."

Boyle hinted at the same thing on February 27 during a chaotic press conference at Pittsburgh's Hilton Hotel. He announced the union was establishing a four-man fact-finding commission to investigate the murders. He was forced to do this, he told a throng of skeptical reporters, because he was frustrated. Only "the whole truth," he shamelessly maintained, "can clear our union of any taint or guilt."

Boyle was tired of hearing "ugly allegations" and "wild charges" that he was somehow personally involved in the killings. He promised he would turn over to the government's prosecutors any evidence the commission uncovered. The besieged union president also warned that he planned to sue for libel any of his detractors who could not back up what they alleged. When a reporter tried to question him, a burly man dressed in a brown suit poked him in the back and told him to shut up.

While Boyle was planning his Potemkin village show trials, Jess Costa was planning real ones. Costa was the district attorney for Washington County, Pennsylvania, and realized that the murderers' trials were going to attract national and international attention. On March 1, 1970, he asked the best prosecutor in Pennsylvania to come to Washington County.

That was Richard Aurel Sprague, who was no stranger to murder and mayhem. He had seen plenty of both in the city of "brotherly love": Philadelphia.

FIFTEEN

A Whole Cage Full of Tigers

S prague's long string of sensational convictions of gang members, blackmailers, and cop killers earned him a reputation as the most feared and respected prosecutor in Philadelphia. That hardly matched his physical appearance: at only five foot seven, with a potbelly and the beginnings of a double chin, Sprague looked as plain as a loaf of white bread. Those who met him for the first time noticed his poker face and sad, hound-dog eyes. He always wore conservative blue or gray business suits, paired with understated ties always adorned with a clip bearing the seal of the city of Philadelphia.

Sprague had no political ambitions. This made him a rarity in a big city's prosecutor's office. He focused more on trying his cases than talking about them in front of a camera.

After serving in the United States Navy's submarine service during World War II and graduating from Temple University, Sprague attended the University of Pennsylvania's law school, where he was an indifferent student. He practiced briefly with a small law firm handling commercial transactions before he joined the Philadelphia County's Volunteer Defenders Association in 1956. The Association, which defended the city's indigents accused of crimes, changed Sprague's life.

He fell in love with the city's dingy courtrooms, which were full of raw human drama. His daily courtroom battles forced him to master the rules of evidence and become an expert cross-examiner. Sprague perfected the art of asking short, precise, rapid-fire questions designed to expose inconsistencies and overwhelm his opponents.

The Philadelphia County District Attorney's Office took note of Sprague's victories against its prosecutors. It hired him in 1958 after three of its lawyers resigned in one day.

By the time of the Yablonski murders, Sprague had supervised or handled over 15,000 criminal cases, more than 450 of which were murder cases. His conviction rate was astonishing. He had sought first-degree murder convictions in sixty-four cases and got what he asked for in sixty-three. Juries had agreed with his call for the death penalty more than twenty times.

Sprague's methods were unorthodox. He never scribbled a note. While other lawyers focused on their legal pads, he watched the defendant, looking for telltale signs of guilt or listening for contradictions. He retained every word of testimony and was absolutely humorless in the courtroom.

Sprague delivered his closing arguments to juries in his booming voice without a scrap of paper or a break in a sentence. He conveyed to them his burning sense of righteous indignation.

A Philadelphia judge who witnessed Sprague in action marveled over his ability to pounce on his opponents' witnesses and tear their stories apart. "Some men are like a tiger," he observed. "Dick Sprague is like a whole cage full of tigers—leashed and caged, thank God. But you can feel the power." In 1966, District Attorney Arlen Specter promoted Sprague to be his First Assistant. This promotion placed him in charge of the office's day-to-day operations and its 140 lawyers.

By 1970, Sprague's peers considered him not only the best prosecutor in Philadelphia but also in Pennsylvania. So did Frank P. Lawley Jr., the state's deputy attorney general. He called Jess Costa, the district attorney of Washington County, shortly after the Yablonskis' bodies were discovered. Costa had been complaining for weeks that federal authorities were freezing him out of the case.

Lawley knew the county had little serious crime; Costa served as its chief prosecutor only two days a week. His five assistants also worked part-time, and spent the rest of the week representing clients in their private law practices.

Lawley also knew that Costa had tried only four murder cases. He suggested to him that Washington County appoint Sprague as its special prosecutor to try the Yablonskis' killers.

A more vain, politically ambitious man would have kept the cases for himself, but Costa understood his own limitations. He also knew Jock Yablonski. He wanted his killers convicted. Costa called Sprague in late February 1970 and asked him to take over the prosecutions.

Sprague did not hesitate. The murders were a prosecutor's dream: they were especially vicious, and their trials offered a national stage. They were also intriguing. From what he had read in the newspapers, he suspected that Gilly, Martin, and Vealey were hired assassins, not burglars. The three cut-rate killers were only the tip of the iceberg. The real questions were: who hired them, and why.

Arlen Specter consented to letting Sprague prosecute the killers after he agreed to continue performing his duties as First Assistant. Sprague hammered out another agreement with Attorney General John Mitchell. He wanted to direct and control the FBI agents assigned to the murders. Mitchell gave Sprague the federal authority he needed by naming him his special assistant.

On March 1, 1970, Costa announced Sprague's appointment as Washington County's special prosecutor. Eleven days later, Sprague flew to Cleveland to confer with United States Attorney Robert Krupansky. The government's chief lawyer in Ohio was not encouraging. He believed Silous Huddleston was the key to unlocking the case, but he thought that the old man, one of the UMWA's most devout disciples, would never betray his union masters. Sprague was agnostic. He wanted to see all the evidence first.

On March 14, Sprague went to Yablonski's boarded-up farmhouse in Clarksville. He inspected the two bedrooms where the killings happened, questioned Yablonski's two sons for hours about what kind of people their slain parents and sister had been, and climbed to the killers' two vantage points.

He also spent time learning about Clarksville and the people who lived there. He knew a lot about picking juries in Philadelphia, but he did not know anything about the inhabitants of southwestern Pennsylvania's coal country. He even circled the area in a state police helicopter to get a feel for its geography.

Sprague flew back to Cleveland three weeks later. Vealey threatened to retract his January 21 confession unless the special prosecutor offered him a deal. He and the other four murder suspects were preparing to fight their extradition from Ohio to Pennsylvania. Vealey promised to testify against the others in exchange for no death penalty and a life sentence in prison.

Sprague shook his head. He refused to bargain with Vealey. That night, the puffy-faced killer slept in leg irons that the special prosecutor had ordered. Sprague's intransigence astonished not only Vealey, but Krupansky and the FBI. They were accustomed to winning a defendant's cooperation by promising to ask the judge for a reduced sentence after he testified truthfully.

Sprague wanted to send a message to the killers—and his prosecution team. He alone was in charge, and he wanted justice, not a bundle of watered-down plea bargains.

He realized he was taking a huge gamble by rebuffing Vealey's offer, but he saw something no one else did when he looked in the killer's eyes. Vealey was scared of him, and he was even more afraid of dying in the electric chair. Sprague sensed he would eventually crumble.

While Sprague waited for Vealey's willpower to wilt, two brothers were making their own plans to revive their slain father's dream of a democratic and clean union.

SIXTEEN

Their Father's Sons

Chip Yablonski was lucky to be alive. On December 30, 1969, he had woken up in the same bed his sister was murdered in early the next morning. Barely two months before, two rough-looking men with hillbilly accents had knocked on the door of his house in Bethesda, Maryland. Chip did not know, as he lied to them about where his father was, that both men were fingering loaded pistols stuffed in their coat pockets, or that one of them wanted to fire-bomb his house and kill everyone in it.

Ever since Ken Yablonski found the three decomposing bodies on January 5, 1970, the two brothers believed that Tony Boyle and the UMWA were behind the murders. They had not been shy about saying it, especially to the press. Boyle and his cronies had reacted angrily, labeling the two men's charges as wild and reckless. Chip now slept with a pistol under his pillow, while his wife tossed and turned at night. He told a West Virginia newspaper reporter, "They won't get me like they got my father."

Everyone who knew the two brothers knew they would not let their father's reform movement die with him. Shortly after the funerals, the brothers formed a pact. They were not going to rest until they had toppled Tony Boyle from his throne.

Their most daunting challenge was keeping their father's cause in the public eye. They faced stiff competition. The war in Vietnam was not going well: nearly 9,500 Americans had been killed in 1969. Americans were also distracted by bad economic news, as inflation began eating away at their disposable income.

The brothers refused to be discouraged. One month after the burials, Ken Yablonski told a group of dissident coal miners that he and his brother were picking up their father's fallen torch. "We don't deserve to be called Jock's sons," he said, with tears in his eyes, "if we don't continue his fight." They had little time to mourn.

Their first chance came when the United States Senate's Subcommittee on Labor launched a far-ranging investigation of the 1969 election and the Department of Labor's handling of Yablonski's complaints about it. George Meany, the septuagenarian head of the AFL-CIO, almost derailed the investigation before it started. He opposed any congressional probe into the UMWA, arguing it would harm all labor unions.

The savage murders roused Congress out of its torpor. Meany grudgingly accepted this political reality, but he fought to steer any hearings to the most favorable forum he could find. Democratic congressional leaders bowed to his pressure. They chose the United States Senate's Subcommittee on Labor to hold the hearings. Harrison A. Williams Jr., a liberal prolabor Democrat from New Jersey, was the committee's chair.

They selected Williams's subcommittee over Senator John B. McClellan's powerful Permanent Subcommittee on Investigations, a body with a long history of spectacular labor hearings. McClellan's hearings into the Teamsters and their links to organized crime in the late 1950s dominated the front pages of all the big city dailies. By the time he finished in 1959, polls showed that Americans considered "labor union problems" to be among the top eight challenges facing the country, on the same footing as defense and education. Meany successfully argued that any investigation led by McClellan, a conservative Democrat from Arkansas, would be just an excuse "to put the screws to labor."

On February 5, 1970, Williams summoned Chip Yablonski to

testify as his subcommittee's leadoff witness. His carefully prepared testimony electrified the hearing room and garnered national attention. He charged Boyle with mounting a reelection campaign riddled with financial irregularities, voting fraud, and outright terror. He bitterly observed that his father never would have run if he had known his campaign was going to cost the lives of his wife and daughter.

The younger Yablonski was no softer on the departments of Labor and Justice. He accused both of dragging their feet when his father begged for their help. Joe Rauh, sitting beside him, had said much the same about the Department of Labor on January 13 when he sent a letter to Secretary Shultz lambasting him for doing nothing to stop Boyle from stealing the election.

Rauh did not stop there, writing that he and the Yablonski family believed that the Department of Labor's failure to investigate the insurgent's well-founded complaints contributed directly to the three murders.

Chip Yablonski's riveting testimony kept his martyred father's cause alive in the press. A month later, Secretary Shultz breathed new life into it. He concluded that Boyle had used widespread fraud to steal the election.

Shultz's investigators determined that Boyle had denied Yablonski the right to post observers at polling places, failed to allow some locals to vote at all, used embezzled union money to pay for his campaign, declined to ensure miners could cast their votes in secrecy, and subjected reform-minded voters to "penalty, discipline or improper interference or reprisal." The investigators also accused the UMWA of failing to keep proper financial records.

The government filed suit on March 5, 1970. Department of Justice lawyers asked the federal judge presiding over the case to overturn the election and order a new one under Shultz's supervision. It had taken the Department of Labor's 230 investigators sixty days, 4,400 interviews, and $500,000 of taxpayers' money to verify what Yablonski and Rauh had told their Secretary months before.

The Yablonski brothers held a press conference the next day. While they welcomed the government's lawsuit, they pointed out it contained almost nothing that their father and Rauh had not spoon-fed the Department of Labor before the murders. The brothers told reporters they could never forgive Shultz for his "inexcusable inaction" during the campaign.

Tony Boyle could not forgive Shultz, either. On March 9, he strode into the National Press Club's grand ballroom in Washington, D.C., to face the city's press corps. He told his closest aides he was going to set the record straight.

Boyle did anything but. After raising his hand and solemnly swearing to "Almighty God" to tell the truth, he read a rambling fourteen-page statement that tore into his critics and the Department of Labor. He called the deaths of the Yablonskis "criminal" and "tragic," but he denied playing any role in them or knowing anyone who had. He complained angrily that those who questioned his honesty were part of the "totalitarian liberal establishment."

Boyle was especially upset by Secretary Shultz's decision to void his election victory over Yablonski. He called it "perhaps the cheapest fraud ever exercised by the United States government on the American labor movement." He charged that the federal government was trying to disenfranchise the country's coal miners. As he scowled into the news cameras, he snarled that he once believed "only Communists were capable of such duplicity."

Boyle's tirade convinced none of the reporters who gathered to listen to him. His answers to their questions only eroded his credibility. They were filled with lies and outright evasions, diluted by poor memory, and littered with non sequiturs.

Reporters were not the only ones who studied Boyle's poor performance. Yablonski's followers were emboldened by the government's lawsuit and Boyle's failure to win any converts to his denials. They began to forge a rank-and-file movement strong enough to beat him after the new election was announced.

On April 1, 1970, hundreds of miners flocked to Clarksville to attend a memorial service for their slain leader. April 1 was a traditional miners' holiday; on that day in 1898, the union's miners won their first contract limiting their workday to eight hours. Most of the miners in Clarksville came from Pennsylvania, West Virginia, Kentucky, Ohio, Indiana, and Illinois. They caucused in the basement of a church, only blocks away from Yablonski's empty farmhouse. They formed the Miners for Democracy Steering Committee.

In death, Yablonski had become the force for reform that he longed to be in the last half year of his life. The reformers organized raffles and raised money from private foundations to sustain their new party and to underwrite the *Miner's Voice*, their own newspaper.

All of this had taken considerable courage. Many of those who came to honor Yablonski worried they might be the next targets of Boyle's assassins. They carried loaded guns, equipped their yards with high-beam floodlights, and bought ferocious dogs.

Losing their lives was only one of their worries. They knew Boyle was going to try to strip them of their jobs, health insurance, and pensions. They predicted correctly that he planned to charge them with dual unionism—the formation of an independent movement inside the UMWA. John L. Lewis had used this devastating charge to purge several of his most strident foes from the UMWA.

Rauh understood the risks these men were taking. He believed only the federal courts could protect their uprising and guarantee their rights to take part in it. If the 1960s had been about anything, it had been the federal courts' enormous power to right historic wrongs and expand individual rights. Rauh wanted the courts to weigh in now on the side of the reformers.

In late April 1970, he founded the Miners' Project, a tiny public-interest law firm dedicated to defending the rights of the Miners for Democracy in court. The Miners' Project worked under the umbrella of Marian Wright Edelman's Washington Research Project, another public-interest litigating group, which specialized in assisting poor children. Rauh had to find his own funding and office space, but Edelman agreed to provide the Miners' Project with oversight, copying, and bookkeeping services.

In the beginning, Chip Yablonski and Clarice Feldman, who had worked with him at the National Labor Relations Board and who had helped Rauh during the waning days of Jock Yablonski's campaign, were the Miners' Project's only lawyers. The number of lawyers doubled to four in 1971, when two former United States Supreme Court law clerks joined the team, and by late 1972 the staff swelled to fifteen, many lured from the country's top law schools.

Rauh financed their initial work with $50,000 in foundation grants. He was well known in wealthy liberal circles because of the key roles he had played in founding Americans for Democratic Action, and his work for the NAACP and the Leadership Conference on Civil Rights. Rauh had little trouble raising the money from such benefactors as the Field and Abelard foundations and a host of wealthy New Yorkers. The press's coverage of the murders and of Chip Yablonski's Senate testimony also attracted donors who were drawn to the fight to combat union corruption. By 1972, the Miners' Project's annual budget had ballooned to $150,000—or over $920,000 in today's dollars.

Rauh turned the Miners' Project loose on Boyle. The Project's lawsuits against him kept the reform movement alive while its members waited for a new election. In its first seven months, the Project filed a motion in federal court to allow the Miners for Democracy to intervene in the government's pending election lawsuit, leaned on federal inspectors to enforce the recently passed 1969 Federal Mine Safety Act, opposed coal operators' injunctions ordering miners to return to work inside unsafe mines, and thwarted President Nixon's nomination of J. Richard Lucas, a professor and the head of the department of mining engineering at Virginia Polytechnic Institute, to head the Bureau of Mines because he had owned $200,000 of coal mining stock.

Its attorneys also filed a lawsuit in Pittsburgh urging that "bogus" locals—those with fewer than the required ten working members—be disbanded, and that pensioners be transferred to working locals. While they waited for that verdict, they aided Ken Yablonski in his defense of Miners for Democracy candidates who were running to unseat Boyle's handpicked slate of candidates in the union's District 5's December 1970 elections.

Boyle threatened to expel the proreform candidates and their supporters from the UMWA for sponsoring campaign literature that criticized the incumbents. Ken Yablonski and Miners' Project's lawyers relied on the Landrum-Griffin Act's "free speech" section to put a stop to that. Undeterred, Boyle established a commission to try the reformers for "dual unionism." He claimed that the Miners for Democracy were attempting to supplant the UMWA as the true bargaining representative for the miners. An emergency hearing held on a Sunday morning in a federal judge's living room ended Boyle's kangaroo court.

On December 14, 1970, the Project's lawyers persuaded the Department of Labor to seize the ballot boxes in District 5 after they accused Boyle's candidates of tampering with the election's absentee ballots. The small public-interest law firm was well on its way to achieving Rauh's goals of giving the reform movement a voice in the federal courts while distinguishing the UMWA as the most sued labor union in the United States.

While the two brothers took on large-scale union corruption, they still wanted personal justice. In early May 1970, they met in Philadelphia with Richard Sprague.

The special prosecutor let them see all his files on the murders. He cross-examined the Yablonskis for two full days on every scrap of paper in his possession, and was particularly interested in any gaps they identified. By the time the family members left on a Sunday evening, they were convinced that Sprague was the right man to bring the assassins to justice. He told them that he intended to peel off the layers of the crime like the layers of an onion.

Sprague strongly suspected the union was behind the murders, but others were not so sure. Secretary of Labor George Shultz was one of the most prominent doubters. He insisted to Senator Williams's subcommittee on May 4, 1970—even though a federal grand jury sitting in Cleveland had indicted the Gillys, Vealey, Martin, and Huddleston for violating Yablonski's rights as a union member by killing him— that there was no connection between the UMWA's election and the murders.

Shultz's comment appalled Ralph Nader. "In a civilized country," he bitterly told reporters after the Secretary's testimony, "George Shultz would be in jail."

United States Attorney Robert Krupansky was also shocked by Shultz's testimony, and called the Department of Justice in Washington to confirm what the Secretary actually said. He worried that Shultz's comment jeopardized the cases he was building against the Yablonskis' killers.

Krupansky did not have to worry. Two days later, a Washington County grand jury deliberated for only an hour before it indicted Gilly, Vealey, and Martin for first-degree murder and conspiracy. Huddleston and Lucy were indicted on the same charges under a Pennsylvania law that made the instigators of a murder as liable as those who actually pulled the trigger. That same day, contractors began to install bulletproof glass and steel mesh on the Washington County jail's windows. The county was readying itself for the biggest murder trials in its 180-year history.

Sprague decided to try each defendant separately. He planned to take down the killers and those who hired them one by one.

SEVENTEEN

Peeling the Onion

While the news of the five indictments in Pennsylvania was troubling, Tony Boyle knew Richard Sprague was a long way from tying him to the Yablonskis' murders. Only Pass and William Turnblazer, the president of District 19, knew he had ordered Yablonski's assassination. He was safe as long as they did not talk. There was nothing in the UMWA's bloodstained history that indicated they would.

For half a century, a wall of silence had protected the union's architects of mayhem and murder, as impenetrable as the Mafia's omertà. Boyle believed this immutable code would keep his co-conspirators and those reporting to them from confessing.

Sprague believed that, too. By November 1970, he was sure that Boyle was involved in the murder plot and that he had relied on his chain of command to execute it. The key to prosecuting him lay in breaking this chain's links, welded together by fear and ignorance.

He first had to get his hands on the killers. A state court in Ohio ordered their extraditions to Pennsylvania, but Gilly and his co-defendants appealed the rulings. The glutted docket of Ohio's Eighth District Court of Appeals ensured that he and the others would not be brought to Washington County's courthouse anytime soon.

While Sprague paced back and forth like a caged tiger in Pennsylvania, a federal prosecutor in Washington, D.C., launched his own legal assault on Tony Boyle.

Thomas Henderson Jr. was affable, soft-spoken, and scholarly. Like Sprague, he did not fit the stereotype of the tough-guy prosecutor. He graduated in 1966 near the top of his class at the University of Alabama Law School, and joined the Department of Justice after a chance meeting with then-Senator Robert F. Kennedy inspired him to enter public service. The tall redhead spent his first four years as a federal prosecutor in Philadelphia, putting Mafia capos behind bars.

In 1970, he transferred to the Department of Justice's Organized Crime and Management-Labor Section, where he ferreted out corruption in labor unions. Charles Ruff, his chief, who later served as the White House counsel who defended President Bill Clinton in his 1999 impeachment trial, assigned him to work on the Yablonski murders. While Sprague prepared for five first-degree murder trials in Washington County, Ruff directed Henderson to prosecute any violations of federal law he could prove Boyle and the union had committed.

Henderson eagerly accepted his new assignment. Atrocities such as the Yablonskis' killings could not go unpunished. "It is extremely important to show the public," he said in one of his rare meetings with the press, "that this type of professional murder will not go unchallenged by government, to show that people can feel secure in their homes."

Armed with the broad subpoena powers of federal grand juries sitting in Pennsylvania, Virginia, and the District of Columbia, Henderson sifted through the UMWA's tangled financial affairs. Boyle had silenced Yablonski in part to keep him from revealing what Henderson was now finding. And the federal prosecutor was finding a lot.

On August 5, 1970, Henderson persuaded a federal grand jury in Pittsburgh to indict Mike Budzanoski, the president of the UMWA's District 5 and an ardent Boyle loyalist, and John Seddon, District 5's secretary-treasurer, on charges of filing false expense accounts and diverting union money to fund Boyle's reelection campaign. Another federal grand jury sitting in Virginia did the same six months later to

Ray Thornbury, a UMWA official in District 28 and another strong Boyle supporter.

Pass did not want any more federal investigators poking around in District 19's records. On December 29, 1970, a fire gutted the district's two-story headquarters in Middlesboro, Kentucky. The fire department believed the blaze started in an office copy machine "that had flammable liquid around it." Pass claimed the fire was an accident and that no records were destroyed, but several sought by a federal grand jury sitting in Cleveland were never found.

The Department of Justice landed an even more punishing blow on Boyle on March 2, 1971, when a Washington, D.C., federal grand jury indicted him and two other high-ranking union officials on thirteen counts of illegally funneling $49,500 in embezzled union funds to friendly Democratic and Republican political candidates. The largest sum—$30,000—went to the 1968 presidential campaign war chest of then-Vice-President Hubert H. Humphrey.

The Corrupt Practices Act and the Landrum-Griffin Act prohibited the UMWA from contributing directly to political candidates—only the union's members could do so, voluntarily. The UMWA's rank-and-file members knew nothing about these contributions until they read about the indictments in the newspaper.

Boyle faced thirty-two years in prison if he was convicted. He resigned as a paid director of the National Bank of Washington, which the UMWA controlled. He issued a statement claiming the government forced him out because he fought too hard for his mine workers.

Justin McCarthy, editor of the *United Mine Workers Journal*, leaped to his patron's defense. He accused the Department of Justice of having a personal vendetta against Boyle. "I don't think Tony Boyle is any Abraham Lincoln or Jesus Christ," he whined to reporters. "But I don't think he has ever done a dishonest thing in his life."

United States District Court Judge Gerhard Gesell disagreed. On April 28, 1971, he ruled that the trustees of the union's Welfare and Retirement Fund had systematically mismanaged its assets for nearly two decades. He found the union, the fund's trustees, and the UMWA-controlled National Bank of Washington guilty of conspiring to keep as much as $75 million of the fund's cash in noninterest-bearing accounts at the bank. The bank and the union had benefited from this "free" use of the money while depriving the union's retirees of pensions and medical care. The judge ordered the UMWA to remove all the fund's assets from the bank.

Gesell's ruling came in a suit filed in August 1969 by a group of disgruntled retired and disabled widows, mostly from West Virginia and Kentucky, who charged that a massive conspiracy had denied them their health care benefits and pensions. While he did not find Boyle personally guilty in the conspiracy—he became a trustee on June 23, 1969, after John L. Lewis died—Judge Gesell ordered him to resign from the board of trustees because of his "insensitivity to fiduciary standards." He criticized Boyle for raising retirees' pensions from $115 to $150 a month while coal markets were declining and for using the fund as a way to win their votes in his reelection campaign against Yablonski.

Boyle's woes mounted after a jury convicted Budzanoski and Seddon, his District 5 loyalists, on May 6, 1971, and another convicted Thornbury in District 28 a month later. His stranglehold on the union was loosening.

Sprague planned to try Claude Vealey first. He hoped that his conviction and a death sentence would jolt the others into telling him who paid for Jock Yablonski's execution. Vealey had confessed just one day after the FBI arrested him, but he had threatened to withdraw his confession after Sprague refused to bargain with him. Since then, he had fought Sprague's efforts to extradite him from Ohio to Pennsylvania.

On December 8, 1970, an Ohio appellate judge denied Vealey's last appeal. Later that day, he found himself handcuffed in the back seat of a Pennsylvania State Police car, speeding through the gathering darkness toward the Washington County courthouse.

President Judge Charles Greenleaf Sweet of the Court of Common Pleas arraigned him on January 4, 1971. He charged Vealey with three counts of murder and a fistful of lesser charges including burglary, larceny, robbery, and conspiracy. Sweet was a former colonel in the United States Marine Corps who had fought at Guadalcanal and Okinawa and a graduate of Harvard Law School. A large, beefy man, Judge Sweet ran a disciplined, no-nonsense courtroom. Attorneys who appeared in front of him knew they needed to be prepared. "If you were stupid," one Washington County lawyer told a reporter after Sweet died in 1999, "he would tell you." Appellate courts seldom overturned his rulings.

Sprague believed that Sweet was the perfect judge to preside over Vealey's trial, but the killer never gave him the chance. On June 23, 1971, Vealey pleaded guilty to three counts of first-degree murder. Cooperation seemed like a better option than the electric chair. Sprague agreed to drop the lesser state charges of burglary and larceny, but he made no other promises. Vealey could still receive a death sentence, but that was far less likely if he cooperated and told the truth.

Joe Masterson, the FBI agent who had arrested him seventeen months before, stepped inside the witness box and read aloud Vealey's January 21, 1970, confession. The killer's matter-of-fact account of the murders sent chills through the courtroom.

Buddy Martin was next. He lost his extradition battle in early July 1971, and Ohio authorities immediately transferred him to Washington County to face three counts of first-degree murder. He appeared before Judge Sweet on July 9. Martin told the judge he was innocent.

Sprague, who believed in the Old Testament's blood-for-blood creed as much as Albert Pass, never wavered from his assessment that Martin was nothing more than a stone-cold killer. He had pumped two bullets into Charlotte's head, one into Marg's lungs, and probably at least two more into Jock's wrist and torso. Sprague was sure the cherubic-looking assassin would never cooperate, and he was not going to waste his time trying to convince him. He needed to send

Martin to the electric chair. He wanted to put the fear of God into the others awaiting trial and send a blunt message that they were facing a prosecutor who was as hard as they were.

Martin's trial started on November 3, 1971, in "Little" Washington, Pennsylvania, a small city tucked away in the soft coal fields about forty miles southwest of Pittsburgh. Its turn-of-the century Beaux-arts courthouse had stained-glass windows and a gold dome with a statue of George Washington perched on top of it. The region's polluted air and harsh weather had taken a toll on both.

It took Sprague and Mark J. Goldberg, Martin's lawyer, nearly a week to settle on a jury of seven women and five men. Sprague was pleased with the jury's composition. Most of those seated were old enough to be the parents of Yablonski's two sons, who sat in the courtroom's first row. Even better, none of them opposed the death penalty.

Goldberg, just five years removed from law school, was trying only his second criminal case. Sprague, meanwhile, had converted the local Ramada Inn into his trial headquarters, where he spent count-less hours carefully preparing his witnesses. He had brought with him dozens of boxes full of documents and exhibits tied to each witness's testimony. He had arrived with these in a municipally owned shiny black Chrysler New Yorker that the Philadelphia press dubbed the "Batmobile."

The special prosecutor grilled his witnesses on what they were going to say in court and how they were going to say it. No detail was small enough to escape his attention. He scolded witnesses whose answers were not precise enough, were too larded with insignificant details, or veered too far away from the exact question he asked. Sprague was like a Broadway producer staging a masterful play. He painstakingly fash-ioned their collective testimony into a dramatic, logical story a jury could easily follow.

From the start, Sprague worried about Martin's boyish appearance. He did not want the jurors sympathizing with him because he looked too young to be a murderer. Sprague was right to worry. Martin's freshly scrubbed face was dotted with pimples, and his gold-rimmed glasses, slicked-back hair, and dark blue suit made him look like a college freshman instead of a vicious killer.

Many female onlookers thought he resembled James Dean, the heartthrob movie star who was killed in a car crash at only twenty-four years old. Sprague wanted to sear a different image of Martin into the jurors' minds.

A little over a decade earlier, the teenaged killer Charles Stark-weather, with his fourteen-year-old girlfriend in tow, had terrorized Nebraska and Wyoming during a sadistic murder spree that claimed eleven lives. As he smiled and joked with his captors, Starkweather looked like the kid next door. A Nebraska jury saw something else, putting him to death in the electric chair in 1959. Sprague wanted his jury to do the same thing to Martin. If Charlie Starkweather was a baby-faced killer, so was Buddy Martin. Sprague saddled the innocent-looking murderer with that moniker within the first five minutes of the trial.

The twelve jurors sat riveted on November 9, 1971, as Sprague began his opening statement. He started by telling them, in short, tension-filled sentences, about the horrors that went on in the Yablonski farmhouse during the early morning hours of December 31, 1969.

"They walked around downstairs. They could see the Christmas tree in the corner and the Christmas cards on the wall. They went upstairs and turned right. In the bedroom on the right Charlotte Yablonski was asleep. In the bedroom on the left the Yablonskis were asleep. The baby-faced killer stepped into Charlotte's bedroom. There were curlers in her hair. She was shot in the top of her head. The person who did that was this defendant," Sprague pointed at Martin, "the baby-faced killer!"

He repeated this message with his first two witnesses. Ken Yablonski, his face pinched in grief, told the jurors about how shocked and horrified he was to discover his family's bloated bodies. Claude Vealey, the man who reloaded and fired four times at his defenseless father, followed him to the witness stand.

Vealey, despite a close shave, starched white shirt, sharply creased trousers, and polished brown shoes, still looked like the thug he was. The special prosecutor wasted no time. After Vealey admitted his own role in the murders, Sprague asked him if he saw anyone else in the courtroom who took part in the killings. "Yes," Vealey replied, "Aubran Martin."

In a low voice, with beads of sweat rising on his large, balding head, Vealey told the jury how he, Martin, and Gilly broke into the Yablonskis' Clarksville home and shot the three victims while they slept in their second-floor bedrooms. He testified that Martin shot the curled up, sleeping young woman twice in the head, and then emptied his still-smoking pistol into her mother and father. The two old comrades from Cleveland's hillbilly underworld frequently stared at one another while Vealey was on the witness stand, but neither said a word to the other.

Goldberg was not able to poke any holes in his story. He did no better with the other eighteen witnesses Sprague called in rapid-fire succession the first day of the trial. These ranged from Dr. Ernest Abernathy, who described the victims' gunshot wounds, to Chip Yablonski, to whom Sprague showed a lined yellow legal pad with "Annette Gilly, 1965, 1846 Penrose, East Cleveland, Ohio," written on it. Chip identified the handwriting as his father's. Yablonski had recorded Lucy's name and address on December 18, 1969, after speaking with the Ohio Department of Motor Vehicles.

Sprague was always in control of the courtroom. He limited his direct examination to quick, precise questions, asking many of his witnesses just five or six. Under Pennsylvania's rules of evidence governing criminal trials, Goldberg was confined to asking questions related only to the topics brought up by the special prosecutor, and to matters bearing directly on any of the government's witnesses' ability to tell the truth. Sprague's focused questions prevented Goldberg from straying from the prosecution's tightly crafted script.

Goldberg's only hope was to put Martin on the witness stand. It was painful to watch. While Martin appeared composed on the surface, he was not. He had tried to kill himself eleven months before by overdosing on tranquilizers. Committing suicide was better than waiting to die on death row, he probably reasoned, but his jailers had gotten him to the hospital in time to save his life.

After admitting to having participated in seventy-five burglaries since he was fifteen years old, Martin spun an elaborate lie. He told the jurors that Gilly and Vealey had promised him $2,000 to take part in a robbery in LaFollette, Tennessee. When they left Cleveland, he realized they were traveling in the wrong direction. It was only then that Gilly told him they were going to Clarksville to break into the Yablonskis' farmhouse.

Martin testified that Gilly told him to wait outside and act as a lookout. While Gilly and Vealey went into the farmhouse, he lay down in the front seat and went to sleep. Martin said he never heard any shots, and he did not know anyone in the house had been killed until he heard it on his car radio a day or two after he returned to Cleveland. He admitted that he did not tell the police because Gilly warned him to keep quiet because "high people, important people, were backing this up." Martin was afraid they might kill him and his family if he said anything.

His client's account pleased Goldberg, but Martin had just committed a massive legal blunder. He confessed that he had taken part in a burglary in which three people were killed. Under Pennsylvania's felony murder rule, anyone who participated in a burglary leading to a murder was as guilty of the killing as the ones who actually pulled the triggers. By admitting that he was the lookout, he was as guilty of slaying the Yablonskis as Gilly and Vealey.

Sprague could not believe his luck, but he wanted more than for Martin to be convicted of a capital offense. He wanted to be sure the jury would vote to execute him. To that end, the special prosecutor had to convince the jurors that the baby-faced killer's life was not worth saving.

When his turn to question Martin came, Sprague forced him to concede that he sometimes carried a gun when he broke into houses, that he saw Vealey carry a rifle into the Yablonskis' farmhouse, and that he and Vealey had practiced firing the .38 revolver and M1 carbine in Gilly's basement before they left for Clarksville.

Sprague destroyed what little was left of Martin's defense when he called his rebuttal witnesses. Two of them were convicts who had shared jail cells with Martin. One testified that Martin had admitted to receiving $1,700 for shooting the Yablonskis, while the other said the killer had bragged to him that he had shot Charlotte and "finished off" her mother and father.

It took the jury only one hour and twenty-three minutes on November 13 to convict Martin of first-degree murder. He paled when Judge Sweet read the verdict but otherwise showed no emotion, other than shifting a pen he was holding from one hand to the other.

It took them only forty more minutes the next morning to sentence him to die in the electric chair. Martin no longer looked like a choirboy. As if he were giving his middle finger to the jury, he wore sunglasses, multicolored trousers, a garish golden shirt, and a bright yellow ascot. He smiled when the jury's foreman read aloud the verdict. He patted Goldberg, who stared forlornly at the floor, gently on the shoulder, as if to comfort him. Martin basked in his notoriety.

Sprague was characteristically taciturn. "Well," he told Arthur Lewis, a former reporter for the *Philadelphia Inquirer*, "that is one down. Now I'll get the rest of those murdering bastards, maybe even Tony himself."

Paul Gilly was next. He never considered asking Sprague for a deal. He had his wife and father-in-law to think about, and anyway, it would be his word against Vealey's. Gilly's criminal record was nothing compared to Vealey's. He was respectable. Any jury could see that. He had owned a small painting company and two houses before he sold them to pay his lawyers.

But Gilly was wrong. In his opening remarks to the jury of seven men and five women on February 28, 1972, Sprague called Gilly "the captain of the ship," the director of the Yablonskis' murders. The special prosecutor put on another masterful show.

His first witness was Ken Yablonski. He told the jurors about the "odor of death" he smelled when he went to his family's home on January 5, 1970. He was followed by Jean Slosarik, the last person to see the family alive, just hours before they were killed, when she sat and chatted with Marg and Charlotte around the farmhouse's big Christmas tree.

James Charles Phillips, whose long sideburns descended from his rust-colored pompadour, stepped into the witness box next, escorted by a squadron of sheriff's deputies. A month before, a grand jury in Cleveland had indicted him for raping his girlfriend's four-year-old daughter. As unsavory as he was, Sprague used him to sketch the murder plot's early outlines. Phillips held the jury spellbound as he described, in his quiet drawl of the Tennessee hills, his trips with Gilly and Vealey to Washington, D.C., Bethesda, Maryland, and across Pennsylvania as they hunted their elusive quarry. Sprague put thirty more witnesses in front of the jury before he sat down.

Paul Gilly's lawyers begged him to testify in his own defense, telling him it was either the witness chair or the electric chair. He refused. He relied solely on character witnesses, most of them family members. His lawyers rested their case after presenting an hour of testimony.

It took the jury five hours on March 1 to convict Gilly on three counts of first-degree murder. It took the jury less than two hours the next morning to sentence him to die in the electric chair, after Sprague reminded them that it was Gilly "who hired two rattlesnakes to exterminate" the Yablonskis.

Gilly, who sat motionless, his left elbow resting on the arm of his chair, while the knuckles of his left hand supported his chin, suddenly bolted to his feet when he heard his death sentence, shouting, "I have something to say! Oh my God! What have you done to me!" before deputy sheriffs wrestled him out of the courtroom.

Lucy Gilly was next in Sprague's crosshairs, but she was not like her husband. She was not going to be strapped into an electric chair, or grow old in a steel cage. Lucy was going to free herself, no matter what it cost.

EIGHTEEN

Lucy and Silous

Lucy Gilly was a survivor. When she was only six years old, the flame in the gas heater in the motel room she shared with her mother went out. Deadly carbon monoxide filled the room's air; unable to get out or raise the window, she lay on the floor, her face pressed to a crack underneath the door, while her mother suffocated.

Lucy was going to find another crack now. She was only thirty-two years old, and she had a teenage son to reclaim from her sisters.

Prison was awful. When the FBI first arrested her on February 5, 1970, its agents transported her to filthy Cuyahoga County jail in Cleveland. She was one of only a handful of female prisoners, something not lost on the leering guards or the sex-deprived inmates.

When that jail became too dangerous, state authorities moved her to the Stark County jail outside Canton, Ohio—which was even worse. The Stark County jail's conditions were so harsh that state judges routinely gave prisoners four days of credit for each day they actually served. To protect her, Lucy's jailors placed her in solitary confinement.

Left alone, she became consumed by her fears of dying in the electric chair. Pennsylvania had not electrocuted a male prisoner since 1962, and it had been even longer since it had executed a female prisoner: Corrine Sikes, an African American maid with a borderline IQ, died in Pennsylvania's electric chair in 1946, after a jury convicted her of stabbing to death the woman she worked for.

But these statistics gave Lucy little comfort. Between 1915 and 1962, Pennsylvania had electrocuted 350 people. Worse, she knew Richard Sprague was a strong supporter of the death penalty. He had sent over twenty men to Pennsylvania's death row, including her husband.

Lucy was afraid of Sprague. In August 1971, her lawyers contacted Thomas Henderson at the Department of Justice, promising that she would implicate an unnamed UMWA official if the government would set her and her father free. Her husband's freedom was not part of her deal. Henderson told her she needed to talk with the special prosecutor; the Department of Justice had no jurisdiction over her state murder charges.

Rebuffed, Lucy clung to the hope that her father's mystical belief in the UMWA would save them. Huddleston had told her that the union's power was limitless. He also warned that its hit men would kill them both if she talked.

Paul Gilly's conviction on three counts of first-degree murder and his death sentence erased her hopes. The union had done nothing to save her husband, and Sprague was going to send her to the electric chair if she lost in her trial. The UMWA's death threats were meaningless now. Sprague was going to kill her first.

Lucy knew she had to strike a deal with him—and Sprague needed her as much as she needed him. From his first day on the case, he never believed the Yablonskis' three killers had acted alone or for their own reasons. They were puppets. He was not interested in prosecuting only those at the bottom. He needed Lucy to lead him to the puppet masters. She could start with her father.

Moreover, Sprague realized that his case against Lucy was paper-thin. She was not one of the killers. She was a distant accessory, who fielded phone calls from her father and husband and borrowed the car the killers drove on December 30 to Clarksville. Neither Huddleston nor Gilly was going to testify against her.

On March 22, 1972, he ordered the FBI to bring her to Philadelphia. Sprague checked her into a heavily guarded room at the Sheraton

Hotel, three blocks from his sixth-floor office in City Hall. She agreed to cooperate three days later, after he promised her that he would not send her to the electric chair if she told him the truth. Lucy was confident in her highly developed powers to manipulate and deceive. She readily agreed. She was set on telling him as little as possible. Her battle of wills with Sprague was about to begin.

Sprague knew that the assassination plot had taken nearly six months to unfold; he needed to hear Lucy's entire story, not a heavily edited, self-serving version of it. He girded himself for a long, drawn-out struggle. He brought in the FBI's Joe Masterson and William Logan Curtis, as well as two lie detector experts, to knock down her defenses, ordering them to question and polygraph her daily.

From her hardbacked chair, she tried to manipulate Masterson and Curtis with half-truths and her cold stare. She admitted Gilly took a lot of trips during the fall of 1969, but she claimed she did not know where. When they pressed her for more, she cried, pouted, and then acted coquettish. After spending several hours with her, the two experienced field agents began to anticipate her lies: Lucy would move her feet.

With the polygraphers, she switched her strategy from lying to withholding information. "She was made of iron," Joseph Brophy, the chief of the Philadelphia district attorney's polygraph unit, later recalled. "Part way through the test, she told us she had willed that she would forget all the details of the case."

Lucy finally broke during their eighth day of questioning, after Sprague threatened to send her back to jail and to the electric chair. Soaked with sweat and convulsed with sobs, she told them everything she knew. She signed a twenty-two-page confession on April 4.

"I just wanted my daddy to love me," Lucy tearfully told the agents. "I guess he doesn't love me anymore!" Sprague declined to discuss with reporters what she said, except to say, "People talk when things get tight."

Later, the press had a field day speculating about the powerful psychological hold Huddleston must have had on his daughter. "She hates him for what he did to her," one paper quoted a member of Sprague's prosecution team saying. "Her father scared her. And yet she wanted to please him."

If that was her goal, she failed miserably.

Word trickled back to Huddleston in the Washington County jail that his daughter was cooperating with Sprague. The old enforcer could hardly believe it. He had warned her about what the union did to traitors. He knew what he was talking about; he had beaten enough of them senseless.

Sprague worried about the same thing. He was taking no chances with his star witness's life. On April 11, 1972, Lucy arrived at the Washington County courthouse in a motorcade of state and local police cruisers, their lights flashing and sirens wailing. No fewer than ten state troopers and deputy sheriffs sprang out first, carrying submachine guns, riot guns, and pump-action shotguns. Their eyes nervously scanned the nearby rooftops for union snipers before they formed a tight scrum around her and hustled her into Judge Charles Sweet's second-floor courtroom.

Lucy, who stood nearly five foot ten in high heels, wore a dark blue suit and a white blouse. Two years in jail had returned her platinum shoulder-length hair to its natural dirty-blonde color, and had turned her skin pasty white. Whispered comments about her sheer black hose and fluffy white blouse from the mostly all-male press corps ranged from lewd to awestruck.

She stared at the floor as she pleaded guilty to three counts of first-degree murder and one count of conspiracy to commit murder, in return for Sprague's promise not to send her to the electric chair. Three state policewomen sat behind her during the proceedings while another thirty uniformed and plainclothes state, local, and county law enforcement officers lined the courtroom's walls.

Sprague pointed out to Judge Sweet that Lucy still faced three life sentences. Sweet sat back in his chair and reminded Lucy as she signed her guilty pleas that there was no going back now. "You realize," he said, looking down at her, "you're taking an irrevocable step, and it is all done now." Lucy answered softly, "Yes."

It was all done for William Prater, too. The next day, Thomas Henderson read Lucy's statement to a federal grand jury sitting in Pittsburgh. Prater, the only UMWA official she had talked with personally about Jock Yablonski's assassination, was implicated.

The grand jury indicted him on three counts of conspiring with Yablonski's killers, obstructing justice, and violating the rebel leader's civil rights as a union member by killing him. The FBI arrested him while he was driving to a shopping center. His wife and two of their seven children looked on tearfully as two agents handcuffed him and put him into the back seat of their car.

On April 13, two lawyers wheeled into Judge Sweet's courtroom a gentle-looking man with snow-white hair who spoke with a thick accent from the Tennessee mountains. It was only when Silous Huddleston curled up his lips in a sardonic smile, or when his gray eyes lost all expression behind their steel-rimmed glasses, that he gave any hint of being one of the UMWA's most ruthless hatchet men and longest-serving terrorists.

His lawyers had brought him before Judge Sweet to ask him to grant their sixty-three-year-old client bail, and to release him before his trial started in four days because of his failing health. They argued Huddleston was no flight risk. The lawyers told the judge that the haggard man sitting in the wheelchair before him suffered from emphysema, black lung, acute bronchitis, and a bad heart. His doctor gave him less than a year to live. Huddleston needed fifteen minutes to recover from just walking up one flight of stairs.

Sprague listened to their pleas for mercy impassively. When his turn came to tell the judge why the coughing and wheezing elderly man should stay in jail, he obliterated Huddleston's carefully crafted public image as everyone's frail grandfather. He called FBI Special Agent William Logan Curtis to the witness stand and asked him to read aloud Lucy Gilly's twenty-two-page statement implicating herself and her father in Jock Yablonski's murder.

Huddleston leaned forward in his wheelchair, fixated on every word Curtis read. He heard his daughter's words spell out his role, explaining how he had talked her husband into joining the plot and how Gilly had hired Vealey and then Martin to assassinate Yablonski. She maintained, though, that Huddleston was not the master plotter. "When this murder was initially set up, Paul and I were not supposed to know that we were dealing with anyone other than my father. My father was supposed to deal only with Bill Prater and he in turn with Albert Pass."

Huddleston's eyes never left Curtis's face. His lips parted in a bitter smile as Lucy's words of betrayal washed over him and he slowly shook his head as if he could not believe what he was hearing. She had not only sold him out, but the union, too.

As Huddleston looked on in amazement, Curtis then paused, took a deep breath, and as if on cue from Sprague, stunned the hushed courtroom with Lucy's next words: "My father told me that the Yablonski murder had the approval of the big man. To me that meant Tony Boyle, president, United Mine Workers." Most of what Lucy admitted was hearsay, but her words made clear that the union had ordered Yablonski's execution.

Edward Carey, the UMWA's acerbic general counsel, downplayed Lucy's claims. He told a small knot of reporters who were waiting for him the next morning outside New York City's Biltmore Hotel that the union's leaders deplored the killings of the Yablonskis. "We look with disfavor on this type of behavior," he claimed, without a trace of irony.

On April 15, a Washington County grand jury indicted Prater on three counts of first-degree murder. It had been slightly over twenty-six months since the FBI arrested Gilly, Vealey, and Martin for the three killings.

Huddleston's cockiness was fading. When the FBI first had suspected him of being involved in the killings, he had enjoyed taunting his federal pursuers almost as much as he did beating up scabs. "You all are going to feel pretty silly," he chided Joe Masterson during an interview at the Cuyahoga jail, "when you realize you have the wrong man."

He had even toyed with the Department of Justice's Thomas Henderson. Huddleston told the federal prosecutor that he might be willing to talk and point to others in the union if he could first meet with J. Edgar Hoover or Richard Kleindienst, the new attorney general of the United States. His outrageous demands did not stop there: he wanted to be released immediately from jail and paid the $50,000 reward Boyle had offered for the capture and conviction of the Yablonskis' killers. Henderson laughed at Huddleston's fanciful offer.

Huddleston had continued to hold out even though the stale air circulating through Cuyahoga County's jail made his every breath labored. His move to Washington County was even more punishing. There, he was wracked with coughing fits. One night, he stopped breathing. Emergency treatment saved him. He continued to defy the prosecutors, and death itself. But Lucy's betrayal changed all that.

Something else had changed, too. Huddleston had spent his whole life believing that his highest duty was loyalty to the UMWA. He had beaten strikebreakers with chains, dynamited nonunion coal operators' offices, and even helped kill for it. All that meant nothing now. By April 1972, twenty-three months after he had been first arrested, he finally realized the union had abandoned him, just like his favorite daughter.

Albert Pass had promised Huddleston up to a million dollars for his legal defense, but what little money he had received to pay his lawyers came from William Turnblazer, from Pass, a $100 contribution from Boyle, and the meager amount left over from the murder fund. To raise more, Pass had forced his District 19 field organizers to contribute $200 a month from their paychecks. Even that made Huddleston uneasy: Prater handed over the money to one of the old man's daughters and one of his granddaughters only after he met with them in secluded motel rooms to drink whiskey and have "a good time." The two women's eighteen meetings with Prater had raised only $23,000 to pay his mounting legal bills and keep him quiet.

Huddleston resented the UMWA's betrayal more than he did Lucy's. He believed that his union masters were betting on him to die before he could say anything. He vowed to outlast them all.

On April 17, Huddleston confessed, just as Sprague and his attorneys were picking a jury to try his murder case. He could not face the public spectacle of Lucy testifying against him. He was also worried about her safety. She had stabbed him in the back, but she was still his flesh and blood. He had gotten her into this. He would stand with her now against the union.

He signed a twenty-five-page statement on May 1, 1972, a momentous day for the Yablonski family and the UMWA. Two days later, he appeared before Judge Sweet and pleaded guilty to three counts of first-degree murder. He sat in a chair placed before the judge and played with a bottle of bronchial spray while the FBI's William Logan Curtis read aloud Huddleston's confession, in which he admitted his role in the murder plot.

"I wish to state that I, with several other people, took part in the plans to murder Joseph Yablonski . . . I found a man who agreed to find some other people to commit the murder. I also obtained the money to pay the others before and after the murders."

Huddleston said that Pass and Prater had recruited him to hire the assassins, which he had agreed to do because he was convinced that Yablonski "was controlled by outsiders who wanted to destroy the union." "I was not to receive any money," he added coldly, "only expenses. I would not have done it for money."

When Huddleston confessed what he had done, he told Sprague that he was not going to hold anything back. He kept his word. His confession stated that the money used to pay for the assassination came from a special "Research and Information Fund" set up by Pass and administered by Prater. This was the first solid evidence that the conspiracy to kill Yablonski had extended from the bleak coalfields of Appalachia to the UMWA's gray stone headquarters in Washington, D.C. It destroyed Boyle's denials that the union had had anything to do with the killings.

Huddleston's confession only confirmed what the two Yablonski brothers already believed. "Murder is as institutionalized with the United Mine Workers as it is with the Mafia," they said in a joint statement to reporters. "The order to kill—to kill our whole family if necessary—was as routinely transmitted and carried out as an order to call a strike or settle a grievance." Yet their anguish was tempered.

The bloody tracks of their family's killers were leading closer and closer to Tony Boyle. So was a new election.

NINETEEN

For Jock

Judge William Benson Bryant's time in Washington's courts taught him that well-trained lawyers and sympathetic judges steeped in the protections of the Constitution could end evils such as school segregation and wrongful convictions. He had graduated first in his class at Howard University Law School, become the city's first black federal prosecutor, and then the first black chief judge of its United States District Court. In a legal career that spanned nearly sixty years, Bryant never wavered from his deep faith in the American legal system. He believed it offered people who were wronged their best chance to be treated fairly and humanely.

Joe Rauh knew "Bill" Bryant long before he became a federal judge. Their paths had crossed often in court while defending the rights of underdogs. Rauh admired Bryant's innate sense of fairness. He was elated when the judge was randomly selected to preside over the case to set aside Boyle's 1969 election victory.

But even Bryant's hands seemed to be tied at first. The government's lawyers opposed the Miners for Democracy's motion to intervene in the election case. The judge, bound by legal precedent, reluctantly agreed with their arguments. So did the United States Court of Appeals for the District of Columbia Circuit.

Daniel Edelman, a brilliant young lawyer for the Miners' Project and a former law clerk for Justice Harry Blackmun, believed both lower courts were wrong. On January 17, 1972, the United States Supreme Court agreed with Edelman's arguments and ruled that Miners for Democracy could participate in the lawsuit. Joe Rauh and Clarice Feldman, one of the reformers' lawyers, were in Judge Bryant's court the very next morning, examining and cross-examining witnesses.

On May 1, the same day Silous Huddleston signed his confession, Judge Bryant handed down a thirty-three-page opinion that found the evidence of Boyle's wrongdoing in the 1969 election "too strong to resist." He wrote that Boyle had used both the UMWA's money and its machinery to defeat Yablonski. He overturned Boyle's victory and ordered a new election.

Rauh was ecstatic. "The walls of justice are closing in on Tony Boyle," he told the *New York Times* after he read the judge's opinion. He and the Yablonski brothers were determined to close them in on him completely.

Rauh's legal work in support of the civil rights movement made him a master at fashioning creative and broad legal remedies. He knew Tony Boyle and the Department of Labor too well to agree to the typical court order entered in union election cases that merely overturned the results and directed that a new election be held under the Secretary of Labor's supervision. Rauh and the Miners' Project's lawyers instead proposed to Judge Bryant that he implement strict controls that would rein in all the pervasive violations of law he had outlined in his May 1 opinion.

Judge Bryant, who understood the broad remedial powers of the federal courts to right historic wrongs as well as Rauh did, was happy to comply. On June 16, 1972, he departed from the traditionally brief and vague orders other federal judges had issued in Landrum-Griffin election cases and handed down a sweeping one designed to enforce his May 1 opinion. He granted the Department of Labor all the power it needed to oversee a new election, and redressed point by point all the voting irregularities Yablonski and Rauh had complained about, fencing in rail by rail Boyle's ability to steal the next election. He was not going to let Boyle plunder the UMWA's resources, twist arms, and commit fraud to stay in power. The judge ordered the new election to take place before January 1, 1973. His ruling ensured that the new balloting was going to be the most closely regulated in American labor history.

The judge prohibited the union's officers from making financial contributions to candidates, permitted the Department of Labor and Miners for Democracy to put monitors in the UMWA's district offices, and required that complete and accurate membership lists and polling-place locations be made promptly available to all candidates.

Just as important, he barred the union from hiring new staff workers during the campaign without ample justification, and letting workers campaign during work hours. To police this, he required UMWA officers to file daily activity reports. Judge Bryant also opened up the union's twice-monthly newspaper, the one publication nearly every miner read. He gave all competing candidates equal space in its pages to spell out and advocate for their platforms.

Jock Yablonski's followers started to prepare for a new election as soon as they read the judge's opinion. On May 4, 1972, Chip and Ken Yablonski sat behind a mound of microphones inside the Pan American Room at Washington, D.C.'s Mayflower Hotel. Their martyred father had done the same thing nearly three years before at a closely guarded press conference when he announced he was challenging Boyle for the UMWA's presidency. The two brothers told a large throng of reporters that Miners for Democracy was going to hold a meeting on May 7 in Charleston, West Virginia, to begin planning a rank-and-file convention.

The delegates were going to have plenty to talk about. That same month, Chip Yablonski won coal miners in the UMWA's District 2 the right to elect their own officers. His victory forced another federal judge to do the same thirteen days later for seven more districts containing 84,000 miners. That lawsuit, filed by the Department of Justice, had been pending for eight years. This was a crippling blow to

Boyle. The UMWA's district officers were no longer going to owe their allegiance to him, because he could no longer handpick them.

On May 27, 1972, 387 coal miners from fifteen of the UMWA's now twenty-four districts in the United States and Canada gathered on a grassy lawn in front of Wheeling College's field house in West Virginia's northern panhandle. By the second day, their ranks had swelled to 463. This was the first rank-and-file convention in modern American labor history. The Black Lung Association and the Disabled Miners and Widows of Southern West Virginia, two other reform groups, had banded together with Miners for Democracy to send delegates.

J. Davitt McAteer, a former student at the college and the author of a scathing study on the lack of coal mine health and safety in West Virginia, convinced the liberal Jesuit school to host the convention. Finding a place to hold it had not been easy. Every convention hall in the state was afraid of upsetting big coal operators.

Monsignor Charles Owens Rice, who had officiated at the Yablonskis' funerals, gave the opening prayer. He stood at a dais behind a photograph of Yablonski and a quote from one of the assassinated rebel's most prophetic speeches: "It is time someone spoke up regardless of what the sacrifice may be." Rice reminded the delegates of the bloody sacrifices that had brought them there. He predicted their victory in December's voting.

Rauh gave the keynote speech. He told his audience that he kept a picture of Yablonski in his law office and beneath it, another of the murdered family's three graves. These reminded him that he could not rest until Boyle was overthrown. "With God's help," he assured the delegates, "we shall overcome!"

Rauh's speech galvanized the delegates. They approved a thirty-four-point platform that focused on mine safety—coal would be mined safely or not at all—cut the salaries and benefits of top union officials, ended nepotism, boosted pensions, demanded sick pay, and supported full autonomy for all districts. They included a "Miners' Bill of Rights."

These provisions ended backroom deals between coal operators and union officials and gave the union's rank and file the right to vote on union contracts.

The delegates chose forty-nine-year-old Arnold Miller, a staunch Yablonski supporter who had organized the insurgent's last rally, to be their presidential candidate and standard-bearer, over Mike Trbovich, the Miners for Democracy's national chairman and Jock Yablonski's neighbor. They selected Miller, a disabled coal miner with black lung from Oley, West Virginia, because he came from the union's largest district, and was an Anglo-Saxon. Trbovich, of Slavic descent, was not happy about losing, but he set aside his disappointment for the time being and agreed to become the dissidents' candidate for vice-president. Many miners, especially in West Virginia and Kentucky, believed that only a candidate whose ancestors came from the British Isles or Ireland could win the union's top job.

The delegates chose Harry Patrick, a forty-one-year-old coal mine mechanic, to be their nominee for secretary-treasurer. Patrick was no stranger to coal mining disasters. One of his brothers had been killed in a mine explosion in 1959, and his father had lost a leg in another.

The three men were facing an uphill campaign. The Miners for Democracy's victories had so far been only won in courtrooms—but there was too much at stake to worry about that now. Judge Bryant's order gave them a fighting chance to overthrow an autocratic ruling clique that had made its ouster all but impossible by controlling the union's treasury and its election machinery. Arnold Miller and his two running mates were going to change that or die trying.

From a distance, all one could see of Arnold Ray Miller was his full head of curly silver hair and his lantern jaw. A closer look showed something else—a jagged scar that ran halfway down his head, and a crumpled ear. Miller had served as a combat infantryman in World War II. He fought across North Africa, up the Italian boot, and on the blood-drenched beaches of Normandy. A German machine gun hidden in a northern France hedgerow had sheared off the left side of his face.

He spent two years in Army hospitals, and endured nineteen operations as plastic surgeons struggled to reconstruct his face. They wanted to continue, but Miller had had enough. He went home and back to mining coal, the only thing he knew how to do.

Black lung and arthritis drove him to the surface for good in 1970. The year before, he and a handful of other miners joined with antipoverty activists to form the Black Lung Association. Miller blamed Boyle for his disability. "You don't expect the companies to do much for you," he complained bitterly to a reporter, "but you have the right to expect help from someone who calls himself president of the United Mine Workers." He said Boyle was no better than the Nazi who had shot off half his face.

On July 16, 1972, Miller, who wore simple off-the-rack suits and did not even own a credit card, tucked a sawed-off shotgun and a loaded pistol under the front seat of his car and drove to Harlan County, Kentucky. He was not going to be intimidated. He kicked off his campaign in the heart of District 19, the union's most dangerous precinct. "We have come here to Harlan County and UMW District 19," he told the crowd who gawked at him, "to make it clear that the days of fear are over and that Tony Boyle's reign of tyranny over the good men of this union are [sic] numbered."

He showed his strength during the election's one-month nomination period, collecting the endorsements of 410 locals in the UMWA's most populous districts. Yablonski had gotten only 96. Boyle won the support of 863 locals, but most of his votes came from the union's retirees.

Boyle was a wounded but dangerous adversary. A jury had convicted him two and a half months before on thirteen counts of embezzling money from the UMWA's treasury and violating the Corrupt Practices Act. A federal judge sentenced him to serve two concurrent five-year prison terms, fined him $130,000, and ordered him to pay back $49,000 to the union. He spent six hours in jail while his attorney scrambled to raise his $179,000 bond.

Boyle was now a convicted felon. He had appealed, but if that failed, he was going to prison. None of this bothered Boyle's sycophants serving on the UMWA's International Executive Board. They blamed President Nixon's Department of Justice for their leader's legal problems. They promised him their full support.

So did many of the union's members. Thousands of them still believed that Boyle was a persecuted saint who could do no wrong. He had raised their pay to $50 a day and boosted pensioners' monthly checks to $150. "It takes somebody with guts to run a union," a miner told *Time*. "If they had an archbishop running, I wouldn't vote for him."

The *New York Times* interviewed another Boyle supporter whose comments were even more pointed. "We knowed [*sic*] Tony done wrong . . . but I think it is best to stick with Tony . . . This is a funny thing for a man to say who believes in democracy as much as I do, but we can't afford democracy in this union."

Boyle was no longer able to use wads of union cash to grease the machinery of his reelection campaign, so he fell back on his customary attacks. He accused Miller and his ticket of being puppets manipulated by powerful outsiders. This remained an effective counterpunch among the union's backwoods locals. "I know you won't let anyone take your union away from you!" he bellowed to a southern West Virginia audience. "This is what Adolf Hitler did when he took over and destroyed that country. He started by destroying the labor unions and the labor organizations, and then he destroyed the churches, and then he built those incinerators and he burned his own people. Some of 'em alive!"

He did not stop there. Boyle labeled Miller's followers as "malcontents," "leftists," and "smelly hippies." He branded Miller and his running mates as "the three stooges running on the Moscow Fire Department slate."

Boyle also freshened his ticket. He pushed out George Titler, his seventy-seven-year-old vice-president, and John Owens, his eighty-two-year-old secretary-treasurer, for two younger candidates. Leonard Pnakovich, the union's former safety director, and Wilbert Killion, District 11's International Executive Board member, were still yes-men, but they were much younger and more energetic campaigners.

Miller was his opponent, but Boyle remained haunted by Yablonski's ghost. At rally after rally, Boyle strayed from his scripted campaign message and spewed lies about his slain rival's alleged corruption and disloyalty. He was enraged especially by news stories that called Yablonski a martyr. Though the murders hung over the campaign, many still believed Boyle's claim that he had played no role in them. "Tony Boyle is too smart to do something like that," one West Virginia miner confidently told a *New York Times* reporter.

While Boyle saw Yablonski lurking behind every tree, just as the murdered maverick had predicted on December 4, 1969, during a speech he gave in a cramped auditorium in Summerville, West Virginia, Miller spoke at campaign rallies and appeared on radio and television. He traveled over 100,000 miles across the coalfields, visited more than 400 bathhouses, and talked personally with nearly 60,000 coal miners. "Being loyal to the union," he told any miner within earshot, "does not mean being loyal to Tony Boyle." Miller was no fool. He never campaigned without a heavily armed bodyguard trailing just a few steps behind him.

He needed the protection. Miller was almost assassinated in Whitesburg, Kentucky, after a pack of armed Boyle supporters nearly cornered him and his two running mates in their motel. A gun battle was avoided only after a quick-witted front-desk clerk told the thugs that the reform candidates were not in their rooms.

Afterwards, Miller met with a group of reporters at a restaurant. He told them, only half in jest, that he should sit with his back to the wall. "I'm not known as someone who can't face danger," he said in his Appalachian drawl, "but I think the biggest thing I got to do is stay alive."

Miller's bravery and his quest to purge the union of corruption did not go unnoticed. Former VISTA volunteers, young campaign workers motivated by the civil rights movement, and other highly skilled activists such as Edgar James, who had managed Senator Robert F. Kennedy's presidential campaign in Oregon, and Don Stillman, a former *Wall Street Journal* reporter and a journalism professor at West Virginia University, flocked to Miller's campaign. They infused it with an energy and professionalism it would not have had otherwise.

James employed the strategies he learned from Bobby Kennedy's short-lived presidential campaign. He used targeted mailings and chain phone calls to preach Miller's fundamental message that the average coal miner was the chief victim of the UMWA's complacency and corruption. He and other young Miller supporters relied on sophisticated polling techniques developed by future political consultant Pat Caddell and other students at Harvard University to zero in on what bread-and-butter issues mattered most to miners. They also raised funds from liberal donors, including the Episcopal Church, to mount a hybrid campaign—in part modern and media savvy, and in part old-fashioned, with stump speeches and face-to-face electioneering.

Stillman, a gifted wordsmith, took full advantage of Judge Bryant's order opening the *United Mine Workers Journal* to all candidates. He filled the eight pages allotted to Miller's campaign in the bimonthly newspaper with reasons why the union's miners should vote for the Miners for Democracy's slate. He also wrote many of the campaign's wittier slogans. One of his catchiest was "Let's make the UMWA great again."

Miller benefited tremendously from the large number of younger miners—perhaps as many as 37,000—who joined the union between 1969 and 1972 as prosperity returned to the coalfields. Many of these new members had fought in Vietnam. They were in no mood to be told what to do by the UMWA's corrupt and distant leaders. "I did two years in Vietnam," one said, "and I didn't come home to get wasted under a piece of slate, just because somebody told me to work under [an] unsupported roof."

The voting took place from December 1 to December 8. Over 1,000 Department of Labor observers monitored the weeklong process. Under tight security, they collected all the ballot boxes and took them to Silver Spring, Maryland, to count all the votes. When they were finished, Miller defeated Boyle by just over 14,000 votes. His election victory was the first successful rank-and-file takeover of a major industrial labor union in modern American history. None of Big Labor's leaders sent him a congratulatory telegram.

Miller held a victory press conference on December 15 at a Silver Spring Holiday Inn. With Chip Yablonski beside him, Miller bowed his head and asked for "a moment's silence in memory of our friend, Jock Yablonski."

"I think this is one of the most historic events that ever occurred in the labor movement of this country," Miller told his assembled followers. "It indicates what happens to labor leaders who are not responsive to the membership."

Chip Yablonski was elated. He took enormous personal and professional satisfaction in Miller's victory. The miners, with his and the other reformers' help, had accomplished so much. He knew better than anyone the terrible cost of Boyle's overthrow, but his father's dream of a democratic union had come true.

Judge Bryant certified Miller's victory on December 22. The victor's followers removed the imposing gate at the foot of the stairs of the UMWA's headquarters building. Since John L. Lewis had put it there, this barrier had been used symbolically and literally to block the rank and file's access to their most senior leader.

Bernard Aronson, Miller's press secretary, told a *New York Times* reporter that the reformers felt like they were storming the Bastille. "We all ran through the place, sitting behind desks and trying the leather furniture. It was great!" Miller's victory brought tears to the eyes of hardened men, more used to the sorrows that dogged their dangerous trade than to joyful political celebrations.

But Aronson noticed something much darker. "It was like the

Wizard of Oz," he remembered years later. "There was this screen and a lot of smoke and noise and light coming from above. When we took the screen away we discovered the real secret: nothing was going on up there at all, just a bunch of guys drawing huge salaries." Jock Yablonski had been right all along.

Sixteen days later, a group of coal miners trooped up the hill to Yablonski's windswept grave in the Washington Cemetery. They placed a wreath on it. It was inscribed, "You finally made it, Jock."

The martyr had been vindicated. Now it was up to Richard Sprague to see that he was avenged.

TWENTY

Back to the Beginning

Maxine Little Prater sat quietly with six of her seven children in the front row of Erie County Courthouse's huge Courtroom Number One on March 9, 1973. She was waiting for her husband's murder trial to begin. Nearly ten months earlier, William Prater's lawyer had filed a motion arguing that his client could not receive a fair trial in Washington County because of all the publicity there swirling around the Yablonskis' murders. The Pennsylvania Supreme Court agreed and moved Prater's murder trial 150 miles north to Erie, a tired manufacturing town that squatted next to the lake that gave the city its name.

Maxine stared straight ahead at the Commonwealth of Pennsylvania Seal that covered most of Courtroom Number One's yellow wall behind the judge's bench. Her comfortable, middle-class existence had turned upside down nearly a year ago, after two FBI agents arrested her husband during a family outing to the grocery store. His crippling legal bills had forced her to sell the family's well-kept two-story house and move to a much smaller home in a rougher part of town.

Maxine got her first job, and worked at the Imperial Shirt factory until the company laid her off. She survived now on weekly $27 unemployment checks, food stamps, and handouts from her church. Contributions from some of Prater's fellow field representatives and from William Turnblazer dried up after the union cut their salaries, and Prater's, in early 1973 as a cost-savings measure.

Boyle had kept him on the UMWA's payroll until Joe Rauh complained about it to the Department of Labor, arguing that this was a blatant attempt to buy Prater's silence and a gross misuse of union funds.

Maxine had never asked her husband where he went and what he did during the nights he did not come home. She knew the UMWA was locked in a life-and-death struggle with the region's nonunion coal operators and that her husband was a loyal union man. She never questioned him about the explosions that sometimes rattled her windows before dawn, or even the rumors she sometimes heard about his other women.

A tall woman who attended her Methodist church regularly, Maxine had quietly raised their seven children, minded her own business, and relied on her strong religious beliefs to sustain her. Prater had sworn to her that he had nothing to do with Yablonski's assassination. Maxine had borrowed money and driven their children all the way to Erie to show him and the jury that they believed him.

Tony Boyle had come to Erie, too. His reasons were more selfish. Prater knew too much about his and Albert Pass's murder fund. He was one of District 19's six field representatives who helped launder the money through the phony Research and Information Committee and kick it back to Pass—and the only field representative who knew what Pass had actually done with the money.

Pass himself was already in custody; the FBI had arrested him on May 2, a day after Huddleston signed his confession, at his house in Middlesboro, Kentucky. He was waiting for them with a packed suitcase.

Boyle was determined to stop Sprague from getting any closer to the truth about who paid for Yablonski's murder. That's why he had come to Prater's murder trial in Erie: to lie.

The Pennsylvania Supreme Court selected Judge Edward H. Carney of Erie County's Court of Common Pleas to preside over Prater's trial.

Carney, a former FBI agent who took copious notes during trials, had a reputation as a fair but by-the-book judge.

On Friday, March 9, 1973, Sprague addressed Prater's jury of seven men and five women. It took him eleven minutes to mention the defendant's name. Prater's trial was going to be the first in which who paid for the murders was as important as who carried them out. Sprague wanted the jurors to believe that Boyle was on trial as much as Prater.

In his opening statement, Sprague led the jury step by step through the cold-blooded way the three convicted killers swooped down on the sleeping family during the early morning hours of New Year's Eve 1969, but then pivoted sharply after he described what they had done inside the farmhouse. He told the jurors that this case was really about taking them "back to the beginning." Prater had played an important role in the murders, but he was just a "conduit along the way."

This case really started with Tony Boyle, he explained. This was the first time Sprague told a jury that the former union president was directly behind the three killings. He promised to prove to them that Boyle had used the union's money to pay for Yablonski's assassination.

By now, Sprague's prosecution of the killers was as well rehearsed as a standing-room-only Broadway production. In staccato fashion, he summoned platoons of his usual witnesses to the stand.

But Sprague called his first surprise witness on March 13: Paul Gilly, who wore the same dark suit he had worn at his own trial as he stepped onto the witness stand. He had decided to break his more than three years of silence to testify for the prosecution.

Lucy's betrayal, followed closely by Huddleston's, had eaten away his resolve to keep his mouth closed. Pressure from his two brothers and a nephew finally brought him to the brink of cooperating. On March 10, 1973, they visited Gilly at the Western State Penitentiary and told him that his father and mother were dying. His religious parents wanted him to tell the truth. If he did, they hoped he might be able to go to heaven.

Gilly's eyes welled up with tears as he talked with his brothers and nephew, but he still hesitated. He wanted his sentence reduced. The year before, the United States Supreme Court had ruled that the death penalty as then practiced violated the Eighth Amendment to the United States Constitution. Gilly was not going to die in Pennsylvania's electric chair, but he still faced three consecutive life sentences for murdering the Yablonskis. Sprague was gunning for Tony Boyle; when he and Gilly spoke the following night, he promised Gilly he would ask the judge to give him just one life sentence for first-degree murder, instead of three consecutive ones, if he cooperated.

Gilly agreed. On March 13, he made a dramatic confession to the jury. "I was told by Mr. Prater," he testified, "that Yablonski was breaking up the union and its pension funds. He said Tony Boyle wanted him killed." In just two sentences, Gilly had linked Prater and Boyle directly to Yablonski's assassination.

Sprague pointed at Prater. "I want you to look at the defendant," he instructed Gilly. "Is there any doubt in your mind that he is one of the men who arranged, discussed with you arrangements, for those murders?"

"No sir, there is not," Gilly said as Prater, his pink cheeks now a dark red, stared at him.

H. David Rothman, a veteran criminal defense lawyer who sported a Fu Manchu mustache, represented Prater. He asked Gilly why he had decided to kill Yablonski. "A lot of persuasion [*sic*] of folks you listen to," the one-time Cleveland house painter answered, "and the promise of a pension that my father and a lot of others did not get and could not get."

Edith Roark, Albert Pass's secretary and District 19's bookkeeper since 1948, followed on Gilly's heels. She admitted to typing two letters from Pass to Boyle, asking Boyle to send $20,000 to District 19 to pay for organizing expenses the district had not paid since September 1968. Sprague asked her if there was anything unusual about the two letters. Yes, she replied. All District 19's other requests for funds were sent directly to John Owens, the UMWA's secretary-treasurer. This was the first time in twenty-one years that she had typed letters from Pass asking Boyle for money.

Roark also divulged that that the union had transferred $19,700 into District 19's bank account and that "on September 30, Mr. Pass supplied me with 23 names and amounts and instructed me to make out a check for each one named." She confessed to doing the same thing on October 10, 1969.

Sprague carefully shifted the jury's attention back to Yablonski's killers. He called George Smith Jr. to the witness stand. He still looked every inch the backwoods mountain man. Smith told the jury about Huddleston's attempt to recruit him to dynamite Yablonski's farmhouse in Clarksville. He said Huddleston instructed him to tie a feed sack stuffed full of dynamite to a pole and lean it against one of Yablonski's bedroom windows.

The special prosecutor staged one of his biggest surprises on March 15 when three District 19 field representatives, Noah Doss, George Washington Hall, and Corwin Edward Ross, paraded one after the other to the witness stand. They admitted to taking union retirees to local banks in Tennessee and Kentucky to cash checks for their "organizing work" and kicking back the money to Prater and Pass. All three acknowledged they had lied to the FBI and federal grand juries because they feared what Pass would do to them if they told the truth. One of them said he had not told the truth because he was afraid that Pass would kill him if he did not.

Their admissions had become a lot easier after Huddleston confessed and the FBI arrested Pass. District 19's strongman could no longer threaten to take away anyone's life, job, pension, or health insurance.

Sprague called Silous Huddleston as his next witness. As he sucked on a tube attached to a green oxygen bottle, Huddleston looked much older than his sixty-four years, no longer the brutal union foot soldier he once was.

Huddleston testified that Prater and Pass had tasked him with finding Yablonski's killers, giving him $15,000 to offer as payment. He astounded the courtroom when he explained why Yablonski had to be eliminated.

"Yablonski was controlled by Continental Oil, which was buying up coal land and wanted to get rid of the union and the royalty payments [to the pension fund]. They couldn't do it from the outside, and Jock was being paid to do it from the inside," he told the jurors.

When Rothman cross-examined him, Huddleston admitted that Pass and Prater were the ones who told him about Yablonski's betrayal. When the lawyer asked him why he believed what they said, Huddleston did not hesitate. "If you're not going to believe your leaders," he said, "you're in pretty bad shape."

Sprague wrapped up his case after he called several members of the so-called Research and Information Committee to testify. Henderson had engineered their appearances: shortly after Huddleston acknowledged his role in the assassination plot, Henderson had summoned Dave Brandenburg, a self-ordained preacher and one of the pensioners recruited to Pass's money-laundering scheme, to appear before a federal grand jury in Pittsburgh. He was extremely close to Huddleston; he had hidden $8,000 of the killers' money for him.

On the eve of Brandenburg's testimony, the FBI arranged a reunion between the two old friends in a Ramada Inn on the city's outskirts. They had not seen one another since the FBI arrested Huddleston in February 1970. After they reminisced about the Tennessee hills, Huddleston convinced Brandenburg to return home and persuade the other pensioners to talk to the FBI.

First one and then another told two agents assigned to the FBI's Knoxville field office how they cashed two checks, in September and October 1969, and handed the money back to their field representatives. All those who were still alive confessed.

On March 17, Sprague asked them why they finally decided to cooperate with the prosecutors. One blurted out to the court that "God got ahold of me!" and made him testify. Another claimed that his repeated lying had "just burned up on me so hard." Nearly all admitted they lied because they were afraid of losing their pensions, health insurance, or their lives if they did not give Pass what he wanted.

Rothman could do little to shake their conscience-stricken testimony. The jury found them to be enormously sympathetic witnesses. Rothman had bigger problems, anyway. He was about to put a witness on the stand who had no conscience at all.

Tony Boyle looked dapper and relaxed, not like an ousted union leader and a convicted felon. Rothman questioned him skillfully. Boyle acknowledged that he approved sending $20,000 to Pass in late September and early October 1969, but claimed he authorized this money for a legitimate purpose. Pass said he needed the money to pay union organizers in Kentucky and Tennessee.

Boyle testified that Pass approached him during the union's 1968 convention in Denver with a low-cost plan "to organize the unorganized" miners of District 19. Pass assured him that twenty-five or thirty pensioners could be hired for five dollars a day to "preach the gospel of the union." Boyle approved his idea and "told him to get the work done." He wanted to reward Pass's zealotry.

Boyle claimed their entire conversation took about "five, six, or seven minutes." He added that he discussed Pass's plan later that same day with William Turnblazer Jr., the president of District 19.

When he cross-examined Boyle, Sprague wasted no time in forcing the former UMWA president to admit he was a convicted felon. He appeared dazed by the ferocity of Sprague's question. He mumbled that the jury convicted him because he had donated money to Hubert Humphrey's 1968 presidential campaign.

Sprague bored into him for nearly three hours. He asked Boyle if he had ever looked into how the $20,000 was spent after he heard allegations it had been used to pay for Yablonski's assassination. Boyle admitted he never had. Sprague also got Boyle to deny that he asked Suzanne Richards, his personal assistant, to call Pass on November 27,

1969, and schedule a meeting with him three days later in Madisonville, Kentucky.

Boyle faced a cluster of reporters after the special prosecutor finished grilling him. He complained to the newsmen, "It is I, not Prater,
on trial here." Yablonski, he lectured the reporters, had plenty of enemies. Any one of them, including the Mafia, could have killed him.

On March 22, Rothman summoned Albert Pass to the witness
stand. He scoffed at the accusation that he had plotted with Prater and
Huddleston to kill Yablonski. Then he grinned. He said the dead man
had been good to him; he'd had no reason to kill him. Yablonski had
been chairman of the Nominating Committee for the International
Executive Board Members during the UMWA's 1968 convention in
Denver. The committee had nominated Pass to be District 20's International Executive Board member.

Rothman had planned to call William Turnblazer Jr. next, but the
District 19 president told the lawyer that his client would be better
off if he did not testify. Rothman sensed Turnblazer's hostility. He
dropped his subpoena and scratched him from his list of witnesses.

During a short break in the trial, Henderson spoke with Rothman and learned that Turnblazer was not going to testify. Henderson
alerted Sprague and called the FBI's Knoxville field office, instructing
its agents to interview Turnblazer as soon as Rothman rested his case.

Wallace Estill, the Special Agent in Charge of the FBI's Knoxville
field office, asked Turnblazer to meet him in the United States Post
Office building across the street from District 19's Middlesboro, Kentucky, headquarters. In a brief but emotionally packed meeting, the
soft-spoken FBI agent quizzed him about why he had decided not to
testify in Prater's trial. If he knew something that could help the government, Estill told him, he should cooperate and likely save himself
from significant prison time. Turnblazer, no simple backwoods lawyer,
knew the FBI agent was right.

He agreed to cooperate, ending a lifetime of loyalty to the union.
Turnblazer admitted that the Research and Information Committee

did not exist until after the Yablonskis were murdered and that the money the district's field representatives gave the pensioners and kicked back to Pass and Prater came from embezzled union funds.

While the FBI arranged for Turnblazer to fly to Erie, Prater testified in his own defense. He stuck closely to what Boyle and Pass had told the jury. The former field organizer defended the Research and Information Committee's organizing work and denied that he had ever met Paul Gilly. He admitted he contributed money to Huddleston's defense fund, but he said he did it because he believed his old friend was innocent.

Prater's self-assured manner melted quickly after Sprague asked him about his eighteen motel room meetings with one of Huddleston's daughters and one of the old man's granddaughters. With his wife staring at him, Prater stammered that they had only had a "good time." He denied taking either woman to bed or giving them over $23,000 to pay Huddleston's lawyers and buy his continued silence.

The next day, Sprague called his rebuttal witnesses to testify. They demolished Boyle's credibility. Edith Roark said that she prepared the twenty-three committeemen's expense account sheets after Yablonski had been murdered. Suzanne Richards testified that she called Pass on Thanksgiving and told him to meet Boyle in Madisonville, Kentucky, on November 30, the day the union president ordered Yablonski's assassination postponed until after the election.

Prater received an even worse shock on March 24 when Turnblazer testified for the prosecution. No District 19 coal miner could recall Turnblazer ever disagreeing with anything Pass said or did. Sprague arranged for a special Saturday session for the District 19 president's dramatic testimony.

"Did you and Tony Boyle at any time talk about the formation of the committee?" Sprague asked him.

"No," he replied tersely.

"Did Albert Pass talk to you about it in 1968 or 1969?" asked Sprague.

"No, sir. The subject never came up at the 1968 convention,"

Turnblazer said. In fact, he testified, the committee did not come into being until January 1970, when Pass was trying to account for the money its members allegedly spent.

Rothman's closing argument was more emotional than factual. He argued that the government was out to get Tony Boyle and had railroaded Prater in the process. The Yablonskis, he claimed, were the unfortunate victims of a botched house burglary. The jurors believed none of what he said. They convicted Prater of three counts of first-degree murder on March 26. He sat motionless, his face bluish-gray, as Judge Carney polled the jurors one by one.

Maxine Prater, red-eyed but not crying, wrapped her arms around the couple's sobbing twelve-year-old daughter. The girl, sensing the worst, had started crying before the judge read the jury's verdict. Prater stood up and raised his hand slightly as if to say goodbye to his wife and their stricken children.

The next day, Maxine and their children came to see him. She told her husband she thought he was guilty—the evidence was overwhelming. She urged him to tell the truth. Maxine did not want their children growing up believing their father was innocent.

Prater sat down that night in his cell and hand-wrote a fifteen-page confession, admitting his role in Yablonski's assassination. On April 6, he gave the FBI enough new information to fill sixteen more pages. His confession mentioned Turnblazer thirty-three times. Prater let drop that Turnblazer had contributed $200 a month to pay Huddleston's lawyer. Why, Sprague wondered, had he paid to keep Huddleston's mouth closed? What was Turnblazer still hiding?

Sprague was going to find that out, but he first had to convict Albert Pass.

TWENTY-ONE

The Marker

Albert Pass's trial began on June 4, 1973, in the same courtroom where William Prater had been convicted three months before. Its outcome was never in doubt: the evidence Sprague presented was overwhelming. Would-be spectators had anticipated this. Only a handful of reporters and two members of Pass's family were on hand when Sprague gave his opening statement to the seven-man, five-woman jury on June 11. Boyle was not in the courtroom this time, but Sprague seemed to be as fixated on him as he was on Pass.

"We're close with Pass, but we are not at the beginning. Pass is not the arranger. He is one of the arrangers. It does not stop here," he told the jury.

It took Sprague just four days to call thirty-nine witnesses. Most of them had testified in Prater's trial, and they repeated what they had told that jury. Prater was the only one who did not. He was now the prosecution's star witness.

The trial's highlight came on June 12, when the FBI's William Logan Curtis once again took the witness stand and read Prater's thirty-one-page confession.

"It was in the summer of 1969, May or June . . . Pass told me something had to be done about Yablonski . . . He said Yablonski had to be knocked off or done away with."

Curtis caused a stir in the courtroom when he read Prater's account of a December 17, 1969, meeting with Pass in Harrogate, Tennessee, just two weeks before the Yablonskis were gunned down in their farmhouse.

"At that time, Albert volunteered that Tony Boyle didn't know about the murder plan. Pass also made a similar statement after the murders. I thought it was a strange statement since I didn't ask Pass anything about Boyle.

Pass's face became ashen and his lips tightly drawn when his old comrade in arms then took the witness stand and coolly answered Sprague's rapid-fire questions.

"Look at the defendant—Albert Pass," Sprague commanded. "Is there any doubt in your mind he is the man who contacted you to arrange to have Jock Yablonski killed?"

"None whatsoever," Prater answered, pointing at his co-conspirator. As Pass put his hands together in front of his face as if he were praying, Prater told the jurors that Pass first approached him about joining the murder plot shortly after Yablonski announced that he was running against Boyle for the UMWA's presidency.

For nearly an hour, Sprague carefully guided him through his many meetings with Pass and Huddleston and the money Pass gave him to hand to Huddleston. When Sprague asked him why he had agreed to join the plot, Prater explained that he was the son and grandson of coal miners. The UMWA was his religion. It made him somebody important, and it gave him everything he had. He did not question Pass when he told him that Yablonski planned to destroy the union.

He conceded he had lied at his own trial. "My loyalties were extended to the wrong people at the wrong time but from now on my first loyalty is to my family," he answered when Pass's lawyer cross-examined him.

Huddleston confronted his old boss from the witness stand, too. He told the jury he was the plot's middleman, and did not conceal his bitterness when he testified about what Pass had promised to do for him if he were arrested. "He told me we are prepared to spend $1 million to get you out." Huddleston acknowledged ruefully that not a word of what Pass had promised was true.

Pass did not testify. Harold Gondelman, his lawyer and one of

Pittsburgh's most respected criminal defense attorneys, based his defense on a string of character witnesses. Sprague barely questioned them.

In his closing argument to the jury, Sprague focused on the $20,000 Boyle sent to Pass. "Why did Pass write to Boyle in this instance?" Sprague asked. "Why didn't he write to International Secretary John Owens? Because the international secretary would have asked to see the records of what work these men had done. That is why he went right to Boyle."

But Pass was no mere moneyman. Sprague finished with a dramatic flourish: Pass was the "marker," the man who drew an arrow above the newspaper photograph of Yablonski he gave to Huddleston to mail to Gilly.

"Who is it that literally marked Joseph Yablonski for death? The marker! The person who marked them for extinction, assassination, sits right here. You have a duty to do. Don't flinch from it."

With no new evidence of his own, Pass's lawyer attacked Sprague's case. Gondelman argued that the government's main witnesses were "confessed murderers and perjurers." This was true, but so was his client.

His attack made no difference. The jury deliberated for only five hours. On June 19, it convicted Pass on three counts of first-degree murder. Pass sat stone-faced as his lawyer polled the jury. Each conviction carried a mandatory life sentence in prison. He broke into a broad grin as deputy sheriffs led him out of the courtroom. His apotheosis had come. He had sacrificed everything he had for the union.

Sprague held an informal press conference on the old courthouse's steps. He called Pass's conviction "another step along the way." He reminded the reporters that there was someone above District 19's boss. The trial's testimony proved that "someone in Washington gave the green light to Pass." He promised there would be "at least one more arrest."

When reporters pressed him, Sprague said his next move would speak for itself. They would not have long to wait.

TWENTY-TWO

The Box

Tony Boyle was in a rare good mood. He woke up early on September 6, 1973, and put on a brown pinstripe suit. He had little need to dress up now, but this morning was different. Arnold Miller had fired Edward Carey, the union's general counsel, and replaced him with Chip Yablonski. Boyle was having his deposition taken that morning as part of Carey's several-million-dollar wrongful-discharge lawsuit against the union. He was going to testify that the UMWA had fired one of his most ardent defenders without cause.

The sleekly tailored suit with a fresh rose threaded through its lapel reminded Boyle of the old days, when he was one of the most powerful and feared labor bosses in the United States. That was all gone now, including most of his pension. Miller had slashed it from $50,000 to $16,000 a year, but Boyle was not finished yet. Sprague, despite his bold threats, was no longer snapping at is heels. He had no one left in jail to prosecute for Yablonski's murder. His relentless hunt seemed to have ended with Pass.

As long as Pass and Turnblazer did not betray him, Boyle was sure it would stay that way. He had done what he could to keep Pass's loyalty. He had funneled money to his old brother-in-arms' wife and even kept him on the union's payroll while he was in jail, just as he had William Prater, until Rauh told Judge Bryant about the payments.

He had less confidence in Turnblazer. District 19's president was too mild, too lawyerly. He had none of Pass's toughness and savagery. Turnblazer had broken ranks and testified against Prater in Erie, but he had stopped short of telling Sprague everything he knew about the murders. Boyle hoped the certainty of Turnblazer's going to prison and losing his license to practice law if he told all ensured he would not say any more.

Sprague was focused on Turnblazer, too. He and his team of investigators had stayed behind in Erie the day after Pass's conviction. They had gone over all the trial's testimony and examined any new leads it yielded. Wallace Estill, who ran the FBI's Knoxville field office, sensed that the reserved, soft-spoken lawyer had a conscience, something missing in Pass and Boyle.

He dispatched Henry Quinn to talk with him. Quinn had a relaxed, easygoing manner. He smoked a pipe, could quote scripture, and loved baseball. The FBI agent spent almost a month with Turnblazer, and gradually built a rapport with him. The two men drove for hours through the winding back roads of Tennessee and Kentucky, talking about the Bible, the Cincinnati Reds, and the details of the case.

Quinn and Estill asked Turnblazer to take a lie detector test. He balked. The polygraph was not reliable. He agreed reluctantly to take one only after the agents told him that the government could not help any witnesses it did not trust.

Joseph Brophy, the Philadelphia District Attorney's Office's polygraph expert who had coaxed Lucy into telling all she knew, and J. R. Pearce, an FBI lie detector examiner, hooked up Turnblazer to a polygraph machine and grilled him for hours about what he knew about the murders.

Turnblazer, just as Lucy had done, struggled to minimize his own role in the killings. Brophy and Pearce carefully monitored his breathing, skin sensitivity, blood pressure, and pulse rates—telltale physiological signs that the machine registered. They told him "the box" showed he was lying when he denied meeting with Boyle to discuss Yablonski's assassination.

Turnblazer finally broke on August 3. With tears streaming down his cheeks, he told them what happened on June 23, 1969. After the union's International Executive Board meeting, he was standing in the hall just outside the third-floor meeting room, talking with Pass. Boyle walked up to them. He ordered them to kill Yablonski. Pass jumped at the opportunity. Turnblazer, too afraid of Boyle and Pass to protest and too loyal to the union, joined the conspiracy to assassinate Jock Yablonski.

Turnblazer, who told the two agents that he had not had a full night's sleep since the bullet-riddled bodies of the Yablonskis were found, gave the FBI a thirty-five-page typed statement twenty days later. He admitted he was still shocked by the depth of Boyle's hatred for Yablonski.

On September 5, 1973, Turnblazer was flown to Pittsburgh, and appeared the next morning before a federal grand jury to admit his role in murdering Yablonski. The grand jury indicted him and Boyle for conspiring to violate Yablonski's civil rights by killing him. Turnblazer pleaded guilty to that federal charge forty minutes later. A Washington County judge immediately issued state arrest warrants for both men, charging them with three counts of first-degree murder.

But Sprague did not publicize the warrants. His reason became clear the next morning.

At 11:20 a.m. on September 6, 1973, in a conference room on the fourth floor of the Union Trust Building in Washington, D.C., Chip Yablonski was questioning Boyle about the legal services Edward Carey performed for the union. Yablonski had just shown Boyle a copy of the UMWA's constitution when there was a sharp knock at the door.

Three burly FBI agents stepped into the room and told Boyle that a federal judge in Pittsburgh had just issued a warrant for his arrest. Two of the agents grabbed Boyle's skinny arms and marched him out of the building to their waiting car.

Boyle looked confused. He told a small knot of spectators that he did not know why he was being arrested. The agents drove him to the United States District Courthouse for the District of Columbia. A federal magistrate arraigned him that afternoon. He released Boyle on a $50,000 bond and scheduled a hearing for September 25 on his removal to Pennsylvania.

By now, word had spread among Washington's press corps about Boyle's arrest. A reporter asked him if he was guilty of depriving Yablonski of his civil rights. "No," Boyle answered, "he conspired as much as I did. He campaigned the same way I did." He called the charges "ridiculous." "I never expected this to come through," he said. "I had no forewarning."

Chip Yablonski, in front of the Union Trust Building, smiled with quiet satisfaction. "We've waited a long time," he told the newsmen.

So had Richard Sprague. When he announced Boyle's arrest at a press conference, the special prosecutor let slip for the first time that Turnblazer had named Boyle as the "instigator" of Yablonski's assassination. He wanted to try the seventy-two-year-old former union head as quickly as possible.

Sprague first had to get Boyle to Pennsylvania. This was not going to be easy. On September 24, the eve of his removal hearing, Boyle tried to kill himself, slipping into a coma for three days after gulping down a fistful of sleeping pills. He was determined not to face any murder charges in Pennsylvania.

Charles Moses, the veteran Montana criminal defense lawyer Boyle had hired to defend him, faced the news cameras in front of George Washington University Hospital. Moses said that Boyle believed he had no chance of getting a fair trial in Pennsylvania. "He was also worried about being in jail at his age," Moses told reporters. "I am certain the government will try and use everything they can against him."

Moses was right about that, but even he was taken aback by how quickly the government moved against his client. On December 3, 1973, the United States Supreme Court declined to review Boyle's thirteen Corrupt Practices Act convictions. A Washington County grand jury indicted him two weeks later for murdering the Yablonskis. District Attorney Jess Costa asked federal authorities in Washington, D.C., to extradite Boyle to Pennsylvania.

On December 19, United States District Court Judge Charles R. Richey reduced Boyle's five-year sentence on Corrupt Practices violations to three years, but he sent him to the federal prison hospital in Springfield, Missouri, to serve it. Boyle sat in a wheelchair, dressed in pajamas. He stared vacantly ahead as the judge rebuked him from the bench. He told Boyle that he had "breached the trust" of his union's members.

Two days later, deputy United States marshals strapped Boyle into an airplane seat and flew him to Springfield. His plane touched down briefly in Pittsburgh. A phalanx of local, state, and federal lawmen met Boyle at the airport and drove him through a snowstorm to Washington County, where Judge Charles Sweet was waiting for him. He arraigned him on three counts of first-degree murder, and warned Boyle of what he was about to face. "Now, you are in Pennsylvania, and we have a tradition of hard-nosed but fair justice." Boyle was about to experience both.

Sprague did not object when Boyle's lawyer argued that his client could not get a fair trial in Washington County. He joined with Charles Moses in asking the state's supreme court to pick a new site in one of the state's eastern counties. He was delighted when the justices moved the trial to Media, only fifteen miles from Philadelphia. The small city in Delaware County was practically in Sprague's backyard. The president judge of the county's Court of Common Pleas tapped Francis J. Catania, who had a reputation for being particularly hard on lawyers who asked long-winded questions, to preside over the high-profile trial.

It took Sprague and Moses five days to select a jury of nine men and three women from the venire of 350. The special prosecutor asked each of the prospective jurors whether they would convict the plotter of a murder as easily as the actual killer. Moses asked if any of them had any prejudices against labor leaders.

Boyle's trial was set for March 25, 1974. His cockiness was gone. No other major labor leader in American history had faced what he was about to—twelve jurors who were going to decide if he was guilty of first-degree murder. He walked with short, unsure steps into the high-ceilinged, oak-trimmed Federal period courthouse. His eyes darted back and forth between the prosecution table and the half-filled room of spectators. He waved wanly when he spotted his wife and daughter.

Boyle looked haggard and skeletal in a poorly fitting blue suit, washed-out gray shirt, and a dark tie. Prison had ravaged his health. He suffered from heart disease, chronic anemia, and severe depression. He took his seat beside Moses. He looked straight ahead, as if he were searching for something that was no longer there.

Among the things no longer there were his allies in Big Labor. Until the Washington County grand jury indicted him for murder, Boyle could count on most of the country's top union leaders' steadfast support, much to Joe Rauh's disgust. "One of the great sadnesses of my life," the lawyer had told the *New York Times* in the middle of Arnold Miller's campaign, "is that the labor movement is trying to sweep the Boyle violence and corruption under the rug." They had backed Boyle in his fights with Yablonski and Miller and their steadfast support of him had continued even in the wake of his conviction for making illegal contributions to politicians from the UMWA's treasury.

Murder, though, was something else. Not even Jimmy Hoffa, the International Brotherhood of Teamsters' jailed two-fisted president, had been accused publicly of that. Union solidarity prevented any of them from criticizing Boyle openly, but one by one Big Labor's bosses quietly deserted him. His unbridled ruthlessness had invited too much federal scrutiny and too much bad publicity for them to remain by his side.

In his opening statement before Judge Catania, Sprague addressed the jury for seventy minutes. He stood in front of a large map of Pennsylvania, West Virginia, Kentucky, Tennessee, and the District of Columbia. He told the jurors he was going to use it to trace the assassins' eight trips to kill Jock Yablonski.

Two other attention-getting props lay nearby. Leaning against the prosecution table was the M1 carbine the killers had used to blow a hole in Marg Yablonski's left shoulder when she woke up screaming, and inches away lay their .38 pistol, its white pearl handle gleaming in the courtroom's lights. Shots fired from it had killed all three victims.

Sprague wasted no time. He portrayed Boyle as the head of a chain of command that issued "a brutal and cold-blooded" murder contract, with a deliberate attempt by the union president to insulate himself from the three killers who pulled the triggers.

"This defendant sitting right here"—Sprague pointed at Boyle—"is the man that used the money from the United Mine Workers, the sweat and blood of the miners of America, to pay for murdering Jock Yablonski!"

Sprague promised the jurors they were going to hear from a long train of witnesses who would link Boyle directly to the assassination plot, and told them that Yablonski "signed his own death warrant" when he decided to run for the union's highest office. Boyle slouched in his chair, staring at the courtroom's pink walls.

Charles Moses counterattacked in his opening address, but often meandered. (Sprague objected eight times.) The Montana lawyer claimed that the murder conspiracy was really a local plot hatched in District 19 by some of the same liars Sprague was now calling as his witnesses. Boyle, he assured the jury, had had nothing to do with it.

He maintained that the evidence was going to show that Pass and Turnblazer ordered Yablonski's execution to silence him: Yablonski was threatening to expose their misuse of nearly a million dollars in union funds. Moses promised to produce a Department of Labor audit that proved this. "Sprague's paths," he lectured the jury, "lead not to Tony Boyle but to others convicted in this case."

For the first time that day, Boyle perked up and paid attention. He was going to have to be at his combative best to beat Richard Sprague.

TWENTY-THREE

The Puppeteer

Sprague called forty-eight witnesses to testify. Some were appearing for their first time, many others for their fifth time. They ranged from Red Man tobacco–chewing Kentucky pensioners who had kicked back union checks for organizing work they never performed to straitlaced FBI fingerprint and firearms experts in their starched white shirts. Sandwiched in between were killers, union officials, and a host of bit players, all building blocks in the special prosecutor's case against Tony Boyle. Sprague used much the same trial strategy he had used with Prater.

He started with Ken Yablonski, who described the horrors he encountered inside his parents' isolated farmhouse when he went to check on them on January 5, 1970. Sprague called Paul Gilly next, and questioned him for most of the afternoon. He wanted Gilly's grisly descriptions of the murders to haunt the jurors overnight.

Gilly's testimony provided the trial's first high drama. The thin-faced former house painter admitted that on December 30, 1969, he and two accomplices traveled to Clarksville to kill Yablonski. After he identified Claude Vealey as one of the two accomplices, Gilly came face-to-face with Buddy Martin. The slightly built killer was in chains and handcuffed to two large deputy sheriffs. Moments before, he had gone berserk in the holding cell behind the courtroom and ripped a sink out of the wall by jumping on it.

Martin spat on Sprague's left shoulder as he walked by the prosecution's table. The special prosecutor did not move a muscle. For nearly a minute, he left Martin's spit on his suit jacket, before he slowly wiped it off with his handkerchief. He wanted the jury to see what kind of man had fired two bullets into a sleeping young woman's head. Sprague could not have asked for a better opening scene if he had written it himself.

Martin's shocking performance was not over. He appalled the mostly blue-collar middle-aged jurors when he called Gilly a "lying motherfucker!" and screamed out, "that Goddamned redneck killed both!" before the deputies hustled him out of the courtroom.

Sprague calmly resumed his questioning. After he described in painstaking detail how they had methodically executed the family, Gilly testified that Huddleston told him during the summer of 1969 that Boyle was behind the murder-for-hire plot. Boyle wanted Yablonski assassinated in Washington, D.C., because of that city's high crime rate. He wanted the police to think Yablonski was a victim of an armed robbery that had gone horribly wrong.

Two of Sprague's most powerful witnesses were Prater and Turnblazer. When Prater testified on Thursday, April 5, much of what he said had been heard before, but one thing was startlingly new: he told the jury that Boyle visited him privately in the Erie County jail during his own murder trial and coached him "to stick with your story, even if you are convicted, stick with your story."

An Erie County deputy sheriff corroborated Prater's story, testifying that he saw Boyle talking with Prater late at night on March 17, 1973, for fifteen or twenty minutes in a private room.

When Sprague asked Prater why he finally confessed, he explained, "There were too many people being hurt in this entire thing. I have a wife and seven children, and lying is against my principles."

Sprague closed his case with Turnblazer, whose testimony was even more devastating than Prater's. On the same day that Hank Aaron broke Babe Ruth's thirty-nine-year-old home-run record, the former head of District 19 broke the back of Boyle's legal defense. He revealed that Boyle ordered Pass and him to "take care of Joseph Yablonski."

Turnblazer admitted that he had lied repeatedly about his role in the assassination until he could not stand it any longer. "I got to the point where I couldn't sleep, and it just came out. I had to clear my conscience."

In his thick southern accent, he described the June 23, 1969 meeting inside the UMWA's Washington headquarters that led to Yablonski's murder. Boyle had huddled with Pass and him on the building's third floor after a long and acrimonious International Executive Board meeting. The meeting had ended with Boyle and Yablonski shouting at each other.

"Were you present when orders or directions were given for the assassination of Joseph Yablonski?" Sprague asked.

"Yes," Turnblazer replied.

"Who gave these orders?"

"Mr. Boyle."

When the special prosecutor asked him if he saw in the courtroom the man who ordered Yablonski's execution, the witness pointed directly at Boyle, who sat at the defense table. Boyle stared at Turnblazer. He shook his head slowly, as if he could not believe what he had just heard. His lieutenants were not going to lie for him anymore.

Turnblazer told the jurors one more devastating fact before he stepped down. He said Pass gave him a copy of the minutes from the International Executive Board's January 22, 1970, meeting—the meeting at which the board had given Pass a standing ovation for his report on the fictitious organizing work his Research and Information Committee had done in District 19. Pass had instructed Turnblazer, whom Boyle had ordered to stay away from the meeting, to read the minutes, so that they could tell the grand jury the same story about the committee's origins and its work.

Moses called his first witnesses on April 9: Huddleston, Dave Brandenburg, and Lucy. None helped his client's cause.

He had hoped to lead with Tom Kane, an auditor with the Department of Labor who had produced a 184-page report in October 1970 that showed how much money the UMWA had sent District 19 the year before. Moses wanted to use his testimony to argue that Pass and Turnblazer had a strong motive to kill Yablonski, because the insurgent threatened to blow the whistle on them for stealing the union's money, but Sprague objected.

He argued that a report about District 19's finances had nothing to do with his murder charges against Boyle. Judge Catania agreed, and barred Moses from questioning Kane or introducing his findings.

With his defense in tatters, Moses called Boyle to the witness stand. As he raised his right hand and swore to tell the truth, the air of dejection surrounding him disappeared. Boyle became alert and feisty, once again the powerful union leader who had ruled the UMWA with an iron fist. He had killed to stay in power; he would lie now to stay out of a Pennsylvania prison.

The lies flowed freely from his lips. He denied that Pass was a friend, but he claimed that he and Yablonski had been "very close friends." He testified that while at the UMWA's 1968 convention in Denver, he had approved the creation of the Research and Information Committee. When Moses questioned him about the June 23, 1969 International Executive Board meeting, Boyle said he did not meet with either Pass or Turnblazer after the meeting. Instead, two representatives from the union's District 5 had appeared in the hallway and whisked him down the stairs to his office for another meeting.

Moses shifted his questioning. He asked Boyle how he had felt when he heard his foe was dead. "I became ill at my stomach, and I usually work 14, 15, 16 hours a day," Boyle answered sorrowfully, as he stared into the jury box. "And I went home. I was sick."

Boyle's lying picked up speed. He said it was his idea to post a $50,000 reward for the capture of the Yablonskis' killers, and he denied that he had sat next to Turnblazer during their flight to Pittsburgh to appear before a federal grand jury. Boyle swore he sat beside Edward Carey, the union's top lawyer.

Moses quizzed him on visiting Prater at the Erie County jail. Boyle admitted he had, but only after Prater's lawyers asked him to do it. He said "at least 10 or 12" people were with him and that his conversation with the District 19 field representative lasted for only "seven, eight minutes."

Moses ended his direct examination with an emphatic question: "Did you have anything to do with the killing of Joseph Yablonski, Margaret Yablonski, or Charlotte Yablonski?"

"Did I have anything to do with it?" Boyle replied rhetorically.

"Yes, sir."

"Absolutely not."

"Did you ever talk to Albert Pass or William Turnblazer and suggest to them that they kill Mr. Yablonski?"

"I certainly did not. To the contrary," Boyle answered emphatically as his lawyer sat down.

But Boyle's self-assured air evaporated under Sprague's withering cross-examination. The special prosecutor set his trap for his quarry carefully, making him repeat the lies he had just told and luring him into telling two more.

Boyle denied he gave Pass a copy of the International Executive Board's January 22, 1970 minutes to hand to Turnblazer. He assured Sprague that none of his fingerprints were on the document.

Sprague shredded what little credibility Boyle had left when he called his rebuttal witnesses. His first was Suzanne Richards, Boyle's personal assistant, who told the jury that Boyle sat beside Turnblazer, not Edward Carey, during their May 10, 1972 flight to Pittsburgh. When Sprague questioned her about the union's reward, she said the idea was hers. Boyle's only contribution was to slash it from $100,000 to $50,000.

The special prosecutor then put David Rothman, Prater's lawyer, on the witness stand. He said he never asked Boyle to meet with his client in the Erie County jail. Instead, Boyle had asked him if he could meet with Prater alone, and they did meet, for nearly twenty minutes. Turnblazer followed Rothman, and repeated his earlier testimony that Pass gave him a copy of the minutes from the International Executive Board's January 22, 1970 meeting. He told the jury he had turned the copy over to the FBI.

Sprague, the master showman, saved the best for last. He called Charles Groenthal, head of the FBI's Washington, D.C., Fingerprint Laboratory, to the witness stand. The special prosecutor asked him if he had found any of Boyle's fingerprints on the minutes.

"Yes," he answered.

"That is all," Sprague told the judge.

"Your duty is clear," Sprague told the jury in his closing argument. "There will have been no success in solving the assassination of Joseph Yablonski, Margaret Yablonski, and Charlotte Yablonski if it fails to reach the originator of the assassination itself, W. A. 'Tony' Boyle."

Moses had little to say. Boyle had left him with nothing but lies. He appealed to the jury to have mercy on his sick and elderly client, pointing out that it was almost Easter, a time for forgiveness and redemption. He ended by pleading with them not to believe Turnblazer, an admitted liar and embezzler.

He could have said the same about his own client. The jury deliberated for only four and a half hours on April 11, 1974, before it found Boyle guilty of three counts of first-degree murder. Boyle shook his head and stared at the floor. Three United States deputy marshals and two Delaware County deputy sheriffs led him quickly from the courtroom.

Ken Yablonski's eyes filled with tears. "You don't know how happy I am. There's no words I can express," he told Sprague.

Richard Sprague's four-year hunt was over. He had tracked Jock Yablonski's killers from two bloody bedrooms in southwestern Pennsylvania's coalfields to the leafy suburbs of Philadelphia.

He was characteristically modest. "It was a magnificent job of detection," he told the large pack of reporters who gathered around him. "It shows how effective law enforcement can get people at the top. Too often it is only the little guys who get caught and convicted. We get only the puppets and not the puppeteers. Not this time, thank God."

Chip Yablonski thanked God for Richard Sprague. He never doubted the dogged special prosecutor was going to peel all the layers of the onion, but he was enormously relieved that the pursuit of his family's killers was finally over. Justice had been done.

A Martyr's Cause

"Everything I had ever learned in the history books taught me that martyrs have to die for causes," Lyndon Johnson told historian Doris Kearns after his own presidency had ended: "John Kennedy had died. But his cause was not really clear. That was my job. I had to take the dead man's program and turn it into a martyr's cause."

Just as President Johnson used John Kennedy's murder to force through Congress the groundbreaking 1964 Civil Rights Act, Arnold Miller and his band of reformers used Jock Yablonski's assassination to encode functional democracy into the UMWA's DNA. By the time a jury convicted Tony Boyle in the spring of 1974, Miller's administration had adopted and passed almost every plank of Yablonski's 1969 platform.

Looking back, it is hard to overstate how much Miller and his followers enthralled the country in late 1972 when they came to Washington. They invited high expectations, something in short supply in that year of the Watergate break-in and President Richard Nixon's crushing defeat of Democratic nominee George McGovern.

Miller's reformers proclaimed a new day for America's coal miners. They immediately slashed their own salaries and sold Boyle's gleaming Cadillacs. The advertisement for one of the cars wryly described it as "never having been exposed to the wear and tear of coalfield driving."

Miller's first year in office was dazzling. He purged all of Boyle's loyalists from the International Executive Board and expanded the union's leadership. Levi Daniel became the first appointed African American member of the board in the UMWA's history. At the same time, Miller fired Antoinette Boyle Engebregson, Suzanne Richards, and a host of other top Boyle administrative lackeys.

By the end of 1973, Miller's administration had held free elections in sixteen of the union's districts, overhauled its health-care and retirement systems, and transformed its bimonthly journal into an actual forum where miners could openly and without fear criticize their leaders. The UMWA's new president was determined to show the nation that coal miners could govern themselves. "We have to show that we're not just a bunch of dumbasses," he earnestly told a *Time* correspondent.

Miller's crowning achievement was the union's new constitution.

Joe Rauh's keynote constitutional convention speech on December 12, 1973, captured the enthusiasm and hopes of the time. He reminded the delegates of their role in this "historic battle for union democracy," and how much their victory over tyranny meant to ordinary Americans. Rauh's speech was an open swipe at Richard Nixon's White House. He praised the union for being the first labor organization in the country to call for Nixon's impeachment.

He brought the delegates to their feet when he said the reformers' ouster of Boyle proved "no just cause is a lost cause," even in the face of the "arrogance of power and cynical corruption in high places!"

The delegates took their cue from the civil rights icon's fiery words. After they stood for a minute in silence to remember Yablonski, they rewrote their constitution, creating one of the most progressive charters in organized labor history. Its provisions ensured democratic elections, full district autonomy, and the rank-and-file's ratifications of contracts. Jock Yablonski's blood had washed the union clean of corruption.

Chairman Lou Antal reminded the delegates of what the union

owed the assassinated rebel. "Some men have a reason for living and dying," he told them. "He died for us to go forward."

More successes followed. The next year, the union's five-man bargaining team successfully negotiated and secured the rank and file's ratification of the National Bituminous Coal Wage Agreement of 1974. Thanks to the Arab states' oil embargoes, coal was once again in high demand. An undersecretary of labor who mediated the talks that led to this deal called it the "richest industry-wide contract" in American labor history. The days of Boyle's sweetheart agreements with coal operators were over.

They were replaced with a week of paid sick leave each year, a pension increase of up to $250 a month, the right to walk out over safety issues, company-paid safety training for mine safety committeemen, and company-funded UMWA mine inspections. The new contract also gave the union's miners an average daily wage of $54.39. This boost placed them once again ahead of the country's auto and steel workers.

Their benefits did not end there. Miners who retired after 1976 got a new pension plan of $500 or more a month. This plan was the first to be negotiated under the Employee Retirement Income Security Act of 1974, the federal law that protects the interests of workers and their beneficiaries who are enrolled in pension and health plans provided by private employers. This law was a direct outgrowth of Yablonski's charges that Boyle had misused the UMWA's health and retirement funds to pay for his 1969 reelection campaign.

The Miners for Democracy's successful revolt and their reforms inspired grassroots revolts in the United Steelworkers of America and in the International Brotherhood of Teamsters. In 1974, second-generation steelworker and reformer Ed Sadlowski, with Joe Rauh at his side, won a specially supervised election to become the head of District 31, the largest district then in the United Steelworkers of America. Two years later, a group of young teamsters formed the Teamsters for a Democratic Union. Its members remained a thorn in the sides of the Teamsters' corrupt bosses until that union finally enjoyed its first democratic election in 1991. Their nearly twenty-year wait underscores how difficult rank-and-file movements were to start, much less sustain.

Yet democracy was always a fragile bloom in the coalfields. Arnold Miller faced strong headwinds even before he sat in Tony Boyle's chair. On the day he was sworn in as the union's new president, Miller received a terse telegram from Boyle's sycophants on the UMWA's International Executive Board. The board passed a resolution that morning asserting its "supreme authority" over the union, something that was laughable given its long history as a lapdog for John L. Lewis and Tony Boyle. Miller promptly dismissed all its members, but its pro-Boyle acolytes had fired a loud warning shot that they did not plan to go away.

They did not. Boyle supporters or anti-Miller candidates won nine board seats in 1973. Miller did not meddle in the elections, but this vocal rump, which composed almost one-third of the board, bedeviled him throughout his presidency.

Other serious divisions surfaced. Mike Trbovich was still bitter about not being selected as the Miners for Democracy's presidential candidate and broke with Miller in 1975. He accused him of misusing union funds, having a staff dominated by "leftwing radicals from New York and Boston," and being a poor administrator. A Department of Labor audit cleared Miller of wasting the union's money, but the discord between the two men fractured the union's reform movement.

Miller was also badly hurt by an exodus of talent. Chip Yablonski, Don Stillman, and several other young reformers resigned from their posts in 1975. They had achieved their goals of restoring democracy to the UMWA, purging it of corruption, and winning its rank and file a groundbreaking contract. Miller foundered without them. He was an inexperienced administrator and had never supervised anything bigger than a two-hundred-man local. One West Virginia news editor quipped that Miller could not run a roadside ice cream stand by himself.

His enemies took full advantage of his hands-off leadership and his reluctance to use his gavel. Union board sessions descended into parliamentary anarchy, with his opponents sometimes coming to blows with his supporters. "The meetings," Miller lamented to a *Time* correspondent, "are a goddam circus." *Business Week* compared the UMWA to Portugal after reformers overthrew its dictatorship in 1974.

Miller responded by becoming increasingly paranoid. He believed Brutuses were lurking all around him. He carried a Smith & Wesson .38 revolver tucked into a holster strapped beneath his left shoulder. He feared being assassinated. He moved out of his Washington, D.C., home and secluded himself across the Potomac River in an apartment in neighboring Alexandria, Virginia.

His behavior became more erratic. He changed the locks on the UMWA's headquarters building to keep fired employees out, allegedly ordered the heat turned off in a critic's office, removed the door to his secretary's office, and hired three $20,000-a-year "security men" to patrol the halls of the building.

Miller also backtracked. He leased a nine-passenger Cadillac limousine, telling critics that union officers needed to travel in "proper dignity." He grew averse to conflict. He disappeared from the union's headquarters, driving alone for hours in circles on the Washington Beltway.

When he was present, Miller grew bored in meetings. His handlers found it harder and harder to keep him focused. He drifted into long asides. He preferred talking about hunting raccoons or making moonshine more than he did discussing the intricacies of union contracts or their negotiations.

Things finally came to a head in 1977, when shrinking coal markets ended the coal operators' willingness to concede to the union's demands for further hefty raises and generous benefits. Miller won only 40 percent of the vote in that June's three-way UMWA presidential race.

The union's miners went on strike for 110 days in 1978. Miller asked the members twice to ratify the contract he negotiated, but they refused both times. They finally ratified it, but Miller suffered a stroke and two heart attacks in its wake. This was his last battle: overwhelmed and sick, he finally stepped down in November 1979.

But the divisive 1977 election and the bitter 1978 strike showed something more than a splintered union. They showed how far the UMWA had come. No federal overseers patrolled its polling places or counted its votes. Its open and democratic processes, no matter how ugly, showed that the UMWA had become a labor union truly controlled by its rank-and-file members. Violence and murder no longer stalked its elections or intimidated its coal miners.

Even a short-lived counterrevolution could not undermine the democratic reforms put into place. Sam Church, Miller's tobacco-chewing, two-fisted vice-president during his second term and a one-time Boyle supporter, tried to turn the clock back, but it was too late. Richard Trumka, a union lawyer who had come of age in Miller's administration, defeated Church in 1982.

Trumka, who is now the president of the AFL-CIO, was a product of Yablonski's vision of opening up the union to younger voices and broadening their leadership opportunities. Raw talent now counted for more than blind loyalty. Under Trumka's leadership, and later Cecil Roberts's, the UMWA became the most democratically run large union in the country.

However, democracy could not inoculate the UMWA against powerful economic and political forces it could not control. High inflation wracked the country during Arnold Miller's two administrations and prompted the Federal Reserve to hike interest rates in 1981. These hikes increased the value of the dollar and sent U.S. exports into a tailspin. They devastated the country's manufacturing sector.

High unemployment followed—it climbed to 10.8 percent of the country's workforce in December 1982—and layoffs crippled America's major industrial unions. Workers were more willing to accept lower wages and fewer benefits. It also made them more willing to listen to company warnings that unionization could threaten their jobs.

President Ronald Reagan seemed to prove this in 1981 when he fired and replaced more than 11,000 air traffic controllers who belonged to the Professional Air Traffic Controllers Organization.

These fears and pressures have grown even stronger over time.

The UMWA's membership has shrunk to 95,000 members, only 6,608 of whom work in underground coal mines. Kentucky, once the union's bloodiest battleground, now has no UMWA-organized mines. Albert Pass's District 19 is no more. Only scattered fragments of it remain, including a union local that now inhabits what is left of its old headquarters building. Its members, just about all UMWA retirees, share its space with a Beltone Hearing Aid Center.

Operators argue that safer mines and higher wages have made the UMWA obsolete—claims that have made a lot of old time Kentucky miners especially bitter. "A lot of people right now who don't know what the [union] stands for is [sic] getting good wages and benefits because of the sacrifice we made," a retired coal digger lamented to the *Washington Post*.

Little of what plagues the UMWA is self-inflicted. Plentiful and cheap natural gas, thanks to unregulated shale drilling, has steadily driven down coal prices. New, stricter environmental rules have also compounded coal's problems. Many utilities are phasing out their use of it as a source of power. Coal now supplies just 30 percent of the country's power, down from nearly 50 percent ten years ago.

To compete, the coal industry has moved to the West, a region with a long history of opposing organized labor and supporting right-to-work laws. The sixteen strip mines in Wyoming's Powder River Basin produce 45 percent of the country's coal, but employ only 10 percent of the nation's miners. The average underground miner in West Virginia produces three tons of coal per hour, while the average miner at a strip mine in Wyoming produces nearly twenty-eight.

What has not changed is that coal miners are still dying from black lung. The National Institute for Occupational Safety and Health estimates that one in ten coal miners who have worked in mines for at least twenty-five years have black lung. These statistics are even grimmer in Central Appalachia, where as many as one in five have symptoms of this incurable and progressive disease.

Their predicament has been made all the more dire because the
pension fund that sick and retired miners rely on will be depleted by
2022, unless Congress steps in with legislation to rescue it.

Tony Boyle watched the beginnings of all this from his jail cell in
Dallas, Pennsylvania, where Judge Catania sent him on September 11,
1975, after sentencing him to serve three consecutive life sentences.
"All I can say is I'm innocent," Boyle maintained.

In 1977, the Pennsylvania Supreme Court granted him a new trial.
Its justices held that his lawyer should have been allowed to question Tom Kane, the federal auditor who combed through District 19's
financial records in October 1970.

It made no difference—Sprague, once again, staged a masterful production. On February 18, 1978, a second jury sitting in Media, Pennsylvania, convicted Boyle again of three counts of first-degree murder.
This time, his lawyer argued that Albert Pass planned the killings on
his own, which enraged the one-time District 19 strongman.

Pass broke his code of silence and confessed to the FBI. When
agents asked him why Boyle tapped him to plan Yablonski's murder,
the one-time District 19 kingpin replied tersely: "He knew I was a loyal
union man he could count on to get the job done." He later told them
that he had decided to confess and testify truthfully "in order to relieve
my conscience of the guilt I have felt caused by my sin in participating
in the murders of Joseph, Margaret, and Charlotte Yablonski."

Pass testified against his erstwhile partner in mayhem. Boyle's
betrayal embittered him, and he was desperate to be reunited with his
wife and his invalid daughter; both were on public assistance. Boyle
did not testify this time. He stared vacantly ahead and his face sagged
after the jury convicted him once more. "I am disappointed," he mumbled to a newspaper reporter, but he did not give up. In July 1979, Boyle

filed a motion asking for a third trial before Judge Catania ordered him to serve three consecutive life sentences for the murders. It failed. His claims of innocence were not over, but his trials were.

Tony Boyle died in the coronary unit of Wilkes-Barre General Hospital in Wilkes-Barre, Pennsylvania, on May 31, 1985, from heart and stomach problems, at age eighty-three. Prison officials had moved him there after his health began to rapidly decline. A UMWA spokesman offered the press a brief comment on Boyle's passing: "The death of former UMWA president Boyle marks the final passage in a tragic chapter in the union's history." Boyle's death marked something else, as well. The era in which unions were important enough to kill for died with him.

Richard Sprague, Boyle's tireless hunter, left the Philadelphia district attorney's office in 1974 after clashing with F. Emmett Fitzpatrick, the city's new district attorney. Fitzpatrick fired Sprague after the special prosecutor called him a liar and "the worst district attorney I have seen in 17 years." Sprague practiced law briefly in Philadelphia before he became the chief counsel for the House Select Committee on Assassinations in 1976.

The committee's overseers found Sprague to be too independent, and too difficult to control. He repeatedly crossed swords with his congressional masters over his budget and authority to steer the investigations, and resigned in 1978 to return to private practice in Philadelphia. Now in his nineties, he is a senior partner at Sprague and Sprague, a general trial practice firm, and remains one of the city's most esteemed and sought-after trial lawyers.

Arnold Miller died on July 12, 1985, from black lung, at just sixty-two. Richard Trumka called Miller "a fitting example for all of us in the UMWA." A brave and decent man, he was just as haunted by Yablonski's ghost as Boyle had been. Many within the union and outside it believed that the much more experienced Yablonski would have made a great union president; Miller believed that, too. Inescapable was the fact that he became the union's president only because of a tragic twist of history.

None of the Yablonskis' killers were fitting examples for anyone, but Buddy Martin, functionally illiterate, used his time behind bars to earn an associate arts degree from Pennsylvania State University and learned to paint with charcoal. While incarcerated, he wrote *Caesar's Gladiator Pit*, which compared life in a maximum-security prison to Julius Caesar's Rome. Martin died of stomach cancer on March 10, 1991, at forty-two years old. His rehabilitation went only so far. He went to his grave denying he killed anyone inside the Yablonskis' farmhouse.

Claude Vealey followed him to the grave on January 31, 1999, dying of brain and spinal cancer at the age of fifty-five, after becoming a heavy equipment operator in prison.

Paul Gilly remains behind bars in the Albion State Correctional Institution not far from the shores of Lake Erie. He tried to do something about that on March 16, 1981, when he wrote a startling letter to Tony Boyle. His letter began, "I am sorry that I lied at your trial in order to get me out of prison." Gilly charged that Richard Sprague, in exchange for his perjured testimony against the former union president, had promised "to get me out of jail" in seven or eight years but had lied and backtracked on his pledge.

Judge Charles Sweet asked the Pennsylvania attorney general to investigate Gilly's astonishing claim. On September 30, 1981, Robert Keuch, the state's executive attorney general, issued an eight-page report, which exonerated Sprague of any wrongdoing.

None of this has stopped the convicted house painter from pushing for his release from prison. Gilly still believes he is being "unconstitutionally and unlawfully detained"; he argues he should have been released from prison in January 1991, because the maximum time he should have to serve for a first-degree felony in Pennsylvania is twenty years. No Pennsylvania court, including its highest, has agreed with his legal analysis. He admits the Yablonski murders still haunt him, especially around Christmas.

After confessing, William Prater pleaded guilty to conspiring to violate Yablonski's civil rights and was sentenced to life in federal prison. He died in his cell of a heart attack on August 12, 1989, at seventy years old. He had been confined to a wheelchair after suffering a stroke in 1983.

William Turnblazer fared better than his one-time field representative. After serving a little a little over four years in a federal penitentiary, he was paroled in October 1978. When the Tennessee Supreme Court revoked his license to practice law, he became a tax assessor in Middlesboro, Kentucky. He died on October 6, 2005, at eighty-two years old.

Albert Pass worked in his penitentiary's dental lab and received high marks for his work ethic, attention to detail, enthusiasm, and recommendations. He became a member of the prison's lifers' association and enjoyed playing cards, but he stopped going to church. He believed God had deserted him, just as the UMWA had done. He wrote in his third petition for clemency that he never believed his actions would lead to Jock Yablonski's death, "let alone his wife and daughter." "I don't know," he added sorrowfully, "how Tony Boyle was able to get such a hold on me." He died in prison in 2002 at eighty-two.

Lucy Gilly remained a survivor. On August 17, 1974, Judge Charles Sweet agreed with Richard Sprague's recommendation that she and Silous Huddleston be placed in the federal government's witness protection program. Sweet noted for the record that the father and daughter owed Washington County court costs of $410, but that the county was not going to make any effort to collect it. "We are not even going to know what their names are a month from now," he quipped from the bench.

Both vanished. The *Philadelphia Bulletin* reported in 1981 that the United States Marshal's Service sent them to live in the western United States. Huddleston did not want to live by the program's strict rules, and refused to change his name. "I was born with it, and by God,

I will die with it," he replied irritably when relatives asked him about it. He hated living in a cramped apartment with Lucy and his grandson.

When Lucy threatened to put him in a nursing home, Huddleston rebelled. He got his own apartment, but then drifted to Toledo, Ohio, to live with one of his sons, but his ravaged lungs gasped for air in that polluted industrial city.

Huddleston tried Florida next and then a western desert. He died on August 17, 1981, at seventy-two years old. A tall, blonde woman with colorless eyes attended his funeral. She was listed only as a "friend" by the funeral home; her name was not included on his list of survivors. His tombstone displays a pick and shovel and the seal of the UMWA. Even in death, Huddleston could not let go of the union.

Joe Rauh remained one of the country's foremost civil rights lawyers. He retired from his practice of law in the late 1980s but kept busy as a public speaker on liberal causes and as a lobbyist against the Reagan and Bush administrations' conservative nominees to the Supreme Court. He died on September 3, 1992, at Sibley Memorial Hospital in Washington, D.C., after suffering a heart attack. He was eighty-one years old.

Ken Yablonski continued to serve western Pennsylvania's coal miners as a labor lawyer until he died of a heart attack September 8, 2002, at age sixty-eight. He was the chair of the medical clinic in Centerville, Pennsylvania, that still bears his father's name.

His brother Chip became one of the leading labor lawyers in the United States, though he is now retired, living in Bethesda, Maryland. His father's legacy remains a better-run, more democratic labor union, with more concern for the safety and working conditions of its coal miners.

Jock, Margaret, and Charlotte Yablonski rest on the highest hill in Washington, Pennsylvania's Washington Cemetery. From their graves, one can see the top of the county's courthouse, where two of their killers were tried. In the more than fifty years they have lain there, no other leader of a revolt inside a major American labor union has been gunned down while standing up for the rights of his or her workers. Today, cheap natural gas, nonunion strip-mined coal, global warming, and hollow political promises are much bigger threats to the UMWA, and the men and women who rely on it, than fraud, extortion, beatings, dynamite, and murder.

ACKNOWLEDGMENTS

Many people and institutions made this book possible.

Foremost, I could not have written it without the help of Chip Yablonski, who lived through so many of the gut-wrenching events I describe. He generously allowed me to use his personal papers on his father's 1969 campaign and his rich collection on the Miners for Democracy. I cannot thank him enough for patiently answering my countless questions, correcting many factual errors in an early draft, and for reminding me just how important his father's and the miners' fight for democracy was.

Richard Sprague, who is still one of Philadelphia's most sought-after trial lawyers, was also enormously generous with his time, insights, and case files. He and Ruth Arnao, one of his assistants, were kind hosts during the two and a half days I spent working in one of his law firm's offices reviewing documents and studying the brilliant trial strategies he used to bring the family's killers to justice.

A far-flung network of former MFD member was indispensable, especially Edgar James, Don Stillman, and Bernie Aronson, who all helped engineer Arnold Miller's election victory over Tony Boyle in 1972. Likewise, I am very grateful to Ralph Nader, Steven Yablonski, Fred Barnes, Elmer Schifko, Judge Laurence Silberman, J. Davitt McAteer, Plato Cacheris, and Mason Caudill, who all consented to be interviewed. Their recollections and insights made this book much richer.

I am especially grateful to Joe Masterson, who laid out for me the story of the FBI's massive hunt for the assassins. Joe's recollections, particularly his interrogation of Buddy Martin, provided some of this book's most dramatic moments. Ray Batvinis, a former FBI Special Agent in Cleveland and a first-rate historian of the Bureau, kindly introduced me to Joe.

I want to thank Paul Gilly, whom I interviewed for over four hours at the Albion State Penitentiary on the outskirts of Erie, Pennsylvania. Although his memories sometimes clashed with what he testified to in court, I appreciate his willingness to meet with me.

I also thank the late James R. Luzier, the then owner of the Yablonskis' farmhouse in Clarksville, for permitting me to walk, in July 2016, literally in the killers' footsteps. The bullet hole, which remains in the master bedroom's floor where Jock Yablonski's body lay, still haunts me.

Similarly, I owe a deep debt to John Tarley, one of my old colleagues in the CIA, who introduced me to his uncle, Carlo Tarley, a former miner and leading UMWA official. Dewey Tarley, John's uncle and Carlo's brother, died on November 20, 1968, when Consol Number 9 blew up. Carlo's tour of what was the mine's site and the other tiny mining communities that surround it was critical in my gaining an understanding of that area's geography and of the daily dangers miners face. Carlo was kind enough to introduce me to Reverend Richard Bowyer, who comforted the families during the Consol Number 9 tragedy.

A host of friends and colleagues read my manuscript, commented on it, or otherwise encouraged me to write it. These include Dr. Nicholas Reynolds, Robert Lamb, Robert Freis, David Thomsson, Richard Munday, Kevin Tiernan, Tristan Atwood Coughlin, Larry Barr, Liza Mundy, Bob Harwood, Mark McConnell, Jim Semivan, and Marshall Burke. I am especially grateful to David Ferriero, the Archivist of the United States, who read an early draft of my manuscript and gave me kind words of support.

Thanks, too, to Earl Dotter, a brilliant photographer and chronicler of the struggles of America's working men and women, for tirelessly helping locate several of the pictures that appear in this book. Phil Smith of the UMWA graciously fielded my questions on the current state of the union.

In addition to the persons above, I relied on a host of institutions to write this book. These include the Library of Congress's Manuscript Division, a warm and friendly place to research made all the more so by Lewis Wyman, Bruce Kirby, and Jeff Flannery; the Special Research Center at the University of Kentucky, where Daniel Weddlington greatly facilitated my research; the Eberly Family Special Collections Library at Pennsylvania State University; the West Virginia and Regional History Center at West Virginia University, which is so ably staffed by Lori Hostettler; the Walter Reuther Library at Wayne State University; the Hoover Institution at Stanford University; and the Sherrod Library at East Tennessee State University. I also benefited greatly from the thousands of pages on the murders I received from the FBI's Freedom of Information Act staff. Although FOIA specialists in the federal government are often criticized, their work is as indispensable as it is unheralded.

This book would have been impossible to write without relying on the work of other authors and reporters who have gone before me. I found the following very useful: Trevor Armbrister, Brit Hume, Tom Bethell, Tony Brown, Arthur Lewis, Ben A. Franklin, Curtis Seltzer, Bonnie E. Stewart, Paul F. Clark, Joseph Finley, David Hackett Fischer, Ward Sinclair, John Moody, Laurence Leamer, John Gaventa, Melvyn Dubofsky, Warren Van Tine, and the *Philadelphia Bulletin*'s series on the murders that ran in August 1981, before the newspaper ceased publishing. I also want to thank Nicolo Majnoni, who cheerfully shared with me the fruits of his own research on the Miners for Democracy for the documentary he is preparing on them.

Todd Schuster, my agent, and Elias Altman, one of his associates, did their usual yeomen's work on my proposal, helping me mold and sharpen my chapters' outlines and character sketches. Elias came up with the book's title. Luckily, Todd shopped my proposal to John Glusman, W. W. Norton's vice-president and editor in chief. An accomplished author in his own right, John is as skilled an editor as he is a gentleman. I benefited enormously from his razor-sharp editorial judgments and his keen ear for language and how it should flow.

None of John's work, however, would have been possible without that first put in by Helen Thomaides, his gifted editorial assistant. Helen's structural edits made this book much stronger and a far better read than what I originally presented. I am truly grateful to her for all the long hours she put in to making this book what it is. I also want to thank Nancy Green for her painstaking copy edits. Her meticulous review saved me from many stylistic and factual pitfalls. Any mistakes John, Helen, and Nancy did not catch are attributable solely to me. A shout out in particular to Rebecca Munro, this book's project editor, who kept it on the rails, never missing a beat. I also owe a debt of gratitude to Ingsu Liu for the book cover's beautiful design.

Lastly, I thank my children, Anna and Robin. Writing a book is necessarily a solitary and self-absorbed task. Your love and support made this one possible.

A NOTE ON SOURCES

Most of the information contained in these pages comes from trial transcripts, contemporary newspaper and magazine articles, personal interviews, Federal Bureau of Investigation case files, previously published books on the 1969 election and the murders, and from documents housed at Wayne State University, the Pennsylvania State University, West Virginia University, the University of Kentucky, East Tennessee State University, the Hoover Institution, and the Library of Congress Manuscript Division's extraordinarily rich Joseph Albert Yablonski Legal Case Collection.

Even with all this material, this book is the most challenging writing project I have ever attempted, because the Yablonskis' three killers all told Pennsylvania and federal authorities different stories about how the murders were planned and what happened inside the family's remote farmhouse during the early morning hours of New Year's Eve 1969, and the account that Paul Gilly gave me when I interviewed him differed from the sworn testimony he gave in *Commonwealth of Pennsylvania v. William J. Prater* in 1973 and in *Commonwealth of Pennsylvania v. W. A. "Tony" Boyle* in 1974. To make sense of their conflicting accounts and to bring order to my narrative, I have followed the paths laid out by Special Prosecutor Richard Sprague in the Commonwealth's Brief Contra Defendant's Post-Trial Motions he filed in *Commonwealth of Pennsylvania v. W. A. "Tony" Boyle*, the Charge of the Court Judge Francis Catania gave the jurors in the same case on April 11, 1974, the FBI's YABMUR: Chronology of Suspects' Activities, September 18, 1969 through December 30, 1969, and by Claude Edward Vealey, one of the three assassins, in his January 21, 1970, confession. I have relied on Vealey's account because he gave his version only three weeks after the murders, and his is the least self-serving of all the stories the killers told.

NOTES

Abbreviations

AEP	Albert Edward Pass
AG	Annette "Lucy" Gilly
CAY	Joseph "Chip" Andrew Yablonski
CEV	Claude Edward Vealey
ETSUAA	East Tennessee State University Archives of Appalachia, Knoxville, Tennessee
GJTC SCRC UK	George J. Titler Collection, Special Collections Research Center, University of Kentucky, Lexington, Kentucky
JAY	Joseph Albert Yablonski
JAYLCC MD LOC	Joseph Albert Yablonski Legal Case Collection, Manuscript Division, Library of Congress, Washington, D.C.
JCP	James Charles Phillips
JLRP MD LOC	Joseph L. Rauh, Jr. Papers, Manuscript Division, Library of Congress, Washington, D.C.
MFDC WRL WSU	Miners for Democracy Collection, Walter Reuther Library, Wayne State University, Detroit, Michigan
MS&HA	Mine Safety & Health Administration
PEG	Paul Eugene Gilly
RAS	Richard Aurel Sprague
SH	Silous Huddleston
UMJ	United Mine Workers Journal
UMWA	United Mine Workers of America

UMWA LDR Ser. 3 EFSCL PSU   United Mine Workers of America, Legal
                             Department Records, Series 3: Boyle and
                             Yablonski, 1933–1981, Eberly Family Spe-
                             cial Collections Library, Pennsylvania State
                             University, State College, Pennsylvania
UMWA 1946 H&RFR Ser. 2 Dir's R,   United Mine Workers of America, 1946
1969 UMWA Election, 1969–1971,   Health & Retirement Fund Records, Series
WV&RHC WVU   II. Director's Records, 1969 UMWA Elec-
                             tion, 1969–1971, West Virginia & Regional
                             History Center West Virginia University,
                             Morgantown, West Virginia
WJP   William Jackson Prater
WJT   William Jenkins Turnblazer

Prologue: Kill Them All

1 **rain pelted their windshield:** CEV confession, January 21, 1970, Box 24, 13–14,
JAYLCC MD LOC.

2 **despotic president since 1963:** Boyle became the union's acting president in
late 1962, and its president on January 19, 1963.

2 **four hundred yards away:** Trevor Armbrister, *An Act of Vengeance* (New York:
Saturday Review Press, 1975), 3; Jim Nicholson, "FBI to Investigate UMW Murders," *Philadelphia Inquirer*, January 7, 1970, 1, Box 9, GJTC SCRC UK.

2 **and slip inside unseen:** CEV confession, 14–15.

3 **got in their way:** Testimony of CEV in *Commonwealth of Pennsylvania v. William J. Prater*, 129, Box 15, JAYLCC MD LOC.

3 **in FBI history:** Duane Lockard, *Coal: A Memoir and Critique* (Charlottesville:
University Press of Virginia, 1998), 141.

3 **convicted of first-degree murder:** Tony Boyle was tried twice, once in 1974 and
again in 1978. Boyle was the president of the UMWA when Yablonski was assassinated. Arnold Miller was the union's president when Boyle was convicted on
three counts of first-degree murder in 1974.

3 **out-of-touch leaders:** Ben A. Franklin, "The Martyr Has Been Vindicated," *New
York Times*, December 17, 1972, E2.

4 **some truth to that:** "Big Labor's Membership Pains," *Wall Street Journal*, January 30, 2017, A14.

4 **openly opposed to them:** Melvyn Dubofsky and Warren Van Tine, *John
L. Lewis* (New York: Quadrangle Books/New York Times, 1977), xiv. George
Meany, the powerful head of the American Federation of Labor-Congress of
Industrial Organizations, was violently anticommunist. At the 1967 AFL-CIO
convention, its members voted down an antiwar resolution by a vote of 2,000
to 6.

Chapter One: A Hazardous Business

7 **just eight days away:** Brit Hume, *Death and the Mines: Rebellion and Murder in the United Mine Workers* (New York: Grossman Publishers, 1971), 3; author's interview with Carlo Tarley, August 27, 2017.

7 **to the mine's sooty floor:** Bonnie E. Stewart, *No. 9: The 1968 Farmington Mine Disaster* (Morgantown: West Virginia University Press, 2012), 5–6.

7 **what lay before them:** Laurence Leamer, "The United Mine Workers Holds an Election," *New York Times Sunday Magazine*, November 26, 1972, 40.

7 **the men disappeared underground:** MS&HA Division of Safety, *Informational Report of Investigation Underground Coal Mine Explosion and Fire, Consol No. 9 Mine, November 20, 1968*, March 1990, 5.

7 **for just eight days:** "Appendix A, Victims of Mine Explosion, Consol No. 9 Mine," MS&HA, *Informational Report*.

8 **Recording of "Folsom Prison Blues":** Author's interview with Tarley; Josh Cooper, "The Shaping of Saban, Mining Disaster, School Shooting, Father's Death, Touched Football Coach," *Decatur Daily*, June 30, 2007, legacy.decaturdaily.com/decaturdaily/sorts/saban.

8 **one more shift:** Stewart, *No. 9*, 5.

8 **shifts inside Number 9:** Myra MacPherson, "Death and Life in a Coal Mining Town," *Washington Post*, January 15, 1969, B1.

8 **in Vietnam's steamy jungles:** Stewart, *No. 9*, 43.

8 **the mine's rich seams:** MS&HA, *Informational Report*, 3.

8 **deadly methane gas:** Ibid., 5.

9 **and for good reason:** A. H. Raskin, "John L. Lewis and the Mine Worker," *Atlantic*, May 1963, 54.

9 **average for all workers:** *Coal Mining Fatality Statistics: 1900–2013, MS&HA Fact Sheet-Historical Data on Mine Disasters in the United States*; Hume, *Death and the Mines*, 16; Ben A. Franklin, "The Scandal of Death and Injury in the Mines," *New York Times Sunday Magazine*, March 28, 1969, 27–28; JAY "Statement Announcing Candidacy," May 29, 1969, CAY papers.

9 **into wheezing wrecks:** Letter, Ralph Nader to Senator Ralph Yarborough, April 26, 1969, Box 81, MFDC WRL WSU; Joe McGinniss, "The Yablonski Murders," *Life*, January 23, 1970, 36.

9 **owners to abandon:** Stewart, *No. 9*, 19.

9 **seventy-five feet from the shaft:** Ibid., 36.

9 **this yearly total:** Ibid., 42; Hume, *Death and the Mines*, 6.

9 **the most dangerous jobs:** Stewart, *No. 9*, 30.

10 **one operator in sixteen years:** Drew Pearson, "Mine Tragedy Called Preventable," *Washington Post*, December 2, 1968; Gary Graham, "New Laws Needed, Boyle Tells Miners," *Johnstown Tribune-Democrat*, June 23, 1969, Box 1, UMWA LDR Ser. 3 EFSCL PSU.

10 **to close big mines:** Tom Bethell, *Conspiracy in Coal* (Huntington: Appalachian Movement Press, 1970), 2.

10 **than protecting coal miners:** Franklin, "Scandal of Death and Injury," 27.

10 **safety training in 1968:** 117 *Cong. Rec.—House* 3238, February 18, 1971.

10 **a chilly 35 degrees:** MS&HA, *Informational Report*, 5.

10 **barrels of underground cannons:** Stewart, *No. 9*, 13.

10 **worked in the two mines:** J. Davitt McAteer, *Monongah: The Tragic Story of the Worst Industrial Accident in U.S. History* (Morgantown: West Virginia University Press, 2007), 241.

11 **shut down for hours:** Stewart, *No. 9*, 45–49.

11 **deadly, odorless methane gas:** Ibid., 67.

11 **would soon be dead:** MS&HA, *Informational Report*, 5.

11 **more than twelve minutes:** *In the Circuit Court of Marion County, West Virginia, Michael D. Michaels et al., Plaintiffs v. Estate of Alex Kovarbasich, and Consolidation Coal Company, Civ. Action 14-C-318*, November 6, 2014; Stewart, *No. 9*, 4.

11 **the fan's alarm system:** "Affidavit of Lawrence Leroy Layne, Case 1:14-cv-00212-IMK-MJA, April 30, 2015." Stewart, *No. 9*, 4. Layne is a retired U.S. Bureau of Mines inspector.

11 **the mine's Llewellyn Portal:** MS&HA, *Informational Report*, 21. When a recovery team found the body of Charles F. Hardman in 1969, they discovered that his wristwatch had stopped at exactly 5:27 a.m.

12 **extracted eight more:** Rex Lauck, "Violent Blast Traps 78 Men," *UMJ*, December 1, 1968, 11.

12 **rolling clouds of smoke:** Author's interview with Rev. Richard Bowyer, September 7, 2017. Rev. Bowyer later led family members to the Fork Methodist Church to escape the prying eyes of news cameras.

12 **news about a rescue:** Ibid.

12 **to be nationally televised:** Bonnie Stewart and Scott Finn, "Memo Suggests Cause of 1968 Deaths," National Public Radio, WAMU 88.5, November 18, 2008.

12 **supply of fresh air:** Diana Nelson Jones, "25 Years Ago, Their World Collapsed in a Fiery Explosion," *Pittsburgh Post-Gazette*, November 21, 1993, F1.

13 **"hazards of being a miner":** 117 *Cong. Rec.—House* 2100, February 8, 1971; Joseph E. Finley, *The Corrupt Kingdom*, (New York: Simon & Schuster, 1972), 213.

13 **to make a living:** Author's interview with Don Stillman, July 15, 2018; Hume, *Death and the Mines*, 16.

13 **"husbands were buried alive":** 117 *Cong. Rec.—House* 3238, February 18, 1971.

14 **number 9's roasted portals:** Trevor Armbrister, *An Act of Vengeance* (New York: Saturday Review Press, 1975), 38–39.

14 **Coal Company's bottomless virtues:** Ibid.

14 **"the way he did?":** Ibid., 39. The photo of Lewis was taken in the aftermath of the West Frankfort, Illinois, mine disaster.

14 **day of prayer and thanks:** Author's interview with Rev. Richard Bowyer. The

first air samples were taken on November 22. They already showed that life could not exist in some areas of the mine.

15 **West Virginia's snowy hollows:** Stewart, *No. 9*, 105–7; author's interview with Rev. Richard Bowyer. Many of the families did not celebrate Thanksgiving or Christmas that year. The mine was sealed by November 30. It was reopened in September 1969. Operations to recover the miners' bodies continued until April 1978. Nineteen bodies were never recovered. Number 9 was permanently sealed in November 1978.

15 **as they always had:** Jones, "25 Years Ago, Their World Collapsed," F1; "Peril in the Mines," *Washington Post*, June 15, 1969, 38.

15 **social and economic structure:** James Patterson, *Grand Expectations: The United States, 1945–1974* (New York: Oxford University Press, 1997), 451–52.

15 **demanded change:** Maurice Isserman and Michael Kazin, *America Divided: The Civil War of the 1960s* (New York: Oxford University Press, 2000), 222–23.

16 **their underground mining caused:** Richard Fry, "Making Amends: Coal Miners, the Black Lung Association, and Federal Compensation Reform, 1969–1972," *Federal History*, 2013, 37; J. Davitt McAteer, *Coal Mine Health and Safety: The Case of West Virginia* (New York: Praeger Publishers, 1970), x.

16 **sixty and sixty-four:** McAteer, *Coal Mine Health and Safety*, x.

16 **scientifically documented evidence:** Paul Nyden, *Miners for Democracy: Struggle in the Coalfields* (PhD dissertation, Columbia University, 1974), 690, 692–93.

17 **composed a "Declaration of Conscience":** 1974 *Congressional Directory*, 196. Hechler wrote *The Bridge at Remagen*, a best-selling book about the American army's momentous crossing of the Rhine River in World War II; Armbrister, *Act of Vengeance*, 38; Laurence I. Barrett, "W. Va. Politician Pushed for Coal Miners' Safety," *Washington Post*, December 12, 2016, B5.

17 **dust a miner inhaled:** Barrett, "W. Va Politician Pushed for Coal Miners' Safety," 1974 *Congressional Directory*, 196.

17 **black lung in February 1968:** Ralph Nader, "They're Still Breathing," *New Republic*, February 3, 1968, 15; author's interview with Ralph Nader, March 20, 2017. Nader became obsessed with car safety while studying personal injury cases at Harvard Law School. General Motors retaliated after he wrote his book, hiring private detectives to comb through his private life and harass him, but their thuggish tactics backfired. The car giant sealed the fate of its poorly designed Corvair and catapulted Nader into his role as a modern-day David battling corporate Goliaths.

17 **in early January 1969:** Fry, "Making Amends," 41.

18 **shouted, "That is baloney!":** Armbrister, *Act of Vengeance*, 50.

18 **coal mining safety standards:** Richard Fry, "Fighting for Survival: Coal Miners and the Struggle over Health and Safety in the U.S., 1968–1988," 2010, 75, digitalcommons.wayne.edu.

18 **the state's coal industry:** Nyden, *Miners for Democracy*, 696.

18 **"black-tongue loudmouths:** Fry, "Fighting for Survival," 77.

18 **"camel rider from Lebanon":** Gary Graham, "New Laws Needed, Boyle Tells Miners," *Johnstown Tribune-Democrat,* June 23, 1969, Box 28, UMWA LDR Ser. 3 EFSCL PSU, June 23, 1969; Hume, *Death and the Mines,* 89–90; Fry, "Fighting for Survival," 118.

18 **about to become law:** Nyden, *Miners for Democracy,* 697; Armbrister, *Act of Vengeance,* 52; Alan Derickson, *Black Lung: Anatomy of a Public Health Disaster,* (Ithaca: Cornell University Press, 1998), 161.

Chapter Two: That Bastard Will Rue the Day

20 **blocked his coronary arteries:** Melvyn Dubofsky and Warren Van Tine, *John L. Lewis: A Biography* (New York: Quadrangle Books/New York Times, 1977), 462.

20 **into its high command:** Adrian Lee, Bonnie Cook, Mike Ruane, and Jim Southwood, "Yablonski, He Bet His Life and Lost," *Philadelphia Bulletin,* August 6, 1981, A10. This article was part of a five-part series that the *Bulletin* published in August 1981 just before it went out of business, alleging that Tony Boyle had been railroaded into prison for murdering the Yablonskis. Although the articles were based on some excellent research and reporting, their conclusion that Boyle was innocent of ordering Jock Yablonski's murder was not true.

20 **union in American History:** Dubofsky and Van Tine, *John L. Lewis,* xiii; Robert H. Zieger, *John L. Lewis: Labor Leader* (Boston: Twayne Publishers, 1988), 80–81.

21 **almost $60 a week:** David Kennedy, *The American People in Depression and War, 1929–1945* (New York: Oxford University Press, 1999), 643; "Lewis Heir Faces Revolt," *Business Week,* November 15, 1969, 112; *Wage Chronology: Bituminous Coal Mine Operators and United Mine Workers, 1933–1981,* U.S. Department of Labor, Bureau of Labor Statistics, November 1980, 26.

21 **or burying them alive:** *UMJ,* June 15–July 15, 1976, 5.

21 **were about to die:** A. H. Raskin, "John L. Lewis and the Mine Worker," *Atlantic,* May 1963, 55. The oldest son of a blacklisted Welsh coal miner, Lewis was born on February 12, 1880, in Cleveland, Iowa. He worked in the mines just long enough to know that he wanted to do something else for a living. An aspiring actor, he rose steadily through the UMWA's ranks by holding a series of unelected administrative posts.

21 **"obligation" to the union:** J. Wayne Flynt, *Dixie's Forgotten People* (Bloomington: Indiana University Press, 1980), 132.

21 **the "aristocrats of labor":** *UMJ,* January 1960, 13. Workers in other unions also revered Lewis, especially after his coal miners became organized labor's "battering ram." The UMWA provided the money and the shock troops that founded

what was to become the Congress of Industrial Organizations in 1936, which organized the country's steel, rubber, and auto workers. The CIO brought millions of workers into organized labor's ranks.

22 **their shotgun houses:** John Gaventa, *Power and Powerlessness: Quiescence & Rebellion in an Appalachian Valley* (Urbana: University of Illinois Press, 1982), 121. In the 1960s, many miners added a framed photograph of assassinated President John F. Kennedy.

22 **could save it:** Paul F. Clark, *The Miners' Fight for Democracy: Arnold Miller and the Reform of the United Mine Workers* (Ithaca: New York State School of Industrial and Labor Relations, 1981), 12.

22 **"those of anyone else":** Ibid., 16.

22 **questioned that they did:** Ibid.

22 **swallow six-foot-long logs:** Tom Bethell, *Coal Patrol*, January 1, 1973, 1. Lewis's personal lifestyle was also lavish. He wore expensively tailored suits, rode in chauffeured Cadillacs, and lived in Robert E. Lee's boyhood home in Alexandria, Virginia.

22 **particularly promising future leaders:** Lee, Cook, Ruane, and Southwood, "Yablonski, He Bet His Life and Lost," A1, A10.

23 **he yearned to be:** Laurence Leamer, "The United Mine Workers Holds an Election," *New York Times Sunday Magazine*, November 26, 1972, 40.

23 **speeches with colorful profanity:** 115 *Cong. Rec.—House* 5763, March 3, 1970.

23 **with photographs—of him:** Trevor Armbrister, *An Act of Vengeance* (New York: Saturday Review Press, 1975), 70.

23 **was a social worker:** Ibid.; Paul Nyden, *Miners for Democracy: Struggle in the Coalfields* (PhD dissertation, Columbia University, 1974), 493–94.

24 **leading to his office:** Bethell, *Coal Patrol*, 2, 3. Lewis put up the gate originally.

24 **know he was gone:** Armbrister, *Act of Vengeance*, 69.

24 **someone was stalking him:** "The Fall of Tony Boyle," *Time*, September 17, 1973, 39.

24 **Scots-Irish coal miners:** FBI Investigation at Butte, Box 23, 322–23, JAYLCC MD LOC.

24 *in the British Isles:* *UMW News*, "W. A. Boyle, President," CAY papers.

24 **on his right hand:** Armbrister, *Act of Vengeance*, 66–69.

25 **Ethel Williams, a schoolteacher:** *UMW News*, "W. A. Boyle, President"; Brit Hume, *Death and the Mines: Rebellion and Murder in the United Mine Workers* (New York: Grossman Publishers, 1971), 57.

25 **part of northern Wyoming:** Hume, *Death and the Mines*, 25.

25 **stamp out his local foes:** Armbrister, *Act of Vengeance*, 66; Dubofsky and Van Tine, *John L. Lewis*, 504.

25 **vehemently anti-union coalfields:** Dubofsky and Van Tine, *John L. Lewis*, 504.

25 **if he went to prison:** FBI Interview of Charles Minton, April 8, 1970, Box 24, JAYLCC MD LOC.

25 **the Wise County courthouse:** Joseph Finley, *The Corrupt Kingdom* (New York: Simon and Schuster, 1972), 145.

26 **the accident was "unavoidable":** Roger Hawthorne, "Four Died in 1958 Mine Cave-in," *Billings Gazette*, August 26, 1969, 1–2; Ben A. Franklin, "Boyle's Family's Mining Role Debated," *Louisville Courier-Journal*, September 2, 1969, Box 2, UMWA 1946 H&RFR Ser. 2 Dir's R, 1969 UMWA Election, 1969–1971, WV&RHC WVU.

26 **Pittsburgh's Polish Hill neighborhood:** Lee, Cook, Ruane, and Southwood, "Yablonski: He Bet His Life and Lost," A10; CAY email to author, July 21, 2015. Yablonski's father came from Russian-occupied north-central Poland. He did not want to die fighting in a war between the Czar and the Emperor of Japan over mineral-rich Manchuria. He left the Russian army to join some cousins living in Pittsburgh, Pennsylvania.

26 **Pennsylvania later that year:** Ray Lubove, *Twentieth Century Pittsburgh*, Vol. 1 (Pittsburgh: University of Pittsburgh, 1969), 13. Ludovica Jasinska anglicized her name to "Louise Jasinski."

26 **for their son to enjoy:** Lee, Cook, Ruane, and Southwood, "Yablonski, He Bet His Life and Lost," A10.

27 **rest of his life:** Ibid.

27 **never amount to anything:** James G. Driscoll, "In the Miners' Roughshod Way, Chiefs Tangle for Leadership," *National Observer*, October 24, 1969, Box 1, UMWA 1946 H&RFR Ser. 2 Dir's R, 1969 UMWA Election, 1969–1971, WV&RHC WVU.

27 **Company closed its doors:** JAY résumé, undated, CAY papers; Irving Bernstein, *The Lean Years: A History of the American Worker, 1920–1933* (Chicago: Haymarket Books, 2010), 130.

27 **disputes in American history:** Bernstein, *Lean Years*, 131.

27 **a thickly-muscled chest:** JAY résumé.

27 **got into violent fistfights:** FBI, "JAY LMRDA Investigative Matter," 9, Pittsburgh, Pennsylvania, July 10, 1969.

27 **served eight months:** Ibid., 6; Board of Pardons, Harrisburg, Pennsylvania, Application Number 5638, April Session, 1956, Box 1, GJTC SCRC UK. Governor George N. Leader pardoned Yablonski on July 13, 1956.

28 **fall ruptured his bladder:** *Louise Yablonski v. Vesta Coal Company*, Claim petition, No. 53,579, 1934, 5, 7, CAY papers.

28 **pneumonia two months later:** Certificate of Death, Commonwealth of Pennsylvania, Steve Jablonski, May 27, 1933, CAY papers.

28 **pay weekly child support:** FBI, "JAY LMRDA Investigative Matter," 1. Yablonski and Huffman finally divorced in 1937.

28 **Yablonski was both:** "A Biography of Jock Yablonski," Box 2, MFDC WRL WSU.

28 **District 5 that same year:** Ibid.; Nyden, *Miners for Democracy*, 391. District 5 lay in the heart of Pennsylvania's soft coal region, and it had seen some of the

industry's bitterest organizing battles. It was the proving ground for several of the UMWA's most influential leaders, and Yablonski leveraged its importance to make himself well known to John L. Lewis.

28 **twenty-eight-man College of Cardinals:** FBI, "JAY LMRDA Investigative Matter," 6.

28 **his "right-hand man":** Dubofsky and Van Tine, *John L. Lewis*, 528

28 **country's wealthiest labor union:** Zieger, *John L. Lewis: Labor Leader*, 174. By 1960, the UMWA had only slightly fewer assets—cash reserves, investments, and buildings—than the Brotherhood of International Teamsters, the United Steelworkers, and the United Auto Workers combined.

29 **"no good son of a bitch":** Lee, Cook, Ruane, and Southwood, "Yablonski, He Bet His Life and Lost," A10.

29 **better union president than Boyle:** Author's interview with CAY, November 18, 2017; Charles Owen Rice, "Jock Yablonski the Rebel," in *Fighter with a Heart, Writings of Charles Owen Rice*, edited by Charles McCollester (Pittsburgh: University of Pittsburgh Press, 1996), 170–72.

29 **watch even more closely:** FBI interview of Mike Trbovich, October 28, 1970, Box 23, JAYLCC MD LOC.

30 **been used for decades:** Hume, *Death and the Mines*, 166.

30 **Bituminous Coal Operators' Association:** Armbrister, *Act of Vengeance*, 44

31 **Boyle's name and picture:** Ralph Nader to John L. Lewis, May 22, 1969, Box 81, MFDC WRL WSU; Hume, *Death and the Mines*, 51; "The Dues of Coal Miners Are Being Plundered by Present Leadership of Their Own Union," 115 *Cong. Rec.—House* 36916, December 4, 1969.

31 **in his followers' adulation:** Hume, *Death and the Mines*, 47.

31 **flowing through his veins:** "Mine Union Chief Denounces Foes," *New York Times*, September 3, 1964, A24.

31 **"Little Hitler":** Armbrister, *Act of Vengeance*, 75.

31 **UMWA's most violent precinct:** Testimony of WJT, *Commonwealth of Pennsylvania v. W. A. "Tony" Boyle*, Box 3, 11–174, JAYLCC MD LOC.

31 **father preached on Sundays:** Adrian Lee, Bonnie Cook, Mike Ruane, and Jim Southwood, "A Man with a Motive for a Union Murder," *Philadelphia Bulletin*, August 4, 1981, A8.

32 **bookkeeping and accounting:** AEP, Cumulative Record, Commonwealth of Pennsylvania, Department of Corrections, Box 12, JAYLCC MD LOC.

32 **disciples and vicious enforcers:** Ibid.

32 **police the 1968 convention:** Edgar N. James, "Union Democracy and the LMRDA: Autocracy and Insurgency in National Union Elections," *Harvard Civil Rights-Civil Liberties Law Review*, Vol. 13 (Spring 1978), 328; *Hearings on the United Mine Workers' Election before the Subcomm. on Labor of the Senate Comm. on Labor and Public Welfare*, 91st Congress, 2d Session, 123.

32 **to be recessed temporarily:** *Hearings on the United Mine Workers' Election*, 123.

32 **his one-man rule:** Hume, *Death and the Mines*, 46, 48.

32 **other things to do:** Armbrister, *Act of Vengeance*, 46.

32 **support for civil rights:** *UMJ*, September 15, 1964, 14.

33 **if it did not:** Yablonski considered challenging Boyle in the 1964 election. On a nighttime stroll during the 1964 convention, Yablonski confided to Dr. Lorin Kerr, the union's black-lung expert, that he was mulling over a possible 1964 run against Boyle. Nothing came of this conversation.

33 **on October 8, 1965:** Armbrister, *Act of Vengeance*, 46.

33 **on the UMWA's fringes:** Ibid., 47.

33 **"comes in mighty handy":** Elise Morrow, "Portrait of a Union Boss," *Saturday Evening Post*, February 28, 1948, 25.

34 **on his own life:** Ibid., 114.

34 **in a landslide:** Tom Bethell, *Coal Patrol*, May 20, 1972, 2.

34 **and handpick its officers:** Hume, *Death and the Mines*, 168.

34 **dutifully toed the line:** Armbrister, *Act of Vengeance*, 48.

35 **any appeals or grievances:** James, "Union Democracy," 262; Hume, *Death and the Mines*, 63.

35 **"Union, and Tony, too":** Hume, *Death and the Mines*, 64.

35 **against the Republican Party's nominee:** *UMJ*, September 15, 1968, 5.

35 **"that they deserve!":** Armbrister, *Act of Vengeance*, 48.

36 **insecurity that came with it:** Ben A. Franklin, "Rank and File Rebellion Stirs in Mine Union, Posing Threat to Lewis Legacy," *New York Times*, June 13, 1969, 24.

36 **be his opening act:** "Boyle Campaign Launched," *Morgantown Post*, April 21, 1969, Box 2, UMWA 1946 H&RFR Ser. 2 Dir's R, 1969 UMWA Election, 1969–1971, WV&RHC WVU. All three dropped out of the race.

36 **growing list of troubles:** "2500 Attend Meeting," *Fairmont Times*, April 28, 1969, Box 2, UMWA 1946 H&RFR Ser. 2 Dir's R, 1969 UMWA Election, 1969–1971, WV&RHC WVU.

37 **compensation for black lung:** Ward Sinclair, "Boyle Wins, but UMW Grudge Goes On," *Louisville Courier-Journal*, December 11, 1969, Box 2, UMWA 1946 H&RFR Ser. 2 Dir's R, 1969 UMWA Election, 1969–1971, WV&RHC WVU; Armbrister, *Act of Vengeance*, 55.

37 **resigned from the board:** Armbrister, *Act of Vengeance*, 55–56.

Chapter Three: Free at Last

38 **all her private clients:** Ward Sinclair, "The Troubles of Tony Boyle," *Louisville Courier-Journal*, August 22, 1971, Box 81, MFDC WRL WSU; Press Release, Miners for Yablonski, June 2, 1969, CAY papers.

38 **"Fire them?":** 117 *Cong Rec.—House* 19528, June 11, 1971; Ben A. Franklin, "Rank and File Rebellion Stirs in Mine Union, Posing Threat to Lewis Legacy,"

New York Times, June 13, 1969, A24; Ed Nichols, "Miners Face Moment of Truth," *Logan Banner*, December 3, 1969, Box 2, UMWA 1946 H&RFR Ser. 2 Dir's R, 1969 UMWA Election, 1969–1971, WV&RHC WVU.

38 **"ill-informed saviors of coal miners":** Trevor Armbrister, "The Coal-Black Shame of the UMW," *Readers Digest*, October 1970, 4, Box 116, JLRP MD LOC.

38 **operators ran their mines:** "Anarchy Threatens the Kingdom of Coal," WWVA, Wheeling, West Virginia, broadcast April 19, 1971, transcript, 117 *Cong. Rec.— House* 19525, June 11, 1971.

39 **a year in dividends:** Ralph Nader to Senator Ralph Yarborough, April 26, 1969, Box 81, MFDC WRL WSU.

39 **the bank's board meetings:** Armbrister, "The Coal-Black Shame of the UMW," 3.

39 **only $30 a month:** WTOP Editorial, "The UMWA" May 1, 1969, Box 24, MFDC WRL WSU. By early 1969, over 70,000 retired miners had lost their pensions. Many slid into poverty and never came out of it.

39 **pieces on his findings:** Morton Mintz, "Nader Charges UMW President with Nepotism," *Washington Post*, April 28, 1969, A2; Robert Walters, "Nader Accuses Miners Union of Payroll-Padding, Collusion," *Washington Evening Star*, April 28, 1969, Box 2, UMWA 1946 H&RFR Ser. 2 Dir's R, 1969 UMWA Election, 1969–1971, WV&RHC WVU.

39 **among its twenty-four pages:** Brit Hume, *Death and the Mines: Rebellion and Murder in the United Mine Workers* (New York: Grossman Publishers, 1971), 164. The *Journal* also attacked Congressman Ken Hechler.

39 **the UMWA's coal miners:** Mintz, "Nader Charges UMW President with Nepotism," A2; Leonard Downie Jr., "Loans to Coal Mine Owners by UMW Bank Hit by Nader," *Washington Post*, March 21, 1969, A2.

40 **some automobile safety cases:** Author's interview with Steven Yablonski, April 21, 2017; Bart Barnes, Obituary of "Worth Rowley, Antitrust Lawyer," *Washington Post*, August 26, 1988, www.washingtonpost.com/archive/local/1988/08/26/obituaries.

40 **a meeting with Yablonski:** Author's interview with Steven Yablonski.

40 **country's most brilliant activists:** Ibid.; Hume, *Death and the Mines*, 169.

40 **what that meant:** Author's interview with Steven Yablonski.

40 **"in a goldfish bowl":** Ibid.; Charles McCarry, *Citizen Nader* (New York: Saturday Review Press, 1972), 241.

40 **killed both men:** Frank Porter, "Strong Foe of Union Corruption Slain Gang-Style in San Francisco," *Washington Post*, April 24, 1966, A1; "Second Painters' Officer Murdered in San Francisco Area Union Revolt," *Washington Post*, May 8, 1966, A1.

41 **rank-and-file members:** A. H. Raskin, "Room at the Top," *New York Times*, January 17, 1965, E6; David Witter, *Corruption and Reform in the Teamsters Union*

(Urbana: University of Illinois Press, 2008), 207. The Landrum-Griffin Act grew out of Senate hearings focused largely on the Teamsters.

41 **into a "divided house":** Justin McCarthy, "UMWA Must Have Unity in Ranks," *UMJ*, May 15, 1969, 3.

41 **give his life more meaning:** 115 *Cong. Rec.—House* 5762, March 3, 1970.

42 **Boyle was leading it:** Thomas O'Hanlon, "Anarchy Threatens the Kingdom of Coal," in *Cong. Rec.—House* 44134, December 30, 1970; "Challenge in the Coal Mines: Men Against Their Union," CBS-TV, September 23, 1969; Hume, *Death and the Mines*, 171. Walter Reuther, the president of the United Auto Workers, did the same thing in 1948 after a would-be assassin fired a shotgun through his kitchen window while he reached for a bowl of peaches from his refrigerator. The blast nearly blew off his right arm. While he lay in the hospital, Reuther's mother begged him to resign and end his crusade to clean up the auto workers' union. His answer was as terse as it was forceful: "No, I'm all tied up in this thing, all involved. I must do it."

42 **"have no business there!":** FBI, "JAY LMRDA Investigative Matter," 11.

43 **her two favorite authors:** Donna Lange, "Resident's Play on Golf Tees Off," *Valley Independent*, undated, CAY papers; CAY email to author, July 22, 2017.

43 **"An ultra-modern miss":** State Teacher's College, California, Pennsylvania, Registration for Placement, Margaret R. Wasicek; "A Fantasy of the Affairs of 1933," CAY papers.

43 **on a blind date:** Barbara Cloud, "Playwright Routs Boredom," *Pittsburgh Press*, May 26, 1963, 2, CAY papers.

43 **and an opera lover:** Richard Starnes, "The Yablonski Case," Reuters, undated, Box 2, GJTC SCRC UK.

43 **salty expletives:** Faith Wasicek to Chip and Shirley Yablonski, May 22, 1970, CAY papers.

43 **sixty plays by 1969:** Cloud, "Playwright Routs Boredom."

44 **became the UMWA's president:** Faith Wasicek to Chip and Shirley Yablonski.

44 **after graduating from college:** 115 *Cong. Rec.—House*, March 3, 1970, 3.

44 **largely African American Hill District:** Ibid.

44 **for Monongalia County's poor:** Elizabeth Furfari, "OEO Position Challenge Assumed by 'U' Graduate," undated, CAY Papers; FBI interview of Helen J. Slosarik, January 13, 1970, 36, Box 23, JAYLCC MD LOC.

45 **social and economic justice:** FBI interview of Slosarik.

45 **"they will destroy you":** Trevor Armbrister, *An Act of Vengeance* (New York: Saturday Review Press, 1975), 56; email, CAY to author, July 22, 2017; "Opportunism Barb Tossed at Yablonski," *Beckley Register and Post*, June 7, 1969, Box 1, GJTC SCRC UK.

45 **that position for himself:** Ralph Nader to John L. Lewis, May 22, 1969, Box 81, MFDC WRL WSU.

45 **lead a palace coup:** Morton Mintz, "Nader Asks Lewis to Fight UMW Rule,"
    Washington Post, May 23, 1969, A12.

46 **to Washington in 1948:** Melvyn Dubofsky and Warren Van Tine, *John L.
    Lewis, A Biography* (New York: Quadrangle Books/New York Times, 1977),
    526–27.

46 **the UMWA had declined:** Ibid.

46 **run against Tony Boyle:** Author's interview with Steven Yablonski; Armbrister,
    Act of Vengeance, 59; McCarry, *Citizen Nader*, 241.

46 **with Joseph L. Rauh Jr.:** Author's interview with Steven Yablonski.

47 **homeless, and the disenfranchised:** Wolfgang Saxon, "Joe Rauh, Jr., Ground-
    breaking Civil Liberties Lawyer, Dies at 81," *New York Times*, September 5, 1992,
    10; David E. Rosenbaum, "Joe Rauh: 50 Years, and Counting," *New York Times*,
    January 8, 1985, A16. Rauh was born January 3, 1911, in Cincinnati, Ohio, the
    son and grandson of German-immigrant shirtmakers. He graduated from Har-
    vard, where he was a star student, and its law school. He clerked for Supreme
    Court Associate Justices Benjamin Cardozo and Felix Frankfurter. Rauh
    became the counselor for several New Deal agencies and a charter member of
    President Franklin Roosevelt's Brain Trust. He served in World War II on Gen-
    eral Douglas MacArthur's staff as an expert on lend-lease. Rauh returned to
    Washington after the war and dedicated his well-honed legal skills to champi-
    oning the underdog.

47 **the campaign's chief counsel:** Author's interview with Steven Yablonski; Ben
    A. Franklin, "Board Member Opposes Boyle For Presidency of Mine Union,"
    New York Times, May 30, 1969, Box 1, GJTC SCRC UK.

47 **"when it's over":** "Challenge in the Coal Mines, Men against Their Union,"
    CBS-TV, September 23, 1969; James A. Wechsler, "Waiting for Lewis," *New York
    Post*, June 4, 1969, Box 1, GJTC SCRC UK.

47 **"had to do it":** Keynote Address of Joseph L. Rauh Jr., Miners for Democracy
    Convention, Wheeling, West Virginia, May 27, 1972, 1, Box 67, MFDC WRL
    WSU.

47 **moral fiber he ever saw:** Ibid., 2.

48 **to begin speaking:** Hume, *Death and the Mines*, 172; author's interview with
    Steven Yablonski.

48 **"were supposed to represent":** Author's interview with Ralph Nader, March
    20, 2017. Beverly Moore Jr., then a student at Harvard Law School, helped Nader
    craft Yablonski's platform; Statement by JAY, Member of the International
    Executive Board of the UMWA, Announcing His Candidacy for the Presidency
    of the UMWA, May 29, 1969, CAY Papers.

48 **"riddled with fear":** Ibid.

48 **prisoner of the past:** Ibid.

48 **captured the UMWA's attention:** Franklin, "Rank and File Rebellion Stirs in
    Mine Union,"A2.

49   **coal industry's lobbying money:** Statement by JAY.

49   **county's valleys and hills:** "Boyle Advocates Program for Eliminating Slag Piles," *Beckley Post-Herald,* October 27, 1969, 2.

49   **"lengths they will go":** Hume, *Death and the Mines,* 174.

49   **"cease being an anvil!":** Frank Porter, "UMWA Aide to Run Against His Chief," *Washington Post,* May 30, 1969, A12.

49   **"free at last":** Jeanne M. Rasmussen, "The Miners, What Happens Now?" *Mountain Life and Work,* February 1970, 3.

Chapter Four: Yablonski Ought to Be Killed

50   **Boyle was incredulous:** 115 *Cong. Rec.—House* 35675, November 25, 1969.

50   **through West Virginia's coalfields:** Ibid.; "Joe's Big Hat in Ring," *Fairmont Times,* June 6, 1969, Box 1, GJTC SCRC UK.

50   **Yablonski they could find:** Trevor Armbrister, *An Act of Vengeance* (New York: Saturday Review Press, 1975), 74.

50   **second week of June:** Melvyn Dubofsky and Warren Van Tine, *John L. Lewis: A Biography* (New York: Quadrangle Books/New York Times, 1977), 528.

51   **campaigns fairly and equally:** JAY to W. A. Boyle, June 2, 1969, Box 23, MFDC WRL WSU.

51   **for fraud and theft:** "Items Discussed at Meeting, June 4, 1969," FBI YABMUR investigation. Yablonski had been president of this local since 1934.

51   **leader did not respond:** Spencer Rich, "UMW President Forces Rival from Job Here," *Washington Post,* June 17, 1969, 18.

51   **raised the insurgent's chances:** Rex Lauck, "John L. Lewis is Dead," *UMJ,* June 15, 1969, 3; Robert H. Zieger, *John L. Lewis: Labor Leader* (Boston: Twayne Publishers, 1988), 184.

51   **eating his lunch alone:** Dubofsky and Van Tine, *John L. Lewis,* 522.

52   **praying at Lewis's grave:** "President Emeritus Lewis Dies," *UMWJ,* 1, June 15, 1969.

52   **distribute Yablonski's campaign literature:** Ben A. Franklin, "Court Orders U.M.W. to Give Space to Boyle's opponent," *New York Times,* June 21, 1969, A18; email, CAY to author, November 27, 2017.

52   **more of the UMWA's dollars:** *Proceedings of the IEB,* UMWA International Headquarters, Washington, D.C., June 23, 1969, Box 74, MFDC WRL WSU. Ralph Nader had predicted that Boyle would engineer this.

52   **accused Yablonski of treason:** Ibid., 18–20, 26, 29, 31, 33–34.

52   **had heard enough:** John Gaventa, *Power and Powerlessness: Quiescence & Rebellion in an Appalachian Valley* (Urbana: University of Illinois Press, 1982), 180; Ben A. Franklin, "Yablonski Inquiry Reported to Focus On a Sum of Money," *New York Times,* January 24, 1970, 1.

53   **"Thank you very much!":** *Proceedings of the IEB,* 50–52.

53 **and to spread fear:** Tom Bethell, *Coal Patrol*, No. 24, May 20, 1972, 3.

53 **less than a minute:** WJT confession, August 23, 1973, 8–9, RAS papers. Pass later claimed to the FBI that when Boyle first asked him to oversee Yablonski's assassination, he did not believe Yablonski was really going to run against Boyle. No board member had challenged a sitting president since 1926. He thought it was a "put up" job, orchestrated by Boyle and Yablonski to keep anyone else from running.

54 **mechanizing their mines:** Tom Bethell, "Conspiracy in Coal" (Huntington: Appalachian Movement Press, 1970), 14–21; Curtis Seltzer, *Fire in the Hole* (Lexington: University Press of Kentucky, 1985), 59.

54 **leaving them nothing:** Paul F. Clark, *The Miners' Fight for Democracy: Arnold Miller and the Reform of the United Mine Workers,* (Ithaca: School of Industrial and Labor Relations, Cornell University, 1981), 18; Paul Nyden, *Miners for Democracy: Struggle in the Coalfields* (PhD dissertation, Columbia University, 1974), 470.

54 **agreements with the UMWA:** Dubofsky and Van Tine, *John L. Lewis*, 503. The TVA, following federal regulations, bought its coal from the lowest bidder.

54 **beatings, bullets, and dynamite:** Ibid., 503–4.

55 **assassinating union organizers:** Ibid.

55 **which was a sin:** Arthur Lewis, *Murder by Contract: The People v. "Tough Tony" Boyle* (New York: Macmillan, 1975), 170.

55 **refused to join the union:** Author's interview with Mason Caudill, August 16, 2018; FBI interview of Arlin Gibson, January 25, 1970, Box 24, JAYLCC MD LOC; *White Oak Coal Company v. United Mine Workers*, 318 F.2d 591, 1963.

55 **Mary Harris "Mother" Jones:** Adrian Lee, Bonnie Cook, Mike Ruane, and Jim Southwood, "A Man with a Motive for a Union Murder," *Philadelphia Bulletin*, August 4, 1981, A8.

55 **"name of John L. Lewis":** Elise Morrow, "Portrait of a Union Boss," *Saturday Evening Post*, February 28, 1948, 25; Don Freeman, "The People in Clay and Leslie Seem To Take 'Trouble" Pretty Much in Stride," *Louisville Courier-Journal*, March 15, 1953, 39.

56 **in the head:** "Coal Operator in Court Tells About Attack," *Louisville Courier-Journal*, November 27, 1958, 62.

56 **acquit Van Huss's attackers:** Lee, Cook, Ruane, and Southwood, "A Man with a Motive," A8.

56 **this death and mayhem:** Joseph E. Finley, *The Corrupt Kingdom: The Rise and Fall of the United Mine Workers* (New York: Simon & Schuster, 1972), 154; "Sniper Kills Ex-Mine Operator," *Louisville Courier-Journal*, June 9, 1959, 17; "Mines Plead for More Troopers After New Dynamiting, Gunfire," *Louisville Courier-Journal*, May 21, 1959, 42; Paul Beck, "Decision Today on Mine Troops," *Louisville Courier-Journal*, April 19, 1959, 11.

56 **into the ground in 1955:** Finley, *Corrupt Kingdom*, 35, 156.

56 **sent to any other:** 115 *Cong. Rec.—House* 36916, December 4, 1969; "Transfer of
Funds, District 19, 1966–1969," Box 26, UMWA LDR Ser. 3 EFSCL PSU.

57 **continued to fade:** Lee, Cook, Ruane, and Southwood, "A Man with a Motive," A8.

57 **of its enemies:** AEP prison record. Pass also had two daughters, one bedridden
her entire life with cerebral palsy.

57 **name was first:** Lee, Cook, Ruane, and Southwood, "A Man with a Motive," A8;
AEP confession, 5.

57 **to oversee Wilson's assassination:** SH confession, May 3, 1972, 13, Box 8, JAY-
LCC MD LOC.

57 **enough to do it:** Adrian Lee, Bonnie Cook, Mike Ruane, and Jim Southwood, "A
Jittery Witness Fails to Get His Story Across," *Philadelphia Bulletin*, August 3,
1981, A6.

57 **use of a car to do it:** Ibid.

58 **two years in prison:** Ibid.; Filings, Boyle Retrial in second trial of *Commonwealth of Pennsylvania v. W. A."Tony" Boyle*, RAS papers. Tanner pled guilty
on November 25, 1968. He served his time in an Ohio state penitentiary from
November 1968 until the latter part of 1970.

58 **Boyle's personal payroll:** Ward Sinclair, "The UMW's Last Chance," *Progressive*, 117 *Cong. Rec.* 13101, May 1971.

58 **below his right ear:** Report of J. Edward Madvay, FBI Pittsburgh Field Office
File 159–63, "Unknown Subject; JAY—Victim, July 10, 1969, 4–5, 7.

58 **reluctantly agreed:** Ibid., 6; Director of FBI, From SAC, Springfield, Subject:
Walter Rodell Barr; JAY-Victim LMRDA, May 27, 1970. After Yablonski was
murdered, Barr, a miner, confessed to the FBI that he had punched Yablonski
in the face during the meeting. Barr's account contradicts Yablonski's doctor's findings. Barr was never arrested. Inexplicably, the FBI never interviewed
Yablonski's examining neurologist, who was certain that he was struck from
behind by a karate-like blow. Morris, the FBI later discovered, received a mys-
terious $1,500 payment from the UMWA that summer. There is no evidence
that Albert Pass knew anything about this other apparent plot to assassinate
Yablonski.

58 **his badly bruised neck:** Armbrister, *Act of Vengeance*, 78.

59 **hand and right foot:** Madvay, "Unknown Subject, JAY," 7; "Assaulted, KOd
at Illinois Talks, Yablonski Says," *Pittsburgh Post-Gazette*, June 30, 1969, Box
2, UMWA 1946 H&RFR Ser. 2 Dir's R, 1969 UMWA Election, 1969–1971,
WV&RHC WVU.

59 **prosecuted for the assault:** Ben A. Franklin, "U.M.W. Candidate Charges Beating," *New York Times*, July 3, 1969, 16; Robert Walters, "Locking the Barn Door:
Secretary Schultz and the Miners," *Washington Monthly*, February 1970, 71.

59 **knocked him unconscious:** "Yablonski Hurt at Party, Says George Titler,"
Welch Daily News, Box 1, GJTC SCRC UK.

59 **employing "fascist tactics":** "Boyle Denies Attack on UMW Foe," *Pittsburgh*

Post-Gazette, August 15, 1969, 2; "Fourteen $64,000 Questions for Jock Yablonski," Box 23 MFDC WRL WSU; Press Release, Miners for Yablonski, July 2, 1969, CAY papers.

59 **to do just that:** Brit Hume, *Death and the Mines: Rebellion and Murder in the United Mine Workers* (New York: Grossman Publishers, 1971), 194. Following the attack, Yablonski issued a press statement proclaiming he would stay in the race, adding "They gotta kill me to get me out," Cong. Ken Hechler Press Statement, June 2, 1969, CAY papers.

Chapter Five: Loyal Union Men

60 **to a federal penitentiary:** AEP confession, September 13, 1977, 4, RAS Papers.

60 **chance to strike back:** Adrian Lee, Bonnie Cook, Mike Ruane, and Jim Southwood, "A Man with a Motive for a Union Murder," *Philadelphia Bulletin*, August 4, 1981, A8.

61 **arrived home in Middlesboro:** AEP confession, 6.

61 **only gotten worse:** Armbrister, *An Act of Vengeance* (New York: Saturday Review Press, 1975), 85–86.

61 **scared and worried man:** WJP confession, June 12, 1973, Box 13, 244–45, JAYLCC MD LOC.

61 **not about to start:** Gary Mihoces, "Prater Confesses that Pass told him Boyle not involved in Yablonski Plot," *Associated Press*, June 13, 1973; AEP confession, 6; testimony of WJP, in *Commonwealth of Pennsylvania v. W. A. "Tony" Boyle*, April 5, 1974, 9–162.

62 **traced to the UMWA:** Armbrister, *Act of Vengeance*, 86.

62 **seams of soft coal:** FBI interview of WJP, January 22, 1970, Box 23, 523, JAYLCC MD LOC.

62 **"principle and stark fear":** Adrian Lee, Bonnie Cook, Mike Ruane, and Jim Southwood, "Plotters: Fiery Father, Deceitful Daughter," *Philadelphia Bulletin*, August 3, 1981, A7.

62 **shooting him in the thigh:** Ibid.; FBI interview of Arlin Gibson, January 25, 1970, Box 23, JAYLCC MD LOC.

62 **his own customers that November:** Joseph E. Finley, *The Corrupt Kingdom: The Rise and Fall of the United Mine Workers* (New York: Simon & Schuster, 1972), 271.

62 **twenty-four months of it:** FBI interview of SH, January 22, 1970, Box 23, JAYLCC MD LOC.

63 **aboveground for good:** FBI interview of SH, March 16, 1970, Box 23, JAYLCC MD LOC.

63 **opposed the union president:** FBI interview of Steve Kochis, April 9, 1970, Box 23, JAYLCC MD LOC. In 1969, Kochis dropped his opposition and supported Boyle against Yablonski.

63 **showing them to his family:** FBI interview of SH, February 27, 1970, 177, Box 23, JAYLCC MD LOC.

63 **had to go:** Lee, Cook, Ruane, and Southwood, "Plotters: Fiery Father, Deceitful Daughter," A7; FBI interview of Ronnie Gibson, April 2, 1970, Box 24, JAYLCC MD LOC.

63 **to kill Jock Yablonski:** AG confession to FBI, April 4, 1972, 4, Box 4, JAYLCC MD LOC.

Chapter Six: Hillbilly Hit Men

64 **"Hillbilly Highway" north to Cleveland:** Author's interview with PEG, July 2, 2017; FBI Report, January 31, 1970; FBI Report, February 26, 1970, FBI interview of SH, January 23, 1970; FBI Report, SH Criminal Record, March 16, 1970, Box 23, JAYLCC MD LOC; Arthur H. Lewis, *Murder by Contract: The People v. "Tough Tony" Boyle* (New York: Macmillan, 1975), 147.

64 **America's "underdeveloped country":** Dan Wakefield, "In Hazard," in *Appalachia in the Sixties, Decade of Reawakening,* edited by David S. Walls and John B. Stephenson (Lexington: University of Press of Kentucky, 1972), 10. Appalachia stretches along a mountain range from western New York to northern Georgia. Central Appalachia covers some sixty counties of Kentucky, Tennessee, Virginia, and West Virginia. *See* Wayne Flynt, *Dixie's Forgotten People* (Bloomington: Indiana University Press, 1980), 134.

65 **Southern Appalachian Migrants:** James A. Haught, "Killers Stalk, But Bungle Yablonski Job at Beckley," *Charleston Gazette,* December 28, 1971, Box 9, GJTC SCRC UK.

65 **support her infant son:** Author's interview with PEG; FBI Report, January 31, 1970, Jacksboro, Tennessee, 413, Box 23, JAYLCC, MD, LOC.

65 **she became his bookkeeper:** Author's interview with PEG.

65 **in an underground accident:** Ibid.

65 **on an assembly line:** Ibid.

66 **marriage was falling apart:** Ibid.; Trevor Armbrister, *An Act of Vengeance* (New York: Saturday Review Press, 1975), 89.

66 **was with other men:** Adrian Lee, Bonnie Cook, Mike Ruane, and Jim Southwood, "Paul Gilly, Portrait of a Lifer and Loser," *Philadelphia Bulletin,* August 2, 1981, A12; FBI interview of Arlin Gibson, January 25, 1970, Box 24, JAYLCC MD LOC.

66 **Gilly's pet monkey:** Author's interview with PEG; Armbrister, *Act of Vengeance,* 9, 90; FBI interview of Annette Lucy Gilly, January 19, 1970, Box 23, JAYLCC MD LOC.

66 **one on his shoulder:** FBI interview of Ronnie Gibson, April 2, 1970, Box 24, JAYLCC MD LOC.

66 **only for a while:** Author's interview with PEG; Armbrister, *Act of Vengeance*, 9.

67 **different sort of clientele:** Armbrister, *Act of Vengeance*, 9, 91.

67 **when they migrated:** Ibid.

67 **even the hangman's noose:** David Hackett Fischer, *Albion's Seed* (New York: Oxford University Press, 1989), 606, 611, 623–24, 626–28.

68 **with him when he left:** Ben A. Franklin, "A Violent Trail in Yablonski Case," *New York Times Sunday Magazine*, January 25, 1970, www.nytimes.com/1970/01/25/archives/a-violent-trail-in-yablonski-case.html.

68 **was nine years old:** FBI interview of CEV, January 20, 1970, Box 23, JAYLCC MD LOC; Armbrister, *Act of Vengeance*, 95–96; "Vealey Tells of Hilltop Plot to Kill Yablonski," *Cleveland Plain Dealer*, July 25, 1971, Box 9, GJTC SCRC UK.

68 **refused to press charges:** FBI interview of CEV, January 20, 1970.

68 **He and Lucy reconciled:** Lee, Cook, Ruane, and Southwood, "Paul Gilly, Portrait of a Lifer and Loser," A12.

68 **to kill Jock Yablonski:** Armbrister, *Act of Vengeance*, 94; AG confession, April 4, 1972, 2, Box 4, JAYLCC MD LOC; FBI interview of Katherine Horn, March 17, 1970, Box 24, JAYLCC MD LOC.

69 **she pouted and sobbed:** Author's interview with PEG.

69 **arrested him for the murder:** PEG confession, March 12, 1973, 5, Box 2, JAYLCC, MD, LOC; AG confession, April 4, 1972, 20, JAYLCC MD LOC.

69 **leaving a Cleveland bar:** Author's interview with PEG.

69 **he had never seen:** FBI interview of PEG, March 12, 1973, 4–5; AG confession, 20.

69 **windows with a shotgun:** Testimony of PEG, *Commonwealth of Pennsylvania v. W. A. "Tony" Boyle*, 7–44, Box 2, JAYLCC MD LOC; FBI interview of Katherine Horn, March 17, 1970, 2, Box 24, JAYLCC MD LOC.

70 **a risky house burglary:** FBI interview of PEG, 5.

70 **in the left knee:** Statement of JCP, January 21, 1970, 163, Box 23, JAYLLC MD LOC; RAS papers, JCP's Criminal Record in *Commonwealth of Pennsylvania v. W. A. "Tony" Boyle*; Armbrister, *Act of Vengeance*, 130.

70 **ambush the insurgent there:** WJP confession, June 12, 1973, 266, Box 13, JAYLCC MD LOC.

70 **on the evening news:** Ibid.

70 **"to a million dollars":** SH confession, May 3, 1972, 16.

71 **and September 29, 1969:** FBI Timeline of Pass and Boyle Meetings, undated.

71 **with the child's father:** FBI interview of Aubran Wayne Martin, January 15, 1970, 387, Box 23, JAYLCC MD LOC; Armbrister, *Act of Vengeance*, 111; Martin's Arrest Record in RAS papers, *Commonwealth of Pennsylvania v. W. A. "Tony" Boyle*.

71 **a bottle of beer:** FBI interview of Aubran Wayne Martin.

71 **owner shot pool:** Armbrister, *An Act of Vengeance*, 115.

71 **to buy a horse:** YABMUR, Chronology of Suspects' Activities, September 18, 1969 through December 30, 1969, 1.

71 **see the murder money:** Testimony of WJP, *Commonwealth of Pennsylvania v. W. A. "Tony" Boyle*, 9-172–9-175, Box 2, JAYLCC MD LOC; SH confession, 18.

72 **District 19's bank account:** AEP to W. A. Boyle, September 24, 1969; AEP to W. A. Boyle, September 30, 1969; Secretary-Treasurer to AEP, October 1, 1969; Secretary-Treasurer to AEP, October 3, 1969; UMWA Check 13098, September 30, 1969; UMWA Check 13129, October 3, 1969, Box 26, UMWA LDR Ser. 3 EFSCL PSU.

72 **Bell and Harlan counties:** Testimony of WJP, 9-176–9-180, Box 2. JAYLCC MD LOC; John Gaventa, *Power and Powerlessness: Quiescence & Rebellion in an Appalachian Valley* (Urbana: University of Illinois Press, 1982), 182.

72 **handed the money back:** Gene Confer, Black Lung Committee Expenses, January 26, 1970, U.S. Department of Labor.

73 **to Prater and Pass:** Armbrister, *Act of Vengeance*, 118; Ward Sinclair, "District 19's role in the UMW," *Louisville Courier-Journal*, March 7, 1971, 4.

73 **overruled him:** WJT statement to the FBI, August 23, 1973, 10, Box 4, JAYLCC MD LOC.

73 **challenged his religious beliefs:** Turnblazer was a practicing Catholic.

73 **possibly a lot more:** Testimony of WJT in *Commonwealth of Pennsylvania v. W. A. "Tony" Boyle*, 11-177–178, Box 3, JAYLCC MD LOC.

73 **do the next night:** Testimony of WJP in *Commonwealth of Pennsylvania v. W. A. "Tony" Boyle*, 10-16–10-17.

74 **see the murder money first:** FBI interview of Mrs. Norval Dippel, January 30, 1970, Box 23, JAYLCC MD LOC; WJP confession, 268; FBI Chronology of Suspects' Activities, September 18, 1969, through December 30, 1969, 2.

74 **as cheaply as possible:** WJP confession, Box 13, JAYLCC MD LOC.

74 **free Vealey the next day:** FBI interview of PEG, 5; Testimony of Bernadine Mary Mathews in *Commonwealth of Pennsylvania v. W. A. "Tony" Boyle*, 8-8, Box 2, JAYLCC MD LOC. Martin also participated in this burglary but got away.

74 **man in the middle:** AG confession, 8, 10; testimony of JCP in *Commonwealth of Pennsylvania v. W. A. "Tony" Boyle*, 105–6, Box 2, JAYLCC MD LOC; testimony of PEG, 6–165. Gilly had stolen the briefcase during his and Lucy's burglary of Norval Dippel's home.

74 **towards Washington, D.C.:** Author's interview with PEG; Armbrister, *Act of Vengeance*, 131.

Chapter Seven: Whatever the Sacrifice May Be

75 **how corrupt or thuggish:** "The Men Who Lead Your Union," Miners Committee for Boyle-Titler-Owens, Box 80, MFDC WRL WSU.

75 **July 9 to August 9:** Email, CAY to author, November 27, 2017.

76 **his and Rauh's campaign strategies:** Email, CAY to author, November 28, 2017.

76 **but he never campaigned:** *Hearings on the Mine Workers' Election before the Subcomm. on Labor of the Senate Comm. on Labor and Public Welfare, 91st Congress, 2d Session,* 24; Paul Nyden, *Miners for Democracy: Struggle in the Coalfields* (PhD dissertation, Columbia University, 1974), 500.

76 **or even mining sites:** Justin McCarthy, "UMWA to Vote Dec 9!," *UMWJ,* December 1, 1969, 3; Edgar N. James, "Union Democracy and the LMRDA: Autocracy and Insurgency in National Union Elections," *Harvard Civil Rights-Civil Liberties Law Review,* Vol. 13 (Spring 1978), 330. The United States contained twenty-three districts.

76 **votes by fear and intimidation:** Robert H. Zieger, *John L. Lewis: Labor Leader* (Boston: Twayne Publishers, 1988), 174; James P. Gannon, "UMW Fund Boosts Pensions 30% as Boyle, Facing Union Election, Takes Panel's Helm," *Wall Street Journal,* June 25, 1969, 3.

77 **union's already bulging coffers:** Gannon, "UMW Fund Boosts Pensions 30%," 3.

77 **their own voting blocs:** Ed Cox, "The Miners Play Rough," *New Republic,* August 2, 1969, 14; *Hearings on Mine Workers' Election,* 11. There may have been as many as 760 bogus locals and as many as 290 composed solely of retirees.

77 **forty cents a ton since 1952:** "Probe of UMW Shows Welfare Fund Periled," *Washington Post,* October 17, 1970, A2.

77 **union fact-finding missions:** Don Walker, "UMW's Boyle Will End Up in Prison, Yablonski Tells Rally at Madisonville," *Louisville Courier-Journal,* November 24, 1969, Box 2, UMWA 1946 H&RFR Ser. 2 Dir's R, 1969 UMWA Election, 1969–1971, WV&RHC WVU.

78 **in the UMWA's history:** Kenneth Yablonski's eulogy, May 29, 1970, CAY papers.

78 **in salaries in 1968:** James, "Union Democracy," 332; "Memorandum," June 18, 1970, Box 23, MFDC WRL WSU; "Transfer of Funds, 1969," Box 26, UMWA LDR Ser. 3 EFSCL PSU.

78 **he was dead:** *Hearings on the Mine Workers' Election,* 51.

78 **name appeared once:** Ed Cox, "The Miners Play Rough," 13; James, "Union Democracy," 333.

79 **"his brother union members":** *Election Bulletin,* CAY papers; Cox, "The Miners Play Rough," 13.

79 **all but deserted him:** "Jock Yablonski is Fighting Mad," JAY papers.

79 **had been in Springfield:** Trevor Armbrister, *An Act of Vengeance* (New York: Saturday Review Press, 1975), 79–81; author's interview with Nader, March 20, 2017; author's interview with CAY, Nov 13, 2017.

79 **too thinly as it was:** Author's interview with Nader; "Yablonski's Challenge to Boyle's Presidency of Mine Workers Could Spur Bitter Fight," *Wall Street Journal*, June 2, 1969, Box 2, UMWA 1946 H&RFR Ser. 2 Dir's R, 1969 UMWA Election, 1969–1971, WV&RHC WVU.

79 **felt seduced and abandoned:** Armbrister, *Act of Vengeance*, 81; author's interview with CAY, November 13, 2017; Fred Barnes, "No Saint," *New Republic*, December 16, 1985, 50; author's interview with Fred Barnes, March 29, 2017. Chip Yablonski believes his father would never have run against Boyle without Nader's backing.

79 **came to his rallies:** *Hearings on the Mine Workers' Election*, 11,

80 **"a union in 10 years":** Jeanne Rasmussen, "Jock—a man who could listen," *Miners' Voice*, June 1970, 2.

80 **and his rampant corruption:** Jeanne Rasmussen, "The Miners: What Happens Now?" *Mountain Life and Work*, February 1970, 3.

80 **"to have to answer!":** 115 *Cong. Rec.—House* 5764, March 3, 1970; Cox, "The Miners Play Rough," 13.

81 **defraud them of their pensions:** Press Release, Hawey A. Wells Jr., M.D.; 115 *Cong. Rec.* 22623–22629, July 31, 1969; Joseph E. Finley, *The Corrupt Kingdom: The Rise and Fall of the United Mine Workers* (New York: Simon & Schuster, 1972), 199.

81 **the country's major newspapers:** *Kenneth Yablonski v. UMWA*, Civil Action No. 1799–69, United States District Court for the District of Columbia, August 15, 1972, 2, 4, Box 117, JLRP MD LOC.

81 **without federal intervention:** David Witter, "The Landrum-Griffin Act: A Case Study in the Possibilities and Problems in Anti-Union Corruption," *Criminal Justice Review*, Vol. 27, No. 2 (Autumn 2002), 301; Laurence Silberman and George Driesen, "The Secretary and the Law: Preballoting Investigations Under the Landrum-Griffin Act," *Georgia Law Review*, Vol. 7, No. 1 (Fall 1972), 4–6; author's interview with Judge Laurence Silberman, April 17, 2017.

82 **thirty infractions of the Act:** *Hearings on the Mine Workers' Election*, 38–46,

82 **the votes were counted:** Ibid., 48–50.

82 **Labor and organized labor:** Burton Hall, *Autocracy and Insurgency in Organized Labor* (New Brunswick: Transaction Books, 1972), 5.

82 **more than the election:** A. H. Raskin, "Labor: It Wants A Little More 'Neglect'," *New York Times*, March 8, 1970, E1; Rauh, "LMRDA-Enforce it or Repeal it," 5, *Georgia Law Review*, 647, 1971; Leonard J. Lurie to Joseph Rauh, December 22, 1970, Papers of Laurence H. Silberman, Box 41, Hoover Institution, Stanford University. Nixon's relations with Big Labor improved briefly in 1972. George Meany, the president of the AFL-CIO, refused to endorse Democratic presidential nominee George McGovern because of his opposition to the Vietnam War.

82 **one of federal meddling:** "Forecasters Give Narrow Lead to Boyle in Election," *Raleigh Register*, December 2, 1969, Box 2, UMWA 1946 H&RFR Ser. 2 Dir's R, 1969 UMWA Election, 1969–1971, WV&RHC WVU; Frank Mankiewicz and Tom Braden, "Senate Showdown May Be forced on UMW Election, Yablonski Case," *Washington Post*, July 14, 1970, A15; author's interview with Judge Laurence Silberman, April 17, 2017, Washington, D.C.

83 **the December 9 ballot:** Email, CAY to author, November 27, 2017.

83 **Welfare and Retirement Fund:** Ben A. Franklin, "Yablonski to Run for U.M.W. Office," *New York Times*, August 13, 1969, A30.

83 **"sweet and gentle people":** Robert C. Maynard, "Mines Bureau, UMW Attacked by Yablonski," *Washington Post*, August 12, 1969, A7.

83 **in his living room:** Joe McGinniss, "The Yablonski Murders," *Life*, January 23, 1970, 37.

84 **much less reporting them:** Ibid.

Chapter Eight: The Hunt

85 **was on 15th Street:** AG confession, April 4, 1972, 8, Box 4, JAYLCC MD LOC.

85 **stalking the wrong target:** Testimony of JCP, *Commonwealth of Pennsylvania v. W. A. "Tony" Boyle*, 105–6.

85 **know what she meant:** PEG confession, March 12, 1973, 7, Box 2, JAYLCC MD LOC.

86 **gas station's parking lot:** AG confession, 8; YABMUR, Chronology of Suspects' Activities, 4.

86 **extended his father's life:** FBI interview of CAY, January 23, 1970, Box 23, JAYLCC MD LOC; Shirley Yablonski and Vealey police line-up, April 14, 1970, Canton, Ohio, Box 23, JAYLCC MD LOC; author's interview with CAY and Shirley Yablonski, November 12, 2017.

86 **to quit now:** Testimony of CEV in *Commonwealth of Pennsylvania v. William J. Prater*, 108, Box 15, JAYLCC MD LOC.

87 **and Farmington, West Virginia:** Thomas Dublin and Walter Licht, *The Face of Decline* (Ithaca: Cornell University Press, 2005), 102; "Yablonksi Charges that Anthracite Miners and Pensioners are Second Class UMW Members," Press Release, Miners for Yablonski, July 15, 1969, CAY papers.

87 **instead of on a farm:** Trevor Armbrister, *An Act of Vengeance* (New York: Saturday Review Press, 1975), 134.

87 **scarred soft coal country:** Testimony of CEV, *Commonwealth of Pennsylvania v. Albert E. Pass*, Box 13, 152, JAYLCC MD LOC.

88 **go back to Cleveland:** YABMUR, Chronology of Suspects' Activities, 5.

88 **the borough toward Cleveland:** Statement of JCP, January 22, 1970, Cleveland, Ohio, 8, Box 24, JAYLCC MD LOC.

88 **it wanted him killed:** AG confession, 10.

88 **$9,000 Prater now held:** WJP confession, June 12, 1973, 269–70.

88 **updates on the plot:** AEP confession, September 13, 1977, 15.

89 **away from the house:** Testimony of CEV, *Commonwealth of Pennsylvania v. W. A. "Tony" Boyle*, 7-183–7-188, Box 2, JAYLCC MD LOC.

89 **they put everything back:** Ibid.; SH confession, 23.

89 **off-the-shelf rat poison instead:** AG confession, 11; Discussion of Methods to Murder Yablonski, FBI Summary, January 31, 1970, 195–97, Box 23, JAYLCC MD LOC.

90 **burning to death everyone inside:** Discussions of Methods to Murder Yablonski, 195–97; SH confession, 24; FBI interview of JCP, January 30, 1970, Box 23, JAYLCC MD LOC.

90 **speed back to Cleveland:** YABMUR, Chronology of Suspects' Activities, 8.

90 **and staring at Yablonski:** Jeanne Rasmussen, "The Miners: What Happens Now?," *Mountain Life and Work*, 4; Armbrister, *Act of Vengeance*, 140; "UMW Rivals Trade Barbs in Vote Bids," *Beckley Post-Herald*, November 10, 1969, Box 1, GJTC SCRC UK.

90 **no matter the consequences:** Rasmussen, "The Miners," 4.

90 **rank-and-file members:** Ibid.

91 **"this kind of America!":** Ibid.

91 **had to be killed:** Author's interview with PEG, July 2, 2017.

91 **continued on to Cleveland:** SH confession, 24; CEV confession, January 21, 1970, 9; Jennifer Bundy, "Yablonski Friend Recalls Being Stalked, Killers Followed UMW Activist for Months in 1969," *Associated Press*, December 31, 1994.

91 **poisoning and firebombing him:** Testimony of WJP, *Commonwealth of Pennsyvania v. W. A. "Tony" Boyle*, 10-53–10-54; AG confession, 18–19.

91 **if they had to:** AG confession, 19.

92 **a good murder weapon:** Testimony of PEG, *Commonwealth of Pennsylvania v. W. A. "Tony" Boyle*, 7-25, 7-29; FBI interview of JCP, February 9, 1970, Box 23, JAYLCC MD LOC.

92 **girl was something else:** Author's interview with PEG.

92 **vote count in District 19:** Testimony of WJP, 10-54–10-57; Armbrister, *Act of Vengeance*, 148; Don Stillman, "The Yablonski Murders: A History," *UMJ*, September 1973, 12.

93 **Illinois, and western Kentucky, too:** "Yablonski Promises Sick Leave," *Pittsburgh Post-Gazette*, October 21, 1969; Ed Nichols, "Miners Face Moment of Truth," *Logan Banner*, December 3, 1969, UMWA 1946 H&RFC Ser. 2 Dir's R, 1969 UMWA Election, 1969–1971, WV&RFC WVU; "Yablonski to Speak at Morgantown Rally," *Evening Standard*, October 3, 1969, Box 81, MFDC WRL WSU.

93 **architect of his murder:** Adrian Lee, Bonnie Cook, Mike Ruane, and Jim Southwood, "Yablonski Murder Jury Did Not Get All the Facts," *Philadelphia Bulletin*, August 2, 1981, A10.

93 **Central Appalachia's environmental mayhem:** "Joseph Yablonski and his

Supporters Give Their Position on the Issues," undated, Box 83, MFDC. WRL
WSU; "Joseph Yablonski, I'll Return Control," *Charleston Gazette*, November
14, 1969; "Yablonski Promises Sick Leave," *Pittsburgh Post-Gazette*, October 21,
1969, Box 1, UMWA 1946 H&RFC Ser. 2 Dir's R, 1969 UMWA Election, 1969–
1971, WV&RHC WVU.

93 **backwaters of organized labor:** James G. Driscoll, "In the Miners' Rough-
shod Way, Chiefs Tangle for Leadership," *National Observer*, October 24, 1969,
Box 2, UMWA 1946 H&RFC Ser. 2 Dir's R, 1969 UMWA Election, 1969–1971
WV&RHC WVU.

93 **"I don't like it!":** 115 *Cong. Rec.—House* 5764, March 3, 1970.

94 **middle of the pack:** "Lewis Heir Faces Revolt," *Business Week*, November 15,
1969, 112.

94 **printed 82,000 extra ballots:** Edgar N. James, *Union Democracy and the
LMRDA: Autocracy and Insurgency in National Union Elections*," *Harvard
Civil Rights-Civil Liberties Law Review*, Vol. 13 (Spring 1988), 334.

94 **the Landrum-Griffin Act:** James, *Union Democracy and the LMRDA*, 334;
Rauh to Shultz, December 1, 1969, 115 *Cong. Rec.—House* 36764, December 4,
1969.

94 **and tore it up:** Jeanne Rasmussen, "Coal Miner's Wife," March 1, 1970, 3, Box 3,
Jeanne Rasmussen Papers, ETSU AA; John Moody, "Boyle Gets Support of Ex-
Foe," *Pittsburgh Post-Gazette*, November 3, 1969, A2.

95 **address in Washington, D.C:** "A Test for Coal Miners," "Another Test for Coal
Miners," UMWA 1946 H&RFR Ser. 2 Dir's R, 1969 UMWA Election, 1969–1971,
WV&RHC WVU.

95 **Crime and Racketeering Section:** Memorandum from Leonard J. Lurie
to W. J. Usery, "Summary of Financial Investigation UMWA, LM-000063,"
November 26, 1969, Box 23, MFDC WRL WSU; "Labor Agency Report Criti-
cizes Finances of Miners Union, May Affect its Election," *Wall Street Journal*,
December 1, 1969, A4. George Shultz worried about unduly influencing the
election with the report's release, but he did not want to sit on the explosive
information.

95 **and "union busting":** "Yablonski Predicts UMW Indictment," *Washington
Post*, December 1, 1969; Don Walker, "UMW's Boyle Will End Up in Prison,
Yablonski Tells Rally at Madisonville," *Louisville Courier-Journal*, November
24, 1969, Box 3, UMWA 1946 H&RFR Ser. 2 Dir's R, 1969 UMWA Election,
1969–1971, WV&RHC WVU; *UMWA Press Release*, November 29, 1969, Box
80, MFDC WRL WSU.

96 **into District 19's coffers:** "Yablonski Sues 3 UMW Leaders, Says They Mis-
used Union Funds," *Washington Post*, December 5, 1969, A2; "Yablonski in
U.S. Court: Suit asks Boyle Pay $18 Million to UMW," *Pittsburgh Post-Gazette*,
December 5, 1969, Box 1, UMWA 1946 H&RFC Ser. 2 Dir's R, 1969 UMWA
Election, 1969–1971 WV&RHC WVU.

Chapter Nine: The Most Dishonest Election in American Labor History

97 **did not believe him:** Testimony of CEV in *Commonwealth of Pennsylvania v. William J. Prater*, 176–77, Box 15, JAYLCC MD LOC.

97 **and to be patient:** SH confession, May 3, 1972, 25.

97 **four-year-old daughter:** FBI Chronology of Suspects' Activities, September 18, 1969 thru December 30, 1969, 8. Phillips was convicted on January 18, 1972, for rape of a minor.

98 **peered through the window:** Trevor Armbrister, *An Act of Vengeance* (New York: Saturday Review Press, 1975), 146–47; FBI YABMUR, Chronology of Suspects' Activites, 9.

98 **and squeeze the trigger:** FBI YABMUR, Chronology of Suspects' Activities, 146–47; Armbrister, *Act of Vengeance*, 146–147; testimony of CEV, *Commonwealth of Pennsylvania v. William J. Prater*, 122, Box 15, JAYLCC MD LOC.

98 **stared ahead in silence:** Author's interview with PEG, July 2, 2017; PEG confession, March 12, 1973, 8.

98 **trip to Clarksville:** AEP confession, September 13, 1977, 16; "Mine Union Head Assails Opponent," *New York Times*, December 1,1969, Box 3 UMWA 1946 H&RFR Ser. 2 Dir's R, 1969 UMWA Election, 1969–1971, WV&RHC, WVU.

99 **UMWA retirees their pensions:** Stuart Brown, *A Man Called Tony: The True Story of the Yablonski Murders* (New York: W. W. Norton, 1976), 93.

99 **cold it was outside:** AG confession, April 4, 1972, 9.

99 **"trip to West Virginia":** YABMUR, Chronology of Suspects' Activities, 9.

99 **until after the election:** AG confession, 9; PEG confession, March 12, 1973, 9.

100 **contested UMWA presidential election:** "Lewis Heir Faces Revolt," *Business Week*, November 15, 1969, 110.

100 **charged twice as much:** Memorandum: Contributions to and Expenditures of the Miners Committee for Boyle, Titler, and Owens, June 18, 1970, Box 23, MFDC, WRL WSU.

100 **for working on Sundays:** "Your Program for UMW Progress" and "Straight Ahead with Tony Boyle," Box 80, MFDC WRL WSU; "Boyle Brings Home the Pork Chops," Box 74, MFDC WRL WSU.

100 **"a miner's need":** Roy Lee Harmon, "W. A. 'Tony' Boyle," Box 80, MFDP WRL WSU.

100 **could run for office:** "Boyle Heads Local Labor Day Program," *Logan Banner*, August 29, 1969; "Annual Labor Day Celebration," *Pike County News*, August 28, 1969, Box 3, UMWA 1946 H&RFR Ser. 2 Dir's R, 1969 UMWA Election, 1969–1971, WV&RHC WVU.

101 **for the Holy Grail:** 115 *Cong. Rec.—House* 24078–24079, September 3, 1969.

101 **badly under his rule:** 115 *Cong. Rec.—House* 24078, September 3, 1969.

101 **satisfaction was short-lived:** Brit Hume, *Death and the Mines: Rebellion and Murder in the United Mine Workers* (New York: Grossman Publishers, 1971), 218.

101 **worse things about him:** "Fourteen $64,000 Questions for Jock Yablonski," Box 23, MFDC WRL WSU.

102 **was medically ineligible:** "UMW District President Attacks Candidate Yablonski," *Bluefield Daily Telegraph*, August 25, 1969, 1; "A Union Brother to Jock Yablonski," July 9, 1969, CAY papers.

102 **contributed to union busting:** "Mine Union Head Assails Opponent," *New York Times*, December 1, 1969, Box 2, UMWA 1946 H&RFR Ser. 2 Dir's R, 1969 UMWA Election, 1969–1971, WV&RHC WVU.

102 **"what I was told":** "The Two Faces of Joseph Yablonski," Box 80, MFDC, WRL WSU; James G. Driscoll, "In The Miners' Roughshod Way, Chiefs Tangle for Leadership," *National Observer*, November 24, 1969; William Chapman, "Bitter Contest for Control of UMW Laced by Insults, Promises and Charges," *Washington Post*, December 8, 1969, A1.

102 **UMWA and abolish it:** Ray Martin, "Boyle, Yablonski battle intensifies," *Dominion-Post*, November 2, 1969, Box 2, UMWA 1946 H&RFR Ser. 2 Dir's R, 1969 UMWA Election, 1969–1971, WV&RHC WVU.

103 **blasting Yablonski's treachery:** John Gaventa, *Power and Powerlessness: Quiescence & Rebellion in an Appalachian Valley* (Urbana: University of Illinois Press, 1982), 195–200.

103 **"wherever he goes!":** 115 *Cong. Rec.—House* 5765, March 3, 1970.

103 **not monitor the election:** JLR to George Shultz, December 1, 1969, Box 23, MFDC, WRL WSU.

103 **could guarantee honest voting:** "Control of the Mine Workers," *Washington Post*, December 3, 1969, A14.

103 **street with his enemies:** George Shultz to JLR, December 6, 1969, Box 23, MFDC WRL WSU.

103 **democratic and responsive union:** 115 *Cong. Rec.—House* 5764, March 3, 1970.

104 **widespread fraud:** *Hearings on the Mine Workers' Election before the Subcomm. on Labor of the Senate Comm. on Labor and Public Welfare*, 91st Congress, 2d Session, 27; "A Message from Ralph Nader: Urgent call for Volunteer Observers for December 9th United Mine Workers Election," CAY papers.

104 **pensioners to the polls:** Trevor Armbrister, "The Coal-Black Shame of the UMW," 135–40, *Reader's Digest*, October 1970, Box 116, JLRP MD LOC; "Appendix G, Election Day Violations," Box 23, MFDC WRL WSU.

104 **dependency and retribution:** "Final Report of the International Tellers," *UMJ*, February 15, 1970; Gaventa, *Power and Powerlessness*, 200.

104 **over a month before:** Armbrister, *Act of Vengeance*, 148.

104 **"even pronounce his name":** "UMW Aide Refuses to Testify," *Washington Post*, February 7, 1970, A3.

104 **his home base:** John Moody, "Boyle Pledges to Implement His Promises," *Pittsburgh Post-Gazette*, December 11, 1969, Box 3, UMWA 1946 H&RFR Ser. 2 Dir's R, 1969 UMWA Election, 1969–1971, WV&RHC WVU.

105 **had stolen the election:** *CBS Evening News*, "Tragedy Strikes UMW Official and Family," January 5, 1970.

105 **80 percent or better:** Ben A. Franklin, "Mine Union Change Likely After Vote," *New York Times*, December 14, 1969, 70.

105 **"and the federal government":** Ibid.

105 **"real honest, clean election":** Ward Sinclair, "Boyle Wins, but UMW Grudge Goes On," *Louisville Courier-Journal*, December 11, 1969, Box 2, UMWA 1946 H&RFR Ser. 2 Dir's R, 1969 UMWA Election, 1969–1971, WV&RHC WVU.

105 **to continue fighting:** Statement of Joseph "Jock" Yablonski, December 10, 1969, Box 23, MFDC WRL WSU; Jeanne Rasmussen interview of Jock Yablonski, December 10, 1969, Box 2, Rasmussen Papers, ETSU AA.

105 **talk about their demands:** John Moody, "Boyle Pledges To Implement His Promises," *Pittsburgh Post-Gazette*, December 11, 1969, UMWA 1946 Ser. 2 1946 H&RFC, 1969 UMWA Election, 1969–1971 WV&RHC WVU; *Hearings on Mine Workers' Election*, 78; "Chronology of Yablonski Complaints, UMW Communications and Private Litigation," undated, Papers of Laurence H. Silberman, Box 41, Hoover Institution, Stanford University.

106 **had plenty of proof:** Testimony of Arnold Miller, *Commonwealth of Pennsylvania v. W. A. "Tony"Boyle*, 10–180, Box 2, JAYLCC MD LOC.

106 **who voted for Yablonski:** *Hearings on the Mine Workers' Election*, 82–94; "Statement of B. J. Garten," December 11, 1969, CAY papers.

106 **thirty-five years in the union:** Rasmussen, "The Miners: What Happens Now?," *Mountain Life and Work*, 6–7.

106 **would see him alive:** Tom Bethell, *Coal Patrol*, May 20, 1972, 4.

107 **emotional appeal went nowhere:** "Chronology of Yablonski Complaints," 9; Memorandum for W. J. Usery Jr., "Meeting with Mr. Yablonski and his Counsel Pursuant to Secretary's Letter of December 13, 1959," December 15, 1969, Papers of Laurence H. Silberman, Box 41, Hoover Institution, Stanford University.

107 **the union's Non-Partisan League:** Moody, "Boyle Pledges To Implement His Promises."

107 **inside his Clarksville farmhouse:** AEP confession, 17.

107 **"ahead with the plan":** Ibid; SH confession, 27–28.

108 **had to kill Yablonski:** Armbrister, *Act of Vengeance*, 153; AG confession, 13.

108 **his enemy was assassinated:** FBI Memorandum for the Record, President Boyle's Schedule, undated.

Chapter Ten: I Shall Die an Honest Man

109 **Clarksville the next day:** FBI interview of Kenneth Yablonski, January 10, 1970, 98, Box 23, JAYLCC MD LOC.

109 **never know the difference:** Testimony of CEV, *Commonwealth of Pennsylvania v. Albert E. Pass*, 143, Box 13, JAYLCC MD LOC.

110 **raced back to Clarksville:** Testimony of CEV, *Commonwealth of Pennsylvania v. W. A."Tony" Boyle*, 7-187–7-189.

110 **also looking for work:** FBI interview of Kenneth Yablonski, 99.

110 **wash it all out:** Author's interview with Mason Caudill, August 16, 2018.

110 **at the Blacksville Coal Mine:** FBI interview of Kenneth Yablonski, 99.

110 **the signal to shoot:** AG confession, April 4, 1972, 12; testimony of CEV in *Commonwealth of Pennsylvania v. Albert E. Pass*, 160.

110 **drive back to Cleveland:** FBI interview of George McClellan, January 7, 1970, 110, Box 23, JAYLCC MD LOC; RAS papers, RAS opening in second trial of *Commonwealth of Pennsylvania v. W. A. "Tony" Boyle*, 1–61.

111 **"who want to kill me!":** FBI interview of Kenneth Yablonski, 98.

111 **in his shirt pocket:** FBI interview of Karl Kafton, January 20, 1970, Box 23, JAYLCC MD LOC.

111 **"Ohio CX-457":** FBI interview of George McClellan, 110.

111 **registered to Annette Gilly:** Testimony of Kenneth Yablonski, *Commonwealth of Pennsylvania v. W. A. "Tony"Boyle*, 8-149 Box 2, JAYLCC MD LOC.

111 **was a house painter:** FBI interview of Karl Kafton, 95–97.

111 **plate number and name:** AG confession, 11–12.

111 **needed a different car:** Trevor Armbrister, *An Act of Vengeance* (New York: Saturday Review Press, 1975), 157.

112 **woman owned the car:** FBI interview of Pennsylvania State Trooper Ronald Fortney, January 19, 1970, 103, Box 23, JAYLCC MD LOC.

112 **Executive Board's January meeting:** Letter from JAY to W. A. Boyle, George J. Titler, and John Owens, December 18, 1969, Box 23, MFDC WRL WSU.

112 **"finally rejected that discipline":** Letter from JAY to International Tellers, December 18, 1969, Box 23, MFDC WRL WSU.

113 **through to its end:** Author's interview with PEG, July 2, 2017.

113 **especially in Kentucky and Tennessee:** Testimony of PEG, *Commonwealth of Pennsylvania v. W. A. "Tony" Boyle*, 6-189-19, Box 2, JAYLCC MD LOC; author's interview with PEG.

113 **East Cleveland's hillbilly ghetto:** SH confession, May 3, 1972, 26.

113 **approved all his targets:** FBI interview of George Smith Jr., January 30, 1970, 459, Box 24, JAYLCC MD LOC; FBI interview of George Smith Jr., April 15, 1970, Box 14, JAYLCC MD LOC.

113 **stay at Brushy Mountain:** FBI interview of George Smith Jr., January 27, 1970, 455–56, Box 23, JAYLCC MD LOC.

114 **liked the professional challenge:** Testimony of George Smith Jr., *Commonwealth of Pennsylvania v. W. A. "Tony" Boyle*, 8-33–51.

114 **away from the plot:** FBI interview of George Smith Jr., January 30, 1970, Box 23, 462, JAYLCC MD LOC. Smith was later acquitted of that charge.

114 **had to shoot him:** SH confession, 27.

115 **and investigate its outcome:** Armbrister, *Act of Vengeance*, 160.

115 **request for an investigation:** William Usery Jr. to JAY, December 23, 1969, Box 23, MFDC WRL WSU.

115 **"in clean, democratic unions":** Telegram, JAY to George P. Shultz, December 24, 1969, Box 23, MFDC WRL WSU.

115 **had stolen the election:** Charles McCarry, *Citizen Nader* (New York: Saturday Review Press, 1972), 250.

115 **apartment above the tavern:** Author's interview with PEG.

116 **the swirling Monongahela River:** CEV confession, January 21, 1970, 10–11.

116 **they left for Cleveland:** FBI interviews of Edward Bakewell and George Rubble, January 23, 1970, 113, 116, Box 23, JAYLCC MD LOC; YABMUR, Chronology of Suspects' Activities, 12; AG confession, 13.

Chapter Eleven: Leave No Witnesses Behind

117 **he did not know:** FBI interview of JCP, January 17, 1970, 161, Box 23 JAYLCC MD LOC.

117 **a bag of potato chips:** Testimony of CEV in *Commonwealth of Pennsylvania v. William J. Prater*, 124; PEG confession, March 12, 1973, 9; Trevor Armbrister, *An Act of Vengeance* (New York: Saturday Review Press, 1975), 22; testimony of CEV in *Commonwealth of Pennsylvania v. Albert E. Pass*, 158.

117 **patrons in the buttocks:** Jerry M. Flint, "Murder Charges Filed," *New York Times*, January 23, 1970, 1.

118 **an easy fifty dollars:** Statement of CEV to the FBI, March 4, 1970, Box 24, JAYLCC MD LOC; FBI interview of Roy Lewis, January 20, 1970, Box 24, JAYLCC, MD LOC; Armbrister, *Act of Vengeance*, 20.

118 **could not find Phillips:** Author's interview with PEG, July 2, 2017.

119 **and nagging self-doubt:** Stuart Brown, *A Man Named Tony: The True Story of the Yablonski Murders* (New York: W. W. Norton, 1976), 6.

119 **used and abandoned:** Armbrister, *Act of Vengeance*, 11; "Last Trip Home," email, CAY to author, December 10, 2017.

119 **from his board seat:** Ward Sinclair, "Boyle Wins, but UMW Grudge Goes on," *Louisville Courier-Journal*, December 11, 1969, Box 2, UMWA 1946 H&RFR Ser. 2 Dir's R, 1969 UMWA Election, 1969–1971, WV&RHC WVU.

120 **some of his own actions:** Tom Bethell, *Coal Patrol*, May 20,1972, 4.

120 **his home at night:** *Hearings on Mine Workers' Election before the Subcomm. on Labor of the Senate Comm. on Labor and Public Welfare, 91st Congress, 2d Session*, 29.

120 **may have haunted him:** The Sicilian Mafia practices no such restraint.

120 **operator and his wife:** Author's interview with Elmer Schifko, July 10, 2017.

121 **Robert Redford's Sundance Kid:** FBI interview of Helen J. Slosarik, January 11, 1970, 40, Box 23, JAYLCC MD LOC; email, CAY to author, December 10, 2017.

121 **help her do that:** FBI interview of Slosarik, 38.

121 **was not giving up:** email, CAY to author.

121 **was worried about crime:** Author's interview with PEG.

121 **markets after World War II:** FBI interview of Claude Martin, January 23, 1970, Box 23, JAYLCC MD LOC.

122 **set up as targets:** Testimony of CEV in *Commonwealth of Pennsylvania v. Albert E. Pass*, 162, Box 13, JAYLCC MD LOC; author's interview with PEG.

122 **sister in Akron, Ohio:** YABMUR, Chronology of Suspects' Activities, 13; AG confesssion, April 4, 1972, 13.

122 **"that was it":** Testimony of CEV in *Commonwealth of Pennsylvania v. William J. Prater*, 128, Box 15, JAYLCC MD LOC.

122 **home by 8:00 p.m.:** PEG confession, March 12, 1973, 9, Box 2, JAYLCC MD LOC.

122 **drinkers seven days a week:** CEV confession, January 21, 1970, 13, Box 24, JAYLC MD LOC.

123 **they never saw him:** Testimony of PEG in *Commonwealth of Pennsylvania v. W. A. "Tony" Boyle*, 6-138–139, Box 2, JAYLCC MD LOC.

123 **really wanted to hurt:** Armbrister, *Act of Vengeance*, 25–26.

123 **family's huge Christmas tree:** FBI interview of Slosarik, January 11, 1970, 32.

123 **3:00 a.m. to read it:** Ibid., 33.

124 **Scotch, and went upstairs:** Ibid., 34.

124 **its passage while campaigning:** Armbrister, *Act of Vengeance*, 164–65.

124 **beginning to sleet:** FBI interview of Slosarik, 34–35.

124 **everyone in the house:** Testimony of CEV in *Commonwealth of Pennsylvania v Albert E. Pass*, 166. Gilly told a different story. He said that they decided to do that while climbing the stairs to the family's bedrooms.

124 **still tired from campaigning:** FBI interview of Helen Slosarik, January 13, 1970, 1, Box 23, JAYLCC MD LOC.

124 **tucked underneath her face:** Testimony of Dr. Ernest Abernathy in *Commonwealth of Pennsylvania v. W. A. "Tony" Boyle*, 7–121; FBI, Items of Evidence Found at the Yablonski Residence on January 7, 1970, 50, JAYLCC MD LOC.

124 **Yablonski's tree-lined driveway:** Testimony of CEV in *Commonwealth of Pennsylvania v. Albert E. Pass*, 130.

125 **No one was up:** CEV confession, 14; testimony of CEV in *Commonwealth of Pennsylvania v. Albert E. Pass*, 167.

125 **help or drive away:** Testimony of CEV in *Commonwealth of Pennsylvania v. Albert E. Pass*, 167–68.

125 **never barked:** Ibid., 168–69.

125 **living room's fireplace mantel:** Ibid., 170.

125 **shoot Yablonski and Marg:** Testimony of CEV in *Commonwealth of Pennsylvania v. William J. Prater*, 134, Box 15, JAYLCC MD LOC. Gilly later testified that Martin balked on the stairs and said he did not want to kill the two women. I have omitted this because Richard Sprague, in his detailed history of the murders in Commonwealth's Brief Contra Defendant's Post-Trial Motions in

Commonwealth of Pennsylvania v. W. A. "Tony" Boyle, does not describe this as happening nor does Claude Vealey in his confession or in any of his testimony.

125 **the right, was closed:** Testimony of Vealey in *Commonwealth of Pennsylvania v. Albert E. Pass*, 171.

126 **exited into her mattress:** FBI interview of Dr. Ernest L. Abernathy, January 13, 1970, Box 23, JAYLCC MD LOC.

126 **began to scream:** CEV confession, 16; testimony of CEV in *Commonwealth of Pennsylvania v. William J. Prater*, 134–35,

126 **the carbine jammed again:** Testimony of CEV in *Commonwealth of Pennsylvania v. William J. Prater*, 134–35. Gilly denies shooting anyone that night. He has told different stories over the years. In his confession to the FBI, he admitted to holding the rifle after Vealey accidentally ejected its shells, but he denied shooting anyone with it. Lucy said in her confession that Gilly told her that he fired the rifle at the couple but missed. During his interview with the author, he claimed he remained downstairs during the murders. He also said the rifle never jammed. Sprague argued in his brief that Gilly shot Marg. Her autopsy determined she was shot once in the left shoulder by the carbine. See Commonwealth's Brief Contra Defendant's Post-Trial Motions in *Commonwealth of Pennsylvania v. W. A. "Tony" Boyle*, 23, Box 1, JAYLCC MD LOC; FBI, Items of Evidence Found at the Yablonski Residence on January 7, 1970, 50.

126 **to her left lung:** Testimony of Dr. Abernathy in *Commonwealth of Pennsylvania v. W. A. "Tony" Boyle*, 7-132–7-134, JAYLCC MD LOC.

127 **crumpled to the floor:** Martin's .38 revolver held six bullets. He fired two into Charlotte, one into Marg, and shot at Yablonski three times. The wound to Yablonski's wrist caused a significant amount of blood spray. It was very likely the first wound he suffered. Abernathy testified that Vealey's shot to Yablonski's head was probably the last.

127 **at his helpless target:** CEV confession, 16.

127 **coup de grace:** Testimony of Abernathy in *Commonwealth of Pennsylvania v. William J. Prater*, 68–69, Box 15, JAYLCC MD LOC.

127 **killers' spent shell casings:** CEV confession, 17; PEG confession, 10; author's interview with PEG.

127 **clutching only his pistol:** CEV confession, 17.

127 **burglary gone horribly wrong:** Testimony of CEV in *Commonwealth of Pennsylvania v. Albert E. Pass*, 174–76; CEV confession, 17.

128 **slaughter the family:** CEV confession, 17; FBI Clandestine Entry into the Yablonski House, January 14, 1970, 63, Box 23, JAYLCC MD LOC. Two FBI agents retraced the killers' movements outside and inside the farmhouse. They estimated that it took the killers ten minutes to break into the house and kill the family. The assassins threw away the film canisters and gloves on the outskirts of Clarksville.

128 **easy as he thought:** Author's interview with PEG.

Chapter Twelve: The Work of a Maniac

129 **biggest payday of their lives:** Testimony of CEV in *Commonwealth of Pennsylvania v. Albert E. Pass,* 177, JAYLCC MD LOC.

130 **getaway car to his brother:** AG confession, April 4, 1972, 14.

130 **its wet and muddy floor:** FBI interview of Edna Faye Gilly, January 23, 1970, Box 23, 426–27, JAYLCC MD LOC.

130 **$280 in a couple days:** PEG confession, March 12, 1973, 11.

130 **and some cheap booze:** Testimony of Joseph Dimaura and Donald Bram, in *Commonwealth of Pennsylvania v. W. A. "Tony" Boyle,* 8-24–8-27, Box 2, JAYLCC MD LOC.

131 **something was horribly wrong:** FBI interview of Kenneth Yablonski, January 8, 1970, Box 23, 23, JAYLCC MD LOC; testimony of Dr. Abernathy in *Commonwealth of Pennsylvania v. William J. Prater,* Box 15, 54, JAYLCC MD LOC.

131 **her long raven hair:** Testimony of Kenneth Yablonski in *Commonwealth of Pennsylvania v. Albert E. Pass,* 38–39, Box 12 JAYLCC MD LOC.

132 **on the other line:** FBI interview of William C. Stewart, January 15, 1970, Box 23, 24–27, JAYLCC MD LOC.

132 **"done such a thing?":** Ibid.

132 **and hung up:** SH confession, May 3, 1971, 28.

132 **better way to kill Yablonski:** Ibid., 28–29.

133 **"say Yablonski was murdered":** AEP confession, September 13, 1977, 18; Commonwealth's Brief Contra Defendant's Post-Trial Motions in *Commonwealth of Pennsylvania v. W. A. "Tony" Boyle,* 25, Box 1, JAYLCC MD LOC.

133 **told him to do it:** AEP confession, 18.

133 **slaughtered everyone in Clarksville:** SH confession, 29.

133 **"something was going on":** Author's interview with Elmer Schifko, July 10, 2017.

134 **were dated December 31, 1969:** Testimony of Elmer Schifko in *Commonwealth of Pennsylvania v. W. A. "Tony"Boyle,* 9-15–9-16, Box 2, JAYLCC MD LOC.

134 **on the stairs and turned back:** FBI interview of Stewart, 28.

134 **breech was cracked open:** David Penn, "Farrell's Fitting Tribute," *Observer-Reporter,* May 22, 2004; testimony of Jackson in *Commonwealth of Pennsylvania v. Aubran W. Martin,* 117, Box 10, JAYLCC MD LOC.

134 **in the Hollywood hills:** "Yablonski of U.M.W. Slain with Wife and Daughter," *New York Times,* January 6, 1970, 1.

134 **an "act of vengeance":** "Death of a Miner," *New York Times,* January 7, 1970, 42.

134 **National Airport to Pittsburgh:** Email, CAY to author, December 10, 2017.

135 **"without even knowing it":** "Yablonski of U.M.W. Slain with Wife and Daughter," 1.

135 **"agencies to his charges":** Robert C. Maynard, "Jock Yablonski: An Anvil Who Decided to Become a Hammer," *Washington Post,* January 4, 1970, A4.

135 **arrest of the killers:** Trevor Armbrister, *An Act of Vengeance* (New York: Saturday Review Press, 1975), 187.

135 **walked out of the mines:** Ben A. Franklin, "Inquiry Is Ordered into Mine Election," *New York Times*, January 9, 1970, 1.

135 **told her to be quiet:** Testimony of W. A. Boyle in *Commonwealth of Pennsylvania v. W. A. "Tony" Boyle*, 12–128, Box 3, JAYLCC MD LOC; "Interviews of
Clarice R. Feldman," March 21, 1973, CAY papers.

135 **"his wife and daughter?":** Fred Barnes, "Close Friend Threatened by Phone
Call, *Washington Evening Star*, January 7, 1970; 116 *Cong. Rec—House*, February
16, 1970, 244.

135 **stared into the camera:** 116 *Cong. Rec—House*, February 16, 1970, 244.

136 **FBI To enter the case:** "Yablonski of U.M.W. Slain with Wife and Daughter,"
1; Michael E. Parrish, *Citizen Rauh* (Ann Arbor: University of Michigan Press,
2011), 204; Maynard, "Jock Yablonski: An Anvil," A4.

136 **and fingerprint cards:** Parrish, *Citizen Rauh*, 82.

136 **hired them to justice:** Armbrister, *Act of Vengeance*, 187.

136 **small-town serenity and security:** Ibid.; Parrish, *Citizen Rauh*, 204–5.

136 **overthrow the United States government:** Bryan Burrough, *Days of Rage* (New
York: Penguin Press, 2015), 55, 68, 79.

137 **their "icy indifference":** "Mitchell Orders FBI to Join Inquiry into Yablonski
Slayings," *New York Times*, January 7, 1970, 1 Box 9, GJTC SCRC UK.

137 **the Pennsylvania State Police:** CAY to the author, July 21, 2017; Jim Nicholson,
"FBI to Investigate UMW Murders," *Philadelphia Inquirer*, January 7, 1970, Box
9, GJTC SCRC UK.

137 **by killing him:** Indictment of Gilly, Martin, and Vealey, February 5, 1970, 8. Box
23, JAYLCC MD LOC. *See* 29 United States Code Section 30.

137 **these in tiny Clarksville:** FBI report, "Joseph Albert Yablonski, February 178,
1970," Box 23, JAYLCC MD LOC. Clarksville had about 1,200 residents in January 1970.

Chapter Thirteen: YABMUR

141 **leads in the murders:** Trevor Armbrister, *An Act of Vengeance* (New York: Saturday Review Press, 1975), 184–89.

142 **the remote Appalachian coalfields:** Ibid., 188.

142 **telephones around the clock:** "Mitchell Orders F.B.I. to Join Inquiry into
Yablonski Slayings," *New York Times*, January 7, 1970, 1, Box 9, GJTC SCRC UK.

142 **was briefly a suspect:** "Who Killed Jock Yablonski?," *Bluefield Daily Telegraph*,
January 15, 1970, Box 9 GJTC SCRC UK.

142 **they passed polygraph tests:** Email, CAY to author, October 5, 2018.

142 **"most of his life":** "A Deadly Venom," *Time*, January 17, 1970, Box 9, GJTC
SCRC UK.

142 **nothing to help investigators:** Victor Riesel, "See Cosa Nostra in Yablonski Killings," *Outside Labor*, January 7, 1970, Box 9, GJTC SCRC UK.

143 **at least two killers:** FBI, List of Items of Evidence from the Residence of Joseph Yablonski, January 9, 1970, 1.

143 **had been sexually assaulted:** Ibid., 2.; "Yablonski Autopsy Doctor Dies at 77," *Charleston Gazette*, May 20, 1997; "The Yablonski Massacre," *Inside Detective*, April 1970, 46. Abernathy's autopsies took place at the Washington Hospital in Washington, Pennsylvania.

143 **three victims nine times:** FBI, List of Items, January 9, 1970, 3.

143 **a Cleveland, Ohio, address:** Testimony of Glen Werking in *Commonwealth of Pennsylvania v. W. A. "Tony" Boyle*, 9-63–9-64, Box 2, JAYLCC MD LOC.

143 **Pennsylvania in mid-December:** FBI interview of AG, January 8, 1970, Box 23, JAYLCC MD LOC.

144 **a country-western singer:** FBI interview of PEG, January 8, 1970, 245, Box 23, JAYLCC MD LOC; FBI interview of PEG, January 19, 1970, 313, Box 23, JAYLCC MD LOC. Gilly told the author that this story "just came to me."

144 **the killers to justice:** Commonwealth's Brief Contra Defendant's Post-Trial Motions in *Commonwealth of Pennsylvania v. W. A. "Tony" Boyle*, 41–42.

144 **a political contribution:** FBI interview of W. A. Boyle, January 8, 1970, 6–7, Box 1, JAYLCC MD LOC.

144 **about Yablonksi's unsavory past:** Ibid., 8.

145 **Department of Labor into action:** Mike Trbovich, one of Yablonski's campaign managers, formally challenged the election's results on January 20, 1970.

145 **"connected with the union":** Ben A. Franklin, "Inquiry Is Ordered into Mine Election," *New York Times*, January 9, 1970, 1; "UMWA Asks Labor Dept. Probe of Election," *UMJ*, January 15, 1970, 10.

145 **he was about to:** FBI Identification Record of Aubran Wayne Martin, January 20, 1970, 412, Box 23, JAYLCC MD LOC; Stuart Brown, *A Man Named Tony: The True Story of the Yablonski Murders* (New York: W. W. Norton, 1976), 30.

145 **the three oak coffins:** Ike Pappas, "Full-Scale Probe Looms as Yablonski Is Buried," *CBS Evening News*, January 9, 1970; Ben A. Franklin, "Eulogist Praises Yablonski Cause," *New York Times*, January 10, 1970.

145 **"a damn shame":** "Friends, Foes pay Respects to Yablonski," *Pittsburgh Press*, January 8, 1970, 2.

146 **from the UMWA's treasury:** Joe McGinniss, "The Yablonski Murders," *Life*, January 23, 1970, 36.

146 **on with the lawsuit:** Ibid.

146 **nodded in agreement:** Ibid.; Linda Charlton, "Activist Labor Priest, Charles Owen Rice," *New York Times*, January 9, 1970, 20.

147 **an immediate federal investigation:** Charlton, "Activist Labor Priest," 20; Memorandum for George Herman, Moderator of Face the Nation, September

3, 1971, Box 65, MFDC WRL WSU; Clarice Feldman, "Miners for Democracy," in *Autocracy and Insurgency in Organized Labor*, edited by Burton Hall (New Brunswick: Transaction Books, 1972), 13. Chip and Ken Yablonski asked the UMWA not to send any official representatives.

147 **into the frozen ground:** Laurence Stern, "Yablonskis Buried in Icy Winter Cold," *Washington Post*, January 10, 1970, A1.

147 **the classroom's white walls:** Frank Mankiewicz and Tom Braden, "Yablonski's Followers to Continue Legal Fight against Union Leaders," *Washington Post*, January 13, 1970; GJTC SCRC UK.

147 **"against Boyle goes on!":** Michael E. Parrish, *Citizen Rauh* (Ann Arbor: University of Michigan Press, 2011), 205–6; Armbrister, *Act of Vengeance*, 195; Stern, "Yablonskis Buried in Icy Winter Cold."

147 **"better ask Albert Pass":** Tom Bethell, *Coal Patrol*, May 20, 1972, 5.

148 **Kentucky or Tennessee hills:** Email, Joe Masterson to author, July 16, 2017; Victor Riesel, "Murder to Order," *Inside Labor*, May 5, 1972; Huntley-Brinkley Report, February 9, 1970.

148 **without his lawyer:** FBI interviews of AEP and WJT, January 9, 1970, Box 23, JAYLCC MD LOC.

148 **end of September 1969:** AEP confession, September 13, 1977, 19; WJT confession, August 23, 1973, 17–18.

148 **cellar behind his house:** FBI interview of AG, January 19, 1970, 421, Box 23, JAYLCC MD LOC; SH confession, May 3, 1972, 30.

148 **wanted to harm him:** FBI interview of SH, January 13, 1970, 1112, Box 23, JAYLCC MD LOC.

149 **told the auditors the truth:** Testimony of WJP in *Commonwealth of Pennsylvania v. W. A. "Tony" Boyle*, 10-68, Box 3, JAYLCC MD LOC.

149 **a bar in West Virginia:** FBI interview of JCP, January 17, 1970, 5–6, Box 23, JAYLCC MD LOC.

149 **Cleve Byrge, Phillips's stepuncle:** FBI Summary of Developments in Cleveland, December 17, 1970, Box 24, JAYLCC MD LOC.

149 **do anything like that:** FBI interview of Adelheid Farthing, January 17, 1970, 208, Box 23, JAYLCC MD LOC.

149 **he knew too much:** FBI Summary, 1.

150 **in the city jail:** Ibid.

Chapter Fourteen: We Got Lucky

151 **the driver's forehead:** Email, Joe Masterson to author, May 1, 2018. The FBN became the Bureau of Narcotics and Dangerous Drugs in 1968 and was folded into the newly established Drug Enforcement Administration in 1973.

151 **later, in June 1965:** Author's interview with Masterson, April 29, 2017; email, Masterson to author.

151 **its Cleveland field office:** Email, Masterson to author.

151 **young agent could get:** Ibid.; Richard Gid Powers, *Secrecy and Power* (New York: Free Press, 1987), 403.

152 **an accountant's spreadsheet:** Author's interview with Masterson.

152 **"cold-nosed punk":** Ibid.

152 **Two days before that:** Masterson's interview of Buddy Martin, January 15, 1970, 386, Box 23, JAYLCC MD LOC. Special Agent Raymond J. Michel also participated in Martin's interview.

152 **he added dismissively:** Ibid.

152 **"murder the whole family?":** Author's interview with Masterson.

152 **"in slaughtering the Yablonskis?":** Ibid.

153 **he later admitted:** Ibid.; FBI Summary of Developments in Cleveland, 1.

153 **to defeat Jock Yablonski:** DOL memo from Leonard J. Lurie thru John V. Moran, April 24, 1972.

153 **$7,560 in October:** UMWA, DOL File 46-1577, District 19, February 13, 1972, 1.

153 **mine openings and closings:** John J. Murphy to Henry R. Queen, Election Investigation, UMWA, February 13, 1972.

153 **or itemized expense records:** DOL Examination of Records, January 26, 1970, 5–6.

153 **gave to each member:** Department of Labor, Murphy to Queen, February 13, 1970, 2.

154 **their tiny bank accounts:** DOL, District 19, Research Committee Expenses, 3.

154 **committee's true purpose was:** D. N. William to LMSA-BET, Subject: 46-1577, January 29, 1970; DOL memo from Hollis Bowers to Daniel F. Gill, United Mine Workers, February 17, 1970.

154 **question him about the murders:** JCP statement to the FBI, January 17, 1970, 6, Box 23, JAYLCC MD LOC.

154 **the next murder victim:** Ibid.

155 **gave Gilly at least $4,000:** JCP statement to the FBI, January 17, 1970, 5–6, Box 23, JAYLCC MD LOC.

155 **two houses in Cleveland:** Adelheid Farthing statement to the FBI, January 17, 1970, 207.

155 **staked out the market:** Author's interview with Masterson; FBI interview of Diane Cook, January 20, 1970, 220, Box 23, JAYLCC, MD, LOC.

155 **with Clarksville circled:** FBI Summary of Developments in Cleveland, 2; FBI report on Search of 1846 Penrose Avenue, January 19, 1970, 641, Box 23, JAYLCC MD LOC.

155 **"stunk to high heaven":** Author's interview with Masterson.

155 **long enough to collect it:** Ibid.

156 **knew about the killings:** Ibid.

156 **"way we came in":** CEV confession, January 21, 1970, 16–17, Box 23, JAYLCC
MD LOC.

157 **keep him from testifying:** Ben A. Franklin, "3 Held in Yablonski Deaths; Cleveland Hearing Today," *New York Times*, January 22, 1970, 1; "Crime: A Hand from
the Grave," *Time*, February 2, 1970.

157 **in a planned murder:** "20 called for Yablonski Slaying Probe," *Washington Post*,
January 25, 1970, A3; FBI interview of Carol Richardson, January 26, 1970, 218,
Box 23, JAYLCC MD LOC.

157 **any ties to the union:** Jerry Flint, "Murder Charges Filed," *New York Times*,
January 23, 1970, 1.

157 **in his Clarksville home:** AEP confession, September 13, 1977, 19.

158 **with a standing ovation:** Ibid., 19–20; testimony of Tony Boyle in *Commonwealth of Pennsylvania v. W. A. "Tony" Boyle*, 12-166–12-167, Box 3, JAYLCC
MD LOC.

158 **was telling the truth:** FBI Report, Cleveland, Ohio, January 22, 1970, 265–69,
Box 23, JAYLCC MD LOC.

158 **one of the vantage points:** Ibid.

158 **and studied its layout:** JCP statement to the FBI, January 22, 1970, 169–71, Box
23, JAYLCC MD LOC.

159 **West Virginia on December 18:** FBI interview of Marilyn Jeannie Seely, January 22, 1970, 304, Box 23, JAYLCC MD LOC.

159 **colder on the river:** Author's interview with Masterson, April 29, 2017.

159 **FBI's laboratory in Washington:** Testimony of Kenneth M. Russell in *Commonwealth of Pennsylvania v. W. A. "Tony" Boyle*, 8-167–8-168, Box 2, JAYLCC
MD LOC.

159 **by his son, Paul:** FBI interview of Luther Anderson, January 27, 1970, 566, Box
23, JAYLCC MD LOC.

160 **kept the pistol for himself:** Testimony of Fred Schunk in *Commonwealth of
Pennsylvania v. W. A. "Tony" Boyle*, 8-162–8-163, Box 2, JAYLCC MD LOC; FBI
interview of JCP, January 28–29, 1970, 608, JAYLCC MD LOC; FBI interview of
CEV, February 4, 1970, 272, Box 23, JAYLCC MD LOC.

160 **out of his mind:** FBI interview of Richard Baron, January 27, 1970, 407, Box 23,
JAYLCC MD LOC.

160 **gave Paul Gilly $4,200:** FBI Summary of Developments in Cleveland, 6, 10.

160 **man funding the murders:** Statement of CEV to the FBI, February 4, 1970, 273,
JAYLCC MD LOC.

160 **near the Yablonskis' farmhouse:** FBI interview of Helen Dufalla, January 23,
1970, 118; FBI report of Special Agent John Calvin Darst, February 6, 1970, 142;
FBI interview of Sophia Ross, January 23, 1970, 157, Box 23, JAYLCC, MD, LOC.

161 **license plate number CX-457:** Testimony of Kathy Rygle, *Commonwealth of
Pennsylvania v. William J. Prater*, 71–74, Box 15, JAYLCC MD LOC; YABMUR,
Chronology of Suspects' Activities, 9.

161 **about the Yablonski murders:** Ben A. Franklin, "3 Indicted for Plot in Yablon-ski Death," *New York Times*, January 30, 1970, 1; FBI search of 1846 Penrose Avenue, East Cleveland, February 5, 1970, 673, Box 23, JAYLCC MD LOC. Robert Krupansky later became a federal judge.

161 **talked to the FBI:** "UMW Aide Refuses to Testify," *Washington Post*, February 7, 1970, A3; AG confession, April 4, 1972, 21.

161 **longer than three months:** SH confession, May 3, 1972, 30.

162 **his love for God:** FBI interview of SH, January 22, 1970, 471, Box 23, JAYLCC MD LOC.

162 **gone to the FBI:** FBI interview of Gary Hicks, January 30, 1970, Box 23, JAYLCC MD LOC. Hicks's sister persuaded him to go to the FBI.

162 **because he had "talked":** FBI interview of George Smith Jr., January 27, 1970, Box 23, JAYLCC MD LOC.

162 **the UMWA's secretary-treasurer:** DOL, Henry A. Queen, Chief, Branch of Elections and Trusteeships, Department of Labor, to U.S. Attorney Robert B. Krupansky, February 18, 1970.

162 **once he had read it:** DOL memo, Hollis Bowers to Daniel Gill, United Mine Workers, February 17, 1970.

163 **"this is no exception":** "UMW Aide Sees U.S. Bid to Pin Slayings on Union," *Washington Post*, February 20, 1970, A20.

163 **"less sense than the killers":** "Equal Time for Tony Boyle," *American Labor*, February 1970, in 116 *Cong. Rec.—House* 6703–6704, March 10, 1970.

163 **"that got him killed":** "Titler Brands Yablonski a Thief," *Charleston Gazette*, February 19, 1970, in 116 *Cong. Rec.—House* 4457, February 23, 1970.

163 **"any taint or guilt":** George J. Curilla Jr., "Boyle Creates Fact-Finding Commission," *UMJ*, March 1, 1970, 1.

163 **told him to shut up:** George Lardner Jr., "UMW Plans Yablonski Probe; Boyle Cites Ugly Allegations," *Washington Post*, February 27, 1970, A4.

Chapter Fifteen: A Whole Cage Full of Tigers

165 **the city of Philadelphia:** "The Tiger," *Time*, July 17, 1972, 56; Trevor Armbrister, *An Act of Vengeance* (New York: Saturday Review Press, 1975), 247.

165 **an indifferent student:** Author's interview with RAS, April 8, 2017.

165 **changed Sprague's life:** Ibid.

166 **and overwhelm his opponents:** Ibid.

166 **resigned in one day:** Ibid.

166 **more than twenty times:** Statement of Jess D. Costa, District Attorney for Washington County, Pennsylvania, March 1, 1970, Box 1, JAYLCC MD LOC; "The Tiger," 56.

166 **humorless in the courtroom:** Author's interview with RAS.

166 **and its 140 lawyers:** "The Tiger," 56; Author's interview with RAS.

167 **out of the case:** Armbrister, *Act of Vengeance*, 244; "Prosecutor in Yablonski Case Picked," *Washington Post*, March 1, 1970, Box 9, GJTC SCRC UK.

167 **take over the prosecutions:** Author's interview with RAS.

167 **hired them and why:** Ibid.

167 **his special assistant:** Ibid.

167 **all the evidence first:** Ibid.

168 **killers' two vantage points:** Ibid.

168 **feel for its geography:** Richard Starnes, "The Yablonski Case," Scripps-Howard, Box 2, GJTC SCRC UK.

168 **life sentence in prison:** Ibid.

168 **after he testified truthfully:** Ibid.

168 **watered-down plea bargains:** Ibid.

168 **democratic and clean union:** Ibid.

Chapter Sixteen: Their Father's Sons

169 **"they got my father":** Tom Tiede, "Yablonski Jr. Seeks to Avenge His Father," *Raleigh Register*, February 3, 1971, Box 28, UMWA LDR Ser. 3 EFSCL PSU.

170 **at their disposable income:** Maurice Isserman and Michael Kazin, *America Divided: The Civil War of the 1960s* (New York: Oxford University Press, 2000), 266, 284–85.

170 **little time to mourn:** *Huntley-Brinkley Report*, NBC-TV, February 9, 1970, Box 28, UMWA LDR Ser. 3 EFSCL PSU.

170 **harm all labor unions:** Frank Mankiewicz and Tom Braden, "Senate Showdown May Be Forced on UMW Election, Yablonski Case," *Washington Post*, July 14, 1970, A15.

170 **"put the screws to labor":** Ben A. Franklin, "Yablonski Inquiry Reported to Focus on a Sum of Money," *New York Times*, January 24, 1970, 1; David Witwer, *Corruption and Reform in the Teamsters Union: Working Class in American History* (Urbana: University of Illinois Press, 2008), 157. Williams later went to prison as part of the Justice Department's Abscam bribery investigation.

171 **his wife and daughter:** "Lewis Aides Said to Back Yablonski," *Washington Post*, February 6, 1970, A3; testimony of CAY, *Hearings on United Mine Workers' Election before the Subcomm. on Labor of the Senate Comm. on Labor and Public Welfare, 91st Congress, 2d session*, 7–38.

171 **to the three murders:** Rauh to Shultz, January 13, 1971.

171 **keep proper financial records:** "Vindication for Jock Yablonski," *Time*, March 16, 1970, 29.

171 **told their Secretary months before:** Testimony of George Shultz, *Hearings on Mine Workers' Election*, 343–344; "Filing of Suit and Relief Requested," Papers of Laurence H. Silberman, Box 41, Hoover Institution, Stanford University. The DOJ filed the suit under Titles II and IV of the Landrum-Griffin Act.

172 **during the campaign:** "Yablonski Sons Charge Shultz Didn't Act in '69," *Washington Post*, March 7, 1970, A6.

172 **knowing anyone who had:** Statement of W. A. Boyle, President, United Mine Workers of America, March 9, 1970, 3, Box 2, UMWA 1946 H&RFR Ser. 2 Dir.'s R, 1969 UMWA Election, 1969–1971, WV&RHC WVU.

172 **the "totalitarian liberal establishment":** Don Stillman, "The Yablonski Murders: A History," *UMJ*, September 1973, 12.

172 **"capable of such duplicity":** Ibid., 4.

173 **their own newspaper:** Clarice Feldman, "Miners for Democracy," in *Autocracy and Insurgency in Organized Labor*, edited by Burton Hall (New Brunswick: Transaction Books, 1972), 14; Ben A. Franklin, "Murder of a Miner May Bring Reforms," *New York Times*, January 11, 1970, 164.

173 **and bought ferocious dogs:** Richard Fry, "Fighting for Survival: Coal Miners and the Struggle for Health and Safety in the United States, 1968–1988" (PhD dissertation, Wayne State University, 2010), 168.

174 **$920,000 in today's dollars:** Emails, CAY to author, September 4, 2017, and October 9, 2018; Joe Rauh to Raymond S. Rubinow, March 30, 1971, Box 116, JLRP, MD LOC. The two Supreme Court law clerks were Daniel Edelman and Lew Sargentich.

174 **coal mining stock:** Curtis Seltzer, *Fire in the Hole: Miners and Managers in the American Coal Industry* (Lexington: University Press of Kentucky, 1985), 116.

175 **ended Boyle's kangaroo court:** Email, CAY to author, October 9, 2018. Joe Rauh, Chip Yablonski, and Clarice Feldman represented the reformers at the hearing.

175 **in the United States:** Email, CAY to author, September 4, 2017; "U.S. Seizes UMW Ballots in District 5 Election," *Washington Post*, December 15, 1970, A8.

175 **layers of an onion:** Author's interview with CAY, May 23, 2018.

176 **election and the murders:** *Hearings on the Mine Workers' Election*, 347.

176 **"would be in jail":** Charles McCarry, *Citizen Nader* (New York: Saturday Review Press, 1972), 256.

176 **against the Yablonskis' killers:** Jack Anderson, "UMW Probe Chairman 'Easy' on Labor Friends," Box 9, GJTC SCRC UK.

176 **actually pulled the trigger:** The three killers were also indicted for burglary, larceny, and robbery.

176 **one by one:** Ben A. Franklin, "Five Are Indicted in Yablonski Case," May 7, 1970, *New York Times*, 25.

Chapter Seventeen: Peeling the Onion

177 **to them from confessing:** Arthur H. Lewis, *Murder by Contract: The People v. "Tough Tony" Boyle* (New York: Macmillan, 1975), 19.

177 **by fear and ignorance:** Jack Anderson, "Yablonski: A Theory," *New York Post*, November 21, 1970.

177 **county's courthouse anytime soon:** Powell Lindsay, "Yablonski Questions Still Unanswered," *Knoxville News Sentinel*, December 7, 1970, Box 28, UMWA LDR Ser. 3 EFSCL PSU.

178 **mafia capos behind bars:** Ward Sinclair, "UMW troubles: Loose ends and a federal knot-tyer," *Louisville Courier-Journal*, September 5, 1971, Box 28, UMWA LDR Ser. 3 EFSCL PSU.

178 **the union had committed:** Ibid.

178 **"secure in their homes":** Ibid.

179 **another strong Boyle supporter:** Brit Hume, *Death and the Mines: Rebellion and Murder in the United Mine Workers* (New York: Grossman Publishers, 1971), 254.

179 **were never found:** "Fire May Have Destroyed Records in Yablonski Case," *Charleston Gazette*, December 31, 1970, Box 9, GJTC SCRC UK.

179 **Vice-President Hubert H. Humphrey:** Jim Mann, "UMW's Boyle Is Convicted," *Washington Post*, April 1, 1972, A1.

179 **hard for his mine workers:** Milton Jaques, "UMW's Boyle Quits National Bank Post," *Pittsburgh Post-Gazette*, March 6, 1971, Box 2, UMWA 1946 H&RFR Ser. 2 Dir's R, 1969 UMWA Election, 1969–1971, WV&RHC WVU.

179 **"dishonest thing in his life":** Trevor Armbrister, *An Act of Vengeance* (New York: Saturday Review Press, 1975), 260.

180 **assets from the bank:** Fred Barnes, "UMWA Dictatorship on the Defensive," in *Autocracy and Labor* (New Brunswick: Transaction Books, 1972), 22–23.

180 **reelection campaign against Yablonski:** Ibid.

180 **the union was loosening:** Ibid., 24; "2 Mine Unionists Guilty on Funds," *New York Times*, May 7, 1971, 16.

180 **from Ohio to Pennsylvania:** Lindsay, "Yablonski Questions Still Unanswered."

180 **the Washington County courthouse:** Ibid.

181 **seldom overturned his rulings:** Michael Bradwell, "Political Figure, Respected Jurist Sweet Dies at 81," *Observer-Reporter*, November 1, 1999, B7.

181 **and told the truth:** Vealey guilty plea, Box 19, JAYLCC MD LOC.

181 **chills through the courtroom:** Author's interview with Masterson, April 29, 2017.

181 **he was innocent:** Vealey guilty plea, Box 10, JAYLCC MD LOC.

182 **hard as they were:** Author's interview with RAS, April 28, 2017.

182 **a toll on both:** Stuart Brown, *A Man Named Tony: The True Story of the Yablonski Murders* (New York: W. W. Norton, 1976), 51.

182 **his second criminal case:** Armbrister, *Act of Vengeance*, 263.

182 **dubbed the "Batmobile":** Brown, *A Man Named Tony*, 53.

182 **jury could easily follow:** Author's interview with RAS.

183 **a vicious killer:** Lewis, *Murder by Contract*, 41.

183 **minutes of the trial:** Opening statement of RAS, *Commonwealth of Pennsylvania v. Aubran W. Martin*, Box 10, JAYLCC MD LOC.

183 **"the baby-faced killer!":** Ibid.

184 **to the witness stand:** Testimony of Kenneth Yablonski in *Commonwealth of Pennsylvania v. Aubran W. Martin*, 1–17, Box 10, JAYLCC MD LOC.

184 **"Aubran Martin":** Lewis, *Murder by Contract*, 44; Testimony of CEV in *Commonwealth of Pennsylvania v. Aubran W. Martin*, 19, Box 10, JAYLCC MD LOC.

184 **her mother and father:** Testimony of CEV, 47.

184 **word to the other:** John Moody, "Huddleston Decides to Talk," *Pittsburgh Post-Gazette*, December 5, 1973, 39.

184 **Department of Motor Vehicles:** Testimony of CAY in *Commonwealth of Pennsylvania v. Aubran W. Martin*, 194, Box 10, JAYLCC MD LOC.

184 **prosecution's tightly crafted script:** 225 PA. Code Rule 611, Mode and Order of Examining Witnesses and Presenting Evidence.

185 **to save his life:** "Yablonski Suspect Tries Drug Overdose," *New York Post*, October 8, 1970, Box 28, UMWA LDR Ser. 3 EFSCL PSU.

185 **into the Yablonskis' farmhouse:** Testimony of Aubran W. Martin in *Commonwealth of Pennsylvania v. Aubran W. Martin*, 298, Box 10, JAYLCC MD LOC.

185 **if he said anything:** Ibid., 337; "Mystery Lingers in Yablonski Case," *New York Times*, March 5, 1972, 42.

185 **as Gilly and Vealey:** Judge Charles G. Sweet's instructions to the jury in *Commonwealth v. Martin*, 504, Box 10, JAYLCC MD LOC.

186 **they left for Clarksville:** RAS cross-examination of Aubran W. Martin in *Commonwealth of Pennsylvania v. Aubran W. Martin*, 365–380, Box 10, JAYLCC MD LOC.

186 **her mother and father:** Testimony of Robert Lee Towler and Robert Geyer in *Commonwealth of Pennsylvania v. Aubran W. Martin*, 425–41, Box 10, JAYLCC MD LOC.

186 **one hand to the other:** "Jury Finds Martin Guilty in Yablonski Murder Trial," *Washington Post*, November 13, 1971, A3.

186 **basked in his notoriety:** Ibid.; Lewis, *Murder by Contract*, 123.

186 **"maybe even Tony himself":** Lewis, *Murder by Contract*, 123.

186 **to pay his lawyers:** Author's interview with PEG, July 2, 2017.

186 **another masterful show:** RAS opening statement in *Commonwealth of Pennsylvania v. Paul E. Gilly*, Box 7, JAYLCC MD LOC.

187 **farmhouse's big Christmas tree:** Testimony of Helen J. Slosarik in *Commonwealth of Pennsylvania v. Paul E. Gilly*, 49–50, Box 7, JAYLCC MD LOC.

187 **hunted their elusive quarry:** Testimony of JCP in *Commonwealth of Pennsylvania v. Paul E. Gilly*, 51–90, Box 7, JAYLCC MD LOC.

187 **an hour of testimony:** Testimony of PEG's character witnesses in *Commonwealth of Pennsylvania v. Paul E. Gilly*, 319–40, Box 7, JAYLCC MD LOC.

187 **"to exterminate" the Yablonskis:** "Pa. Jury Convicts Gilly in Yablonski Murders," *Washington Post*, March 2, 1972, A8; Joseph R. Daughen, *Fearless: The Richard A. Sprague Story* (Chicago: American Bar Association, 2008), 116.

187 **out of the courtroom:** Daughen, *Fearless*, 116; PEG statement in *Commonwealth of Pennsylvania v. Paul E. Gilly*, 394, Box 7, JAYLCC MD LOC; Edward Verlich, "Hired by Gilly to Help Kill Yablonski, Vealey Testifies," *Pittsburgh Press*, February 29, 1972, A1.

Chapter Eighteen: Lucy and Silous

188 **while her mother suffocated:** Author's interview with PEG, July 2, 2017; Trevor Ambrister, *An Act of Violence* (New York: Saturday Review Press, 1975) 278.

188 **the sex-deprived inmates:** *Commonwealth of Pennsylvania v. Annette Gilly, Commonwealth of Pennsylvania v. Silous Huddleston*, Hearing on Degree of Guilt and Sentencing, August 17, 1974, 8, Box 4, JAYLCC MD LOC.

188 **in solitary confinement:** Author's interview with Joseph Masterson, April 29, 2017.

189 **including her husband:** "Tough, Honest, and Fired," *Time*, December 30, 1974, 52.

189 **her state murder charges:** Armbrister, *An Act of Vengeance*, 278–79.

189 **she needed him:** Stuart Brown, *A Man Named Tony: The True Story of the Yablonski Murders* (New York: W. W. Norton, 1976), 85.

189 **start with her father:** Hearing on Degree of Guilt and Sentencing, 13–14.

190 **and polygraph her daily:** Author's interview with Masterson.

190 **move her feet:** Ibid.

190 **"details of the case":** "The Tiger," *Time*, July 17, 1972, 56. Brophy was a veteran Philadelphia Police Department officer and the chief of its polygraph unit.

190 **confession on April 4:** Author's interview with Masterson.

190 **"when things get tight":** Author's interview with Masterson; "Yablonski Probe Reopened," *Beckley Post-Herald*, April 5, 1972, Box 2, GJTC SCRC UK.

191 **"wanted to please him":** Adrian Lee, Bonnie Cook, Mike Ruane, and Jim Southwood, "Plotters: Fiery Father, Deceitful Daughter," *Philadelphia Bulletin*, August 3, 1981, A7.

191 **enough of them senseless:** Brown, *A Man Named Tony*, 90.

191 **Sweet's second-floor courtroom:** Author's interview with Elmer Schifko, July 10, 2017.

191 **from lewd to awestruck:** Arthur H. Lewis, *Murder by Contract: The People v. "Tough Tony" Boyle* (New York: Macmillan, 1975), 141–42.

191 **lined the courtroom's walls:** "Mrs. Gilly's Guilty Plea Hints of New Indictments," *Charleston Gazette*, April 12, 1972, Box 2, GJTC SCRC, UK.

192 **answered softly, "Yes":** "Mrs. Gilly's Confession Reportedly Implicates UMW Official," News 4, WRC Television, 7:00 p.m., April 11, 1972, Box 28, UMWA LDR Ser. 3 EFSCL PSU.

192 **back seat of their car:** Armbrister, *Act of Vengeance*, 286.

192 **and longest-serving terrorists:** Lewis, *Murder by Contract*, 145.

192 **one flight of stairs:** Hearing on Degree of Guilt and Sentencing, 11; "Huddleston

Trial Begins Today," *Beckley Post-Herald*, April 17, 1972, Box 2, GJTC SCRC UK.

193 **"in turn with Albert Pass":** AG confession, April 4, 1972, 21, Box 4, JAYLCC MD LOC.

193 **but the union, too:** Lewis, *Murder by Contract*, 153.

193 **had ordered Yablonski's execution:** Ben A. Franklin, "Woman in Yablonski Case Mentions Name of Boyle," *New York Times*, April 14, 1972, 1.

193 **a trace of irony:** Ibid.

193 **for the three killings:** Ibid.

194 **"have the wrong man":** FBI interview of SH, March 16, 1970, 21, Box 23, JAYLCC MD LOC.

194 **Huddleston's fanciful offer:** Brown, *A Man Named Tony*, 90.

194 **betrayal changed all that:** Hearing on Degree of Guilt and Sentencing, 10.

194 **like his favorite daughter:** FBI interview of Arlin Gibson, January 22, 1970, summarized in FBI Summary of Developments in Cleveland, 7, Box 23, JAYLCC MD LOC.

195 **and keep him quiet:** Don Stillman, "The Prater Trial," *UMJ*, April 1, 1973, 4; AEP confession, September 13, 1977, 21.

195 **now against the union:** Hearing on Degree of Guilt and Sentencing, 20.

195 **"and after the murders":** SH confession, May 3, 1972, 13, Box 8, JAYLCC MD LOC.

195 **"done it for money":** Ibid., 34.

196 **administered by Prater:** Ibid., 33–34.

196 **to do with the killings:** "Bye-bye Boyle?," *Newsweek*, May 15, 1972, 36; "The Yablonski Contract," *Time*, May 15, 1972, 23.

196 **"or settle a grievance":** United Press International, May 4, 1970, Papers of Laurence J. Silberman, Box 41, Hoover Institution, Stanford University.

Chapter Nineteen: For Jock

197 **treated fairly and humanely:** Yvonne Shinhoster Lamb, "Pioneering D.C. Judge Beat Racial Odds with Wisdom," *Washington Post*, November 15, 2005, A23.

198 **examining and cross-examining witnesses:** Email, CAY to author, October 9, 2018. The government's lawyers argued that only the Department of Labor could seek to overturn a union election. While the Supreme Court did not deny the Department's prominent role, it held that Miners for Democracy had the right to intervene and augment the government's case.

198 **ordered a new election:** Juan M. Vasquez, "U.M.W. Election of Boyle Is Upset by Federal Judge," *New York Times*, May 2, 1972, 1.

198 **close in on him completely:** Ibid.

198 **his May 1 opinion:** Email, CAY to author, October 9, 2018.

199 **regulated in American labor history:** Tom Bethell, *Coal Patrol*, May 20, 1972, 4.

199 **advocate for their platforms:** "Order and Opinion of Judge Bryant in Election Case," *UMJ*, July 1, 1972, 2–10.

199 **a rank-and-file convention:** Peter Milius, "Rebels Seek UMW Control," *Washington Post*, May 5, 1972, A16.

200 **no longer handpick them:** Email, CAY to author, September 4, 2017; Juan M. Vasquez, "Judge Bars Seven Mine Union Trusteeships, Opening Way to Long-Sought Elections," *New York Times*, May 25, 1972, 29.

200 **to send delegates:** Paul Nyden, *Miners for Democracy: Struggle in the Coalfields* (PhD dissertation, Columbia University, 1974), 532–33. Wheeling College is now Wheeling Jesuit University.

200 **upsetting big coal operators:** Author's interview with J. Davitt McAteer, June 18, 2018.

200 **victory in December's voting:** MFD Convention Schedule, Box 28, LDR Ser. 3 EFSCL PSU.

200 **"we shall overcome!":** Keynote Address of JLR, MFD Convention, Wheeling, West Virginia, May 27, 1972, 10, CAY papers.

201 **vote on union contracts:** Bethell, *Coal Patrol*, June 1, 1972, 4. The task of assembling hundreds of miners from various states was a logistical nightmare, but even more challenging was devising a system in which they could select candidates and vote on a platform. The elaborate formulae developed by the Miners' Project and staffers from the Black Lung Association ensured that every delegate had a voice but that their votes were apportioned by districts to reflect their makeup and the 1969 election's results adjusted for the violations Judge Bryant found. CAY email to author, October 9, 2018.

201 **the union's top job:** Edgar N. James, *Union Democracy and the LMRDA*: Autocracy and Insurgency in National Union Elections," *Harvard Civil Rights-Civil Liberties Law Review*, Vol. 13 (Spring 1978), 338.

201 **lost a leg in another:** Bernie Aronson, "Miller, Trbovich, Patrick—Biographical Sketches," *Post Herald and Register*, June 11, 1972, 26, Box 27, UMWA LDR Ser. 3 EFSCL PSU.

202 **side of his face:** Ibid.

202 **shot off half his face:** Ibid.; Bethell, *Coal Patrol*, June 1, 1972, 5.

202 **"this union are [sic] numbered":** "Boyle's Opponent Begins Campaign," *Billings Gazette*, July 17, 1972, Box 27, UMWA LDR Ser. 3 EFSCL PSU.

202 **from the union's retirees:** Bethell, *Coal Patrol*, September 15, 1972, 1.

203 **raise his $179,000 bond:** Juan M. Vasquez, "Boyle Convicted in Political Use of Union's Money," *New York Times*, April 1, 1972, 1; Jim Mann, "Tony Boyle Gets 5 Years, Heavy Fines," *Washington Post*, June 28, 1972, A1.

203 **their full support:** George Vecsey, "Boyle, at U.M.W. Rally, Terms 'Outsiders' Key Threat to Union," *New York Times*, September 5, 1972, 12; "Let's Hear It about Tony Boyle," *Washington Post*, July 5, 1972, A22.

203 **"wouldn't vote for him:** "Tough Tony in Trouble?" *Time*, December 4, 1972, 31.

203 **"democracy in this union":** Laurence Leamer, "The United Mine Workers Hold an Election," *New York Times Sunday Magazine*, November 26, 1972, 41. The provision for a $50-an-hour wage was spelled out in the union's 1971 contract with the Bituminous Coal Operators' Association.

203 **"Some of 'em alive":** Ibid.

203 **"Moscow Fire Department slate":** "Tough Tony in Trouble?," 31.

204 **more energetic campaigners:** "Boyle-Pnakovich-Killion, the Pro-union Team," *UMJ*, August 15, 1972, 18.

204 **a *New York Times* reporter:** Ibid.; Vecsey, "Boyle, at U.M.W. Rally, Terms 'Outsiders' Key Threat to Union," 12.

204 **a few steps behind him:** Nyden, *Miners for Democracy*, 562; "Tough Tony in Trouble," 31; author's interview with Don Stillman, July 15, 2018.

204 **not in their rooms:** Curtis Seltzer, *Fire in the Hole* (Lexington: University Press of Kentucky, 1985), 122.

204 **"is stay alive":** "UMW Challenger to Tony Boyle Presses Campaign for Presidency," *Louisville Courier-Journal*, August 17, 1972, 3.

205 **face-to-face electioneering:** Author's interview with Edgar James, February 14, 2018; author's interview with Don Stillman.

205 **"the UMWA great again":** Author's interview with Don Stillman.

205 **"under [an] unsupported roof":** Nyden, *Miners for Democracy*, 562–63; *Officers' Report to the UMWA*, September 1976, 3.

206 **a congratulatory telegram:** George Vecsey, "Mine Workers Begin Balloting," *New York Times*, December 2, 1972, 71; Ben A. Franklin, "Boyle Lost Post by 14,000 Votes," *New York Times*, December 17, 1972, 32.

206 **"our friend, Jock Yablonski":** Ben A. Franklin, "The Martyr Had Been Vindicated," *New York Times*, December 17, 1972, E2.

206 **"responsive to the membership":** Ben A. Franklin, "Boyle Is Ousted by Miners' Votes after Long Fight," *New York Times*, December 16, 1972, A1.

206 **union had come true:** Email, CAY to author, September 30, 2019.

206 **joyful political celebrations:** Ben A. Franklin: "Headquarters of Miners Opened to Rank and File," *New York Times*, January 14, 1973, 58; Franklin, "Miners Now Have Problems of Free Choice," *New York Times*, November 30, 1975, 22.

207 **been right all along:** Seltzer, *Fire in the Hole*, 129. Author's interview with Bernard Aronson, January 25, 2019.

207 **"finally Made it, Jock":** Margie Carlin, "Fresh Winds of Change Blow over Jock's Grave," *Pittsburgh Press*, December 31, 1972, Box 2, GJTC SCRC UK.

Chapter Twenty: Back to the Beginning

208 **behind the judge's bench:** Stuart Brown, *A Man Named Tony: The True Story of the Yablonski Murders* (New York: W. W. Norton, 1976), 128, 147; Arthur H.

Lewis, *Murder by Contract: The People v. "Tough Tony" Boyle* (New York: Macmillan, 1975), 191.

208 **rougher part of town:** Trevor Armbrister, *An Act of Vengeance* (New York: Saturday Review Press, 1975), 302.

208 **handouts from her church:** Ibid.

209 **misuse of union funds:** Ibid.; WJT confession, August 23, 1973, 29, RAS papers; Mary Walton, "Pass, Prater Get Boot from Payroll," *Charleston Gazette*, July 19, 1972, Box 2, GJTC SCRC UK.

209 **that they believed him:** Armbrister, *Act of Vengeance*, 302.

209 **with a packed suitcase:** Ibid., 291.

210 **by-the-book judge:** "Longtime Judge Edward Carney Dies," *Erie Times-News*, September 11, 1998, 10.

210 **"conduit along the way":** RAS opening statement in *Commonwealth of Pennsylvania v. William J. Prater*, 19, 24, Box 15, JAYLCC MD LOC.

210 **witnesses to the stand:** Testimony of Kathy Rygle in *Commonwealth of Pennsylvania v. William J. Prater*, 71–37; testimony of Fred Schunk in *Commonwealth of Pennsylvania v. William J. Prater*, 202–6; testimony of CAY in *Commonwealth of Pennsylvania v. William J. Prater*, 197–98.

211 **if he cooperated:** Armbrister, *Act of Vengeance*, 300–330; author's interview with PEG. Gilly later claimed that Sprague coerced him into pleading guilty by shouting and cursing at him. The Pennsylvania courts have refused to overturn his guilty plea and conviction. The Supreme Court ruled the death penalty as it was then practiced in the United States "cruel and unusual punishment" and unconstitutional in *Furman v. Georgia*, 408, U.S. 238 (1972).

211 **directly to Yablonski's assassination:** John P. Moody, "Yablonski Slayer Testifies," *Washington Post*, March 14, 1973, A6.

211 **stared at him:** Ben A. Franklin, "Boyle Is Implicated by Yablonski Killer," *New York Times*, March 14, 1973, 89.

211 **"and could not get":** Ibid.

212 **on October 10, 1969:** Testimony of Edith Roark in *Commonwealth of Pennsylvania v. William J. Prater*, 460–67; Box 15, JAYLCC MD LOC.

212 **one of Yablonski's bedroom windows:** Testimony of George Smith Jr. in *Commonwealth of Pennsylvania v. William J. Prater*, 507–12.

212 **if he did not:** Noah Doss confession to FBI, June 12, 1972, 18, FBI Prosecutive Summary, Box 23 JAYLCC MD LOC.

213 **he told the jurors:** Testimony of SH in *Commonwealth of Pennsylvania v. William J. Prater*, 696; John P. Moody, "Plotter Says He Believed Yablonski Was in the Pay of a Giant Coal Firm," *Washington Post*, March 17, 1973, A3.

213 **"in pretty bad shape":** Testimony of SH in *Commonwealth of Pennsylvania v. William J. Prater*, 761.

213 **killers' money for him:** John Moody, "The Probe of the Murder Fund," December 4, 1973, *Pittsburgh Post-Gazette*, 49.

213 **talk to the FBI:** Ibid.

213 **who were still alive confessed:** Ibid.

214 **give Pass what he wanted:** Testimony of Bronce Waldroop in *Commonwealth of Pennsylvania v. William J. Prater*, 829, 848; testimony of Clifford Marcum in *Commonwealth of Pennsylvania v. William J. Prater*, 860; testimony of Harvey Huddleston in *Commonwealth of Pennsylvania v. William J. Prater*, 876; testimony of Louis Lowe in *Commonwealth of Pennsylvania v. William J. Prater*, 895; Don Stillman, "The Prater Trial," *UMJ*, April 1, 1973, 11.

214 **to reward Pass's zealotry:** Testimony of W. A. Boyle in *Commonwealth of Pennsylvania v. William J. Prater*, 225, Box 17, JAYLCC MD LOC.

214 **president of District 19:** Ibid., 228; John P. Moody, "Jury Hears Boyle Version of Fund," *Washington Post*, March 21, 1973, A3.

214 **Humphrey's 1968 presidential campaign:** Testimony of W. A. Boyle in *Commonwealth of Pennsylvania v. William J. Prater*, 267–68.

215 **in Madisonville, Kentucky:** Ibid., 290, 302, 305, 307–8.

215 **could have killed him:** Moody, "Jury Hears Boyle Version of Fund."

215 **to kill Yablonski:** Testimony of AEP in *Commonwealth of Pennsylvania v. William J. Prater*, 514, 517, 558, 565; John P. Moody, "Evidence Blocked in Yablonski Case," *Washington Post*, March 23, 1973, A18.

215 **International Executive Board member:** Testimony of AEP in *Commonwealth of Pennsylvania v. William J. Prater*, 558.

215 **his list of witnesses:** Stillman, "Prater Trial," 5.

215 **Rothman rested his case:** John Moody, "Searching for the Missing Link," *Pittsburgh Post-Gazette*, December 6, 1973, 33. Henderson did not want to raise any potential ethics questions or give Prater an issue on appeal if the agents interrogated Turnblazer before Prater rested his case.

216 **from embezzled union funds:** Affidavit of Wallace Estill in *Commonwealth of Pennsylvania v. W. A. "Tony" Boyle*, RAS papers.

216 **old friend was innocent:** Testimony of WJP in *Commonwealth of Pennsylvania v. William J. Prater*, 612–25; Stillman, "Prater Trial," 10.

216 **buy his continued silence:** Testimony of WJP in *Commonwealth of Pennsylvania v. William J. Prater*, 698–707.

216 **until after the election:** Testimony of Edith Roark in *Commonwealth of Pennsylvania v. William J. Prater*, 758, 760; testimony of Suzanne Richards in *Commonwealth of Pennsylvania v. William J. Prater*, 811.

216 **he replied tersely:** Testimony of WJT in *Commonwealth of Pennsylvania v. William J. Prater*, 846.

217 **its members allegedly spent:** Ibid; Stillman, "Prater Trial," 11; "Mine Official Disputes Boyle's Testimony," *New York Times*, March 25, 1973, 65; John Moody, "Searching for the Missing Link," December 6, 1973, *Pittsburgh Post-Gazette*, 33.

217 **polled the jurors one by one:** "Prater Trial," *Washington Post*, March 22, 1973, B21.

217 **and their stricken children:** John P. Moody, "UMW Aide Prater Guilty in Murder of Yablonskis," *Washington Post*, March 27, 1973, A1; Gary Mihoces, "Jury Convicts Prater of First-Degree Murder," *Louisville Courier-Journal*, March 27, 1973, 18.

217 **their father was innocent:** Testimony of WJP in *Commonwealth of Pennsylvania v. W. A. "Tony" Boyle*, 80–82, Box 3, JAYLCC MD LOC; John P. Moody, "Prater Implicates Pass, UMW Funds in Slayings," *Washington Post*, April 11, 1973, A3.

217 **was Turnblazer still hiding?:** "Prater Implicates Pass, UMW Funds in Slayings," A3; Armbrister, *Act of Vengeance*, 311–12.

Chapter Twenty-One: The Marker

218 **as he was on Pass:** Don Stillman "The Yablonski Murder Probe: Where To Now?" *UMJ*, June 15–30, 1973, 5.

218 **he told the jury:** Ibid.

218 **"or done away with":** Confession of WJP in *Commonwealth of Pennsylvania v. Albert E. Pass*, 264, Box 13, JAYLCC MD LOC.

219 **anything about Boyle:** Ibid., 273.

219 **"have Jock Yablonski killed?":** John P. Moody, "Pass Identified as Ordering the Murder of Yablonski," *Washington Post*, June 14, 1973, A3.

219 **for the UMWA's presidency:** Ibid.

219 **to destroy the union:** Stillman, "Yablonski Murder Probe," 6.

219 **lawyer cross-examined him:** Testimony of WJP in *Commonwealth of Pennsylvania v. Albert E. Pass*, 418–19 , Box 13, JAYLCC MD LOC; Moody, "Pass Identified as Ordering the Murder of Yablonski."

219 **had promised was true:** "$1 Million Reported Available," *New York Times*, June 14, 1973, 17.

220 **barely questioned them:** Stillman, "Yablonski Murder Probe," 6.

220 **"went right to Boyle":** "Yablonski Jury Gets Case," *Washington Post*, June 19, 1971, A3.

220 **to mail to Gilly:** RAS closing argument in *Commonwealth of Pennsylvania v. Albert E. Pass*, Box 13, JAYLCC MD LOC, 162.

220 **"Don't flinch from it":** Ibid.

220 **so was his client:** "Yablonski Jury Gets Case."

220 **had for the union:** Arthur H. Lewis, *Murder by Contract: The People v. "Tough Tony" Boyle* (New York: Macmillan, 1975), 302.

220 **"at least one more arrest":** John P. Moody, "Albert Pass Convicted in Yablonski Murder," *Washington Post*, June 20, 1973, A3.

Chapter Twenty-Two: The Box

221 **defenders without cause:** Don Stillman, "Tony Boyle Arrested, Charged in Murders of Yablonski Family," *UMJ*, September 1973, 3.

221 **have ended with Pass:** B. D. Colen and Peter Milius, "Boyle Is Near Death from Pill Overdose," *Washington Post*, September 26, 1973, A1.

221 **Bryant about the payments:** Memorandum from Jeremiah C. Collins to W. A. Boyle and John Owens, Re: Salary Payments to Albert Pass, May 25, 1972, Box 66, MFDC WRL WSU. Collins was a lawyer with Williams, Connolly, and Califano, one of Washington, D.C.'s most prominent law firms. He equated paying Pass while he was in jail with paying him while he was on vacation.

222 **missing in Pass and Boyle:** Affidavit of Wallace Estill, RAS papers.

222 **witnesses it did not trust:** Ibid.; Trevor Armbrister, *An Act of Vengeance* (New York: Saturday Review Press, 1975), 314.

222 **"knew about the murders":** Gayle Ronan Sims, "J. M. Brophy, Police Polygraph Pioneer," *Philadelphia Inquirer*, May 31, 2007. In 1973, Brophy served as the first head of the polygraph unit in the Philadelphia District Attorney's Office.

223 **to discuss Yablonski's assassination:** FBI, Pamela W. Higgins, Memo to the File, Yablonski Investigation, August 2, 1973. The results of polygraph tests are generally inadmissible in most state courts because of questions about their reliability.

223 **to assassinate Jock Yablonski:** WJT confession, August 23, 1973, 9.

223 **Boyle's hatred for Yablonski:** Ibid., 37.

223 **Turnblazer was flown to Pittsburgh:** WJT confession, 34; Don Stillman, "Turnblazer Pleads Guilty," *UMJ*, September 1973, 8.

223 **three counts of first-degree murder:** Don Stillman, "Tony Boyle Arrested, Charged in Murders of Yablonski Family," *UMJ*, September 1973, 4.

223 **knock at the door:** John Herling, "Transcript of an Arrest," *Washington Post*, September 22, 1973, A14.

224 **to their waiting car:** Ibid.

224 **removal to Pennsylvania:** Stillman, "Tony Boyle Arrested, Charged," 6.

224 **"had no forewarning":** Herling, "Transcript of an Arrest," A14.

224 **he told the newsmen:** Peter Milius, "Boyle Seized in Murder of UMW Rival," *Washington Post*, September 7, 1973, A1.

224 **murder charges in Pennsylvania:** Report of Dr. Milton Gusak, December 10, 1973, Box 1, JAYLCC MD LOC; Colen and Milius, "Boyle Is Near Death." Boyle overdosed on sodium amytal.

224 **"everything they can against him":** Colen and Milius, "Boyle Is Near Death," A1.

225 **extradite Boyle to Pennsylvania:** "Boyle Loses Political Gift Law Appeal," *Pittsburgh Post-Gazette*, December 4, 1973, 7.

225 **of his union's members:** Timothy S. Robinson, "Tony Boyle Ordered to U.S. Prison," *Washington Post*, December 20, 1973, A4.

225 **about to experience both:** Arraignment before the Honorable Charles G. Sweet, 6, in *Commonwealth of Pennsylvania v. W. A. "Tony" Boyle*, Box 1, JAYLCC MD LOC.

225 **practically in Sprague's backyard:** John P. Moody, "Boyle Trial to Be Moved to East Pa.," *Washington Post*, January 24, 1974, A3.

225 **preside over the high-profile trial:** Stuart Brown, *A Name Named Tony: The True Story of the Yablonski Murders* (New York: W. W. Norton, 1976), 195.

226 **prejudices against labor leaders:** Commonwealth's Brief Contra Defendant's Post-Trial Motions in *Commonwealth of Pennsylvania v. W. A."Tony" Boyle*, 4, Box 1, JAYLCC MD LOC; William Claiborne, "Trial of Boyle in Yablonski Killings Opens," *Washington Post*, March 26, 1974, A3.

226 **his wife and daughter:** Claiborne, "Trial of Boyle in Yablonski Killings Opens.

226 **was no longer there:** Ibid.

226 **"corruption under the rug":** Laurence Leamer, "The United Mine Workers Holds an Election" *New York Times Sunday Magazine*, November 26, 1972, 42.

227 **remain by his side:** B. J. Widick, "George Meany's Last Hurrah," *Nation*, September 4, 1972, Box 116, JLRP MD LOC; email, Don Stillman to author, January 19, 2019. Only the United Auto Workers spoke out against Boyle and financially contributed to Miller's campaign to overthrow him.

227 **trips to kill Jock Yablonski:** Opening statement of RAS in *Commonwealth of Pennsylvania v. W. A. "Tony" Boyle*, 10–11, Box 2, JAYLCC MD LOC.

227 **who pulled the triggers:** Ibid.; William Claiborne, "Prosecutors Say Boyle Set Murder," *Washington Post*, April 2, 1974, A6.

227 **"for murdering Jock Yablonski!":** Opening statement of RAS, 6–14.

227 **the courtroom's pink walls:** Ibid., 16; "Boyle's Turn at Last," *Time*, April 15, 1974, 36.

228 **"convicted in this case":** Opening statement of Charles Moses in *Commonwealth of Pennsylvania v. W. A. "Tony" Boyle*, 6-56–6-65, 73–79, Box 2, JAYLCC MD LOC; "Boyle's Turn at Last," 36.

Chapter Twenty-Three: The Puppeteer

229 **haunt the jurors overnight:** Testimony of Kenneth Yablonski in *Commonwealth of Pennsylvania v. W. A. "Tony" Boyle*, 6-88, Box 2, JAYLCC MD LOC.

229 **by jumping on it:** Saramma Methratta, "Behind Bars," https://news.psu.edu/story/141463/1988/09/01/research/behind-bars.

230 **had written it himself:** Author's interview with RAS, April 28, 2017.

230 **out of the courtroom:** Testimony of PEG in *Commonwealth of Pennsylvania v. W. A. "Tony" Boyle*, Box 2, 6-132, JAYLCC MD LOC.

230 **had gone horribly wrong:** Ibid., 6-158, 160.

230 **"stick with your story"**: Testimony of WJP in *Commonwealth of Pennsylvania v. W. A. "Tony" Boyle*, 10-74, Box 3, JAYLCC MD LOC.

230 **in a private room**: Charge of the Court in *Commonwealth of Pennsylvania v. W.A. "Tony" Boyle*, 14-63, Box 4, JAYLCC MD LOC.

230 **"is against my principles"**: Testimony of WJP in *Commonwealth of Pennsylvania v. W. A. "Tony" Boyle*, 10-105.

231 **"take care of Joseph Yablonski"**: Testimony of WJT in *Commonwealth of Pennsylvania v. W. A. "Tony" Boyle*, 11-176, Box 3, JAYLCC, MD, LOC.

231 **"to clear my conscience"**: Ibid., 11-201.

231 **"Mr. Boyle"**: Ibid., 11-172.

231 **lie for him anymore**: Ben A. Franklin, "Witness Says He Heard Boyle Order Yablonski Death," *New York Times*, April 9, 1974, 17; ". . . Kill Yablonski, Take Care of Him," *Washington Post*, April 9, 1974, A1.

231 **committee's origins and its work**: Testimony of WJT in *Commonwealth of Pennsylvania v. W. A. "Tony" Boyle*, 11-184-185, Box 3, JAYLCC MD LOC. Boyle had purposely excluded Turnblazer from the meeting.

232 **but Sprague objected**: Adrian Lee, Bonnie Cook, Mike Ruane, and Jim Southwood, "Union's Money Flowed without Records, *Philadelphia Bulletin*, August 5, 1981, A1, A8, A9.

232 **or introducing his findings**: Ibid., A9.

232 **to his office for another meeting**: Testimony of W. A. Boyle in *Commonwealth of Pennsylvania v. W. A. "Tony" Boyle*, Box 3, 12-20, JAYLCC, MD, LOC.

232 **"I was sick"**: Ibid., 12-129.

233 **the union's top lawyer**: Ibid., 12-132.

233 **only "seven, eight minutes"**: Ibid., 12-136–12-139.

233 **his lawyer sat down**: Ibid., 12-139.

233 **into telling two more**: Ibid., 12-143.

233 **were on the document**: Ibid., 12-168–12-170; Commonwealth's Brief Contra Defendant's Post-Trial Motions in *Commonwealth of Pennsylvania v. W. A. "Tony" Boyle*, 31.

233 **from $100,000 to $50,000**: Ibid., 14-114.

234 **over to the FBI**: Ibid., 14-115–14-116.

234 **Sprague told the judge**: Ibid., 14-114–14-118.

234 **"W. A. 'Tony' Boyle"**: "Boyle Case to Go to Jury Today," *Washington Post*, April 11, 1974, A2.

234 **admitted liar and embezzler**: Ibid.

234 **quickly from the courtroom**: Ben A. Franklin, "Jury Finds Boyle Guilty in 3 Yablonski Murders," *New York Times*, April 12, 1974, 65.

234 **he told Sprague**: Ibid.

235 **"this time, thank God"**: James Driscoll, "The Legacy of Jock Yablonski," Box 116, JLRP MD LOC.

235 **had been done**: Email, CAY to author, July 21, 2018.

Epilogue: A Martyr's Cause

237 **"into a martyr's cause"**: Maurice Isserman and Michael Kazin, *America Divided, The Civil War of the 1960s* (New York: Oxford University Press, 2000), 106.

237 **Democratic nominee George McGovern:** Author's interview with Bernard Aronson, January 25, 2019; Bill Peterson, "The Tragedy of the Miners," *Washington Post*, January 16, 1977, B1.

237 **"wear and tear of coalfield driving":** "3 Boyle-Era Cadillacs to Be Sold to Miners," *Washington Post*, February 3, 1973, A2.

238 **top Boyle administrative lackeys:** Peterson,"Tragedy of the Miners," B1; Paul Nyden, *Miners for Democracy: Struggle in the Coalfields* (PhD dissertation, Columbia University, 1974), 539; author's interview with Bernard Aronson.

238 **told a *Time* correspondent:** Paul F. Clark, *The Miners' Fight for Democracy: Arnold Miller and the Reform of the United Mine Workers* (Ithaca: New York State School of Industrial and Labor Relations, 1981), 34; "The New Militancy: A Cry for More," *Time*, November 25, 1974, 36.

238 **call for Nixon's impeachment:** Address by Joe Rauh Jr., *Proceedings of the 46th Consecutive Constitutional Convention of the UMWA*, 317.

238 **"corruption in high places!":** Joseph Rauh Jr., *The Challenge We Face*, December 12, 1973, Box 116, JLRP MD LOC.

238 **clean of corruption:** Ibid.; "Boyle Daughter Loses Post as UMW Lawyer," *Washington Post*, January 31, 1973, A14.

239 **"for us to go forward":** *Proceedings of the 46th*, 5.

239 **coal operators were over:** CAY, "Jock Yablonski's 1969 Campaign for the UMW Presidency: His Son Looks Back 40 Years After His Assassination," *Labor and Working-Class History Association Newsletter*, Spring 2010, 17–18. The team consisted of Chip Yablonski, Rick Bank, Tom Bethell, Richard Trumka, and Bernie Aronson.

239 **auto and steel workers:** Ibid.

239 **1969 reelection campaign:** Michael S. Gordon, "The Employee Retirement Income Security Act of 1974: The First Decade," An Information Paper Prepared for Use by the Special Committee on Aging, United States Senate, 98th Cong. 2d Sess., August 1984, (Washington: Government Printing Office, 1984), 15.

240 **start, much less sustain:** In 1977, with Joe Rauh and Edgar James at his side, Sadlowski ran for the union's presidency. He lost, alleging massive fraud. Rauh appealed unsuccessfully to the Department of Labor and the federal courts. See Herman Benson, *Rebels, Reformers, and Racketeers* (Bloomington, IN: 1stBooks, 2005), 96–112, 198–203.

240 **plan to go away:** Tom Bethell, *Coal Patrol*, January 1, 1973, 7; Peter Milius, "Boyle Bloc Ousted from UMW Board," *Washington Post*, December 23, 1972, A1.

240 **"throughout his presidency":** Ben A. Franklin, "Miners Now Have Problems of Free Choice," *New York Times*, November 30, 1975, 22.

240 **the union's reform movement:** "U.M.W. Strife—Again," *Time*, May 17, 1976, 69; Sara Fitz, "U.S. Auditors Find UMW Books Clean," *Washington Post*, April 16, 1976, A19.

240 **ice cream stand by himself:** Austin Scott, "3 Influential in UMW Reform Are Leaving Union Positions," *Washington Post*, August 14, 1975, A2; Bethell, *Coal Patrol*, January 1, 1973, 5.

241 **its dictatorship in 1974:** "U.M.W. Strife—Again," 69; "The Leaderless Miners Edge toward a National Strike," *Business Week*, October 11, 1976, 98.

241 **in neighboring Alexandria, Virginia:** "U.M.W. Strife—Again," 69.

241 **on the Washington Beltway:** Clark, *Miners' Fight for Democracy*, 92–93, 132; Duane Lockard, *Coal: A Memoir and Critique* (Charlottesville: University Press of Virginia, 1998), 144.

241 **contracts or their negotiations:** Author's interview with Mason Caudill, August 16, 2018.

242 **stepped down in November 1979:** Clark, *Miners' Fight for Democracy*, 112.

242 **intimidated its coal miners:** Ibid.

242 **union in the country:** Curtis Seltzer, "Death of Reform in the U.M.W.," *Nation*, May 31, 1980, 657; Lockard, *Coal*, 146–47. The UMWA has not had a contested presidential election since 1982.

243 **Air Traffic Controllers Organization:** Rich Yeselen, "The Decline of Labor, the Increase of Inequality," talkingpointsmemo.com/features/marchtoinequality/ onedeclineoflabor.

243 **Beltone Hearing Aid Center:** U.S. Department of Labor, "Quarterly Mine Employment and Coal Production Report," Table 20, 2016. Another 4,415 UMWA members work in strip or surface mines. Email from Phil Smith, UMWA, to author, October 9, 2018; author's visit to Middlesboro, Kentucky, August 16, 2018.

243 **lamented to the *Washington Post*:** Dylan Brown, "Coal Mining Union Faces 'Life-and-Death' Test," April 11, 2017, www.eenews.net/stories/1060052929/ print; Dylan Lyons, "No Unionized Mines Left in Kentucky, Where Labor Wars Once Raged," *Washington Post*, September 6, 2015, A4.

243 **50 percent ten years ago:** Timothy Puko and John W. Miller, "Coal Mine to Lay Off About 21% of Workers," *Wall Street Journal*, May 22, 2015, B2.

243 **produces nearly twenty-eight:** Bonnie Berkowitz and Tim Meko, "Appalachia Comes Up Small in Era of Giant Coal Mines," *Washington Post*, May 2, 2017, www.washingtonpost.com/graphics/national/coal-jobs-in-appalachia/.

244 **legislation to rescue it:** "Number of Black Lung Cases among U.S. Coal Miners Continues to Rise," *Fayetteville Tribune*, July 27, 2018, 4.

244 **"I'm innocent," Boyle maintained:** Stuart Brown, *A Man Named Tony: The True Story of the Yablonski Murders* (New York: W. W. Norton, 1976), 225.

244 **records in October 1970:** Peter Milius, "Tony Boyle Wins New Trial in Death of UMW Insurgent," *Washington Post*, January 29, 1977, A4.

244 **"murders of Joseph, Margaret, and Charlotte Yablonski":** AEP confession, September 13, 1977, RAS papers.

245 **not over, but his trials were:** Linda Herskowitz, "Tony Boyle Is Convicted a 2nd Time," *Washington Post*, February 19, 1979, A2.

245 **died with him:** J. Y. Smith, "Former UMW Chief Tony Boyle Dies at 83," *Washington Post*, June 1, 1985, B4; James Haugh, "Revisiting the UMW Cleanup," March 22, 2005, *Charleston Gazette*, A4.

245 **sought-after trial lawyers:** "Tough, Honest and Fired," *Time*, December 30, 1974, 52; Joseph R. Daughen, *Fearless: The Richard A. Sprague Story* (Chicago: American Bar Association, 2008), 141–58.

246 **tragic twist of history:** Bart Barnes, "Arnold Miller, Once Reform President of UMW, Dies at 62," *Washington Post*, July 13, 1985, B6.

246 **inside the Yablonskis' farmhouse:** "Aubran W. Martin, 42, Murderer of Unionist," *New York Times*, March 13, 1991, 25.

246 **equipment operator in prison:** "Killer Claude Vealey Dies at 55," *Washington Post*, February 4, 1999.

246 **backtracked on his pledge:** Adrian Lee, Bonnie Cook, Mike Ruane, and Jim Southwood, "Paul Gilly: Portrait of a Lifer and Loser," *Philadelphia Bulletin*, August 2, 1981, A1.

246 **any wrongdoing:** "Pennsylvania Exonerates in Boyle Trial," *New York Times*, September 30, 1981, A20.

246 **especially around Christmas:** Author's interview with PEG, July 2, 2017; Richard Robbins, "1969 Yablonski Murders Spurred Union Reforms," *Pittsburgh Tribune*, December 27, 2009, A2.

247 **life in federal prison:** "Convict Accuses Ex-Union Official": *New York Times*, June 14, 1973, 17.

247 **a stroke in 1983:** "William Prater; Jailed for Life in Unionist's Murder," August 12, 1989, Associated Press.

247 **at eighty-two years old:** Richard Robbins, "1969 Yablonski Murders Spurred Union Reforms," *Pittsburgh Tribune*, December 27, 2009, A2; "Law License of ex-Official of UMW Revoked," *Bradford (PA) ERA*, November 1, 1974, 10.

247 **"a hold on me":** AEP Education and Training Cumulative Record, Commonwealth of Pennsylvania, Department of Corrections, Box 12, JAYLCC MD LOC; AEP's Third Petition for Clemency, RAS papers.

247 **at eighty-two years old:** AEP Education and Training Cumulative Record; Robbins, "1969 Yablonski Murders Spurred Union Reforms."

247 **quipped from the bench:** *Commonwealth of Pennsylvania v. Annette Gilly; Commonwealth of Pennsylvania v. Silous Huddleston;* Hearing on Degree of Guilt and Sentencing, August 17, 1974, 32, Box 4, JAYLCC MD LOC.

248 **with Lucy and his grandson:** Adrian Lee, Bonnie Cook, Mike Ruane, and Jim Southwood, "Plotters: Fiery Father, Deceitful Daughter," *Philadelphia Bulletin*, August 3, 1981, A1, A7.

248 **not let go of the union:** Ibid.

248 **was eighty-one years old:** Wolfgang Saxon, "Joseph Rauh Jr., Groundbreaking Civil Liberties Lawyer, Dies at 81," *New York Times*, September 5, 1992, 10.

248 **bears his father's name:** "Kenneth J. Yablonski, 68, Labor Lawyer," Associated Press, September 13, 2002.

INDEX